# Arthur Ashe

*Portrait in Motion*

# Arthur Ashe

## Portrait in Motion

### Arthur Ashe
*with Frank Deford*

*Illustrated with Photographs*

Houghton Mifflin Company Boston
1975

Library of Congress Cataloging in Publication Data

Ashe, Arthur.
  Arthur Ashe, portrait in motion.

  1. Ashe, Arthur.  2. Tennis.  I. Deford, Frank, joint author.  II. Title.
GV994.A7A32        796.34'2'0924[B]        74-34465
ISBN 0-395-20429-1

Printed in the United States of America
V 10 9 8 7 6 5 4 3 2 1

To my grandmothers,
*"Ma" Taylor* and *"Big Mama" Cunningham,*
who between them raised twenty children,
and who taught me right from wrong.

# *Preface*

I would like to say a few words which might make it easier for you to appreciate this book.

It is a diary about what I did and the thoughts I had, over the course of a year, Wimbledon to Wimbledon, 1973–74. It is disjointed, the way my life is. Topics that have no relationship to one another follow upon each other. But one of the unique aspects of my life is the juxtaposition of disparate events and people, and so I think it is both accurate and important to maintain this sequential chaos in the diary.

I am not a typical member of the tennis tour and my experiences are by no means conclusive, but they are representative. The only things I haven't mentioned are those that I thought too private. But I think what I left unsaid is merely private; I don't believe the omissions would improve your understanding of me or the world around me.

The book will not help you play tennis. It is not an instructional manual. But I'm sure that it will help you to understand tennis, to appreciate the matches you see and the players who participate in them. The book might even make it possible for you to understand tennis politics . . . along with the eight other people in the world who do.

I have tried not to climb up on a soapbox. But I do lead an unusual life, and am, with my colleagues, privileged to see more of the world than most people. In this year, I played on five continents, made 129 airplane trips, slept in 71 different beds and traveled 165,000 miles. By itself, this sort of quantitative bombast doesn't prove much of anything. But I try to make my travel work for me. Even the dullest tennis players can perceive how interdependent the world is. If I belabor the subject occasionally, please bear with me; I hope it is the only excess you will have to tolerate.

Finally, the book has been, in a sense, therapeutic for me. Writing has forced me to take a closer look at my life and myself. Especially, it has helped me to appreciate two aspects of my career better. The first is that I am very lucky to have the life I do and especially fortunate to be doing something that I like. The second is that so many of the people I know, especially the men I play against, are pretty damn good people.

A.R.A., Jr.

# Contents

# Illustrations

# Arthur Ashe

*Portrait in Motion*

# 1

# The Second Hundred Years Begin

*Monday, June 11, 1973 — Yugoslavia / London*

So much happened today.  It's eerie that today would be the day I decided to begin this diary.  I planned to start it when I arrived in England for Wimbledon, 1973, to carry it through Wimbledon, 1974 — so today was supposed to be an arbitrary place to begin. Instead, it was a day when every part of my life was affected.

First of all: Nikki Pilic.  I had planned weeks ago to go visit him at his home in Yugoslavia.  Happy little sun and fun.  But suddenly Nikki is the thread the whole tennis world hangs on.  Because of him there may not even be a Wimbledon, 1973.  Not for many of us, anyway.  Pilic has been threatened with suspension by the Yugoslav Tennis Association Federation, because it claims that he refused to play Davis Cup for Yugoslavia this year after they say he committed himself to the team.  Nikki says this is not so, and our players union, the Association of Tennis Professionals, has taken up his case.  I am especially involved because I am an officer of the ATP — and one of its founders, for that matter.  If the International Lawn Tennis Association gets Wimbledon to uphold the Yugoslav suspension, we expect to side with him.  Ban him, lose us all. Tennis is exactly a century old, and this, at last, will be the moment when the players stand up for themselves.

And we'll do it this time.  We will.

Secondly, today is also Kathy's birthday. Kathy Benn is my girl friend. We've grown awfully close. She's a free-lance commercial artist from Toronto, and very pretty. Very pretty. She's been with me over here in Europe for the last month.

Thirdly — today, I forgot it was Kathy's birthday.

And then, at last, today was also the day that my Grandmother Cunningham died.

Kathy and I had dinner with Nikki and his wife last night, and then we came over to London this morning. In the afternoon, we went shopping along King's Road, which made her feel better about her birthday. Then we went to Trader Vic's for dinner and gambled for a little while at the Playboy Club. I don't suppose I could have been asleep for more than twenty minutes when my Aunt Marie called from Richmond with the news about Big Mama.

I had a moment's hesitation about whether I should spend the money just to fly over and right back for the funeral, but there was really no decision to make. Big Mama was one of my heroines. I must go.

She was my mother's mother, and she raised ten children, almost single-handedly. The oldest of them was only seventeen when my grandfather died. You hear so much about matriarchal black families — well, Big Mama was a black matriarch but only because she had to be and because she was good at it. She kept the family together, all the while working full-time in the kitchen at a white public school. She was a strong, dear, fine woman. I'll go home.

*Tuesday, June 12 — London*

I ran this morning in Hyde Park; I've run in some of the great parks of the world. I was up by the Inn on the Park, where Howard Hughes lives on the top floor. They say. Then this afternoon, Kathy and I visited a few museums. We started at the Lefevre Gallery, which was showing a collection by Edward Burns. Then we went on to the Tate Gallery and finally to Harrods, where I got carried away and bought a Rembrandt etching. It's entitled *The White Negress,* and it set me back some money. But I'm damned excited. There are only eight of this particular etching in the whole

2

world; after they were run off, they destroyed the plate. So, I own an original Rembrandt, and I'll probably do a lot of bragging.

*Wednesday, June 13 — London / New York*

We left on different planes, me to New York, Kathy to Toronto. It was very painful separating, but I'm a bit relieved too because we've been together the last four weeks, night and day, and that's the longest time I've ever spent with one woman.

*Thursday, June 14 — New York / Richmond / New York*

My father met me at Byrd Field, and we drove over to my Uncle James Cunningham's house in North Side. All my grandmother's surviving children were there. Two are dead: my mother and an aunt. It was fantastic to see all my family again. The last time we were all together was twenty-three years ago, when my mother died in the spring. I think the more family you have, the closer you are.

I was too young to go to my mother's funeral. The only funeral I had ever been to before today was my grandfather's on my father's side. They asked me if I wanted to see my grandmother for the last time, but I said no, I didn't. I don't know why; I regret it now.

The funeral was at Westwood Baptist. Westwood is a suburb of Richmond, a little black enclave set in white environs. It probably grew up because of the need for domestic servants in the area. Big Mama's house was at 93 Glenburne Road. It only had five rooms and one bath, but there was a good-sized back yard and plenty of room to roam around in the neighborhood, or to gather around my grandmother and listen to her talk. She was always full of pithy folk wisdoms that I still remember: if you have small ears, it means you're stingy; if your nose is wet, that signifies you're mean; that sort of thing. Growing up, I spent a lot of happy weekends visiting at 93 Glenburne. I spent all those Sunday mornings at Westwood Baptist too.

I never let on to Big Mama that I had stopped believing in Jesus. I always kept on going to Sunday school and acting in all the church plays. I guess most of my family still assumes that I am a Christian, but I've always been very skeptical. Even for a kid, I

3

had a scientific mind, and there just wasn't any way I could accept the Baptist fundamentalism. One of my most vivid memories, growing up, was in 1953, when I was ten, when President Eisenhower inserted "under God" into the Pledge of Allegiance: ". . . one nation, under God, with liberty and . . ." I remember very clearly thinking at the time, young as I was, that he had no business doing that. What I always hated most about religion was that it was forced on me. But I sure never let on to Big Mama that I was a closet agnostic.

Big Mama's funeral brought me back to Westwood Baptist for the first time in many years, and even with a new wing on the church and a bright young preacher and a reading from the "new" Bible, it seemed as ever. And it was a tremendously moving service too. In the end, when they rolled her down the aisle, my Uncle Reudi, the youngest of her children, just said, "Goodbye, Mama," but that was enough for me. I was gone. I cried like I haven't cried in years. I couldn't stop. I cried until I got outside to my cousin's car. Maybe for the first time in my life I felt something of what I imagine women experience when they are permitted to have a good cry. I felt relieved when the tears finally stopped.

We buried Big Mama in Woodlawn Cemetery, not far from my mother. It was warm and the sky was high clear blue when they buried her. Then I got a flight back to New York and was on the nine P.M. Pan Am to London.

*Friday, June 15 — London*

I slept for a couple hours when I got in this morning, and then had some eggs Benedict. I always stay at the Westbury in London; best eggs Benedict in the world. This afternoon I practiced with Clark Graebner and Buster Mottram, so I was unable to attend Nikki Pilic's hearing. We are trying to get an injunction against the ILTF in the British courts so that Nikki can play Wimbledon.

*Saturday, June 16 — London*

It feels so unlike London, so unlike Wimbledon. For one thing it is uncommonly hot here. I slept under just a sheet last night. For another, the climate for tennis players is even hotter. The press, by and large, has turned against us, and because Wimbledon counts so much as a national institution, what is essentially only a labor-management dispute has been twisted to make it appear that the players are against the English. And me anti-British? Are you kidding? I love this place. London has got to be the most civil, civilized city in the world.

Nikki, of course, is the focal point. Suddenly, he's the most famous tennis player in the world, and a symbol of working-class defiance. That is ironic since, politically, Pilic lies somewhere to the right of Marie Antoinette. He is perhaps the most conservative member of the tour, even old-fashioned and hidebound in many ways. He often wears a polo coat that must be a relic from the 1930s, and his ties are so narrow they could double for shoelaces. Nikki is also the original male chauvinist pig (Bobby Riggs is a feminist by comparison) and a chronic hypochondriac and complainer as well.

Nikki will bitch constantly about American failings when in the States, but then as soon as we reach Europe and something insignificant goes wrong — Nikki can't get his morning toast warm enough, for instance — he will be off, railing at the Europeans for their inefficiency, and praising the U.S. Nonetheless, according to Pilic, our American efficiency is sadly lacking when it comes to discipline. We are all bleeding-heart softies. Nikki's solution to the drug problem, for example, is to shoot all the drug pushers. Coincidentally, this was also his solution to the problem he perceived with long-haired hippies. In fact, he carefully outlined this plan of long-hair extinction to Jeff Borowiak as soon as Jeff joined the tour. At the time, Jeff had hair down to midback. More recently, Nikki also had a solution for plane hijackings. It is: shoot the hijackers. But, luckily for us, he has not yet advanced this proposal for taking care of protesting tennis players.

With it all, though, Nikki is really quite an engaging fellow, and everybody likes him. One of the first times after I met him, he came over in the locker room and put his hand on my head. Just held it there awhile. I didn't know what the hell was going on. Finally he said: "Iss not like steel wool. You know what I mean? Iss not like steel wool at all. Iss soft."

5

But Nikki's personality is extraneous to the issue, because we would be supporting any member of the ATP caught in this bind. What happened is this. For the last few years the Yugoslavian tennis fathers wanted nothing to do with Nikki because he was a dirty rotten capitalist professional. Suddenly they decided Nikki was pure again, though, and asked him to represent the team. He said he would — *if* the other top Yugoslav player, Zeljko Franulovic, was recovered from injuries and could also play and if Pilic had no other commitments. Well, Nikki qualified for the doubles finals of World Championship Tennis with Allan Stone, and Franulovic wasn't recovered sufficiently to play anyway. So Nikki was off the hook — on two counts, for that matter — but the Yugoslav tennis officials maintained he was committed and cried to the ILTF, which somehow convinced Wimbledon to turn down Nikki's entry. The kicker to all of this is that while the players are catching all the heat for threatening to boycott Wimbledon, it was the ILTF, not us, who made Wimbledon the battleground.

Nikki and I went out there to practice today, and ran into Herman David, the chairman of Wimbledon, while we were changing clothes. Mr. David was the leader, in 1968, in opening up Wimbledon to the pros and, in effect, in changing the whole nature of the tennis beast.

The five years since 1968 is a millennium. Already, the kids coming into tennis have no concept what it was like as shamateurism. When I first came to Wimbledon, in 1963, exactly ten years ago, my presence there was dictated by the U.S. Lawn Tennis Association. They decreed who would play and who would not. In the bargain, it was understood that you would play at the specified American events for the rest of the summer. Compensation was 50 pounds, doled out to each player by Bill Clothier of the USLTA. I remember how envious I was of Chuck McKinley and Dennis Ralston, the American one-two, who got the big money, 100 pounds each.

The British players were, like us, ordered about by their association. Most of them had to play "county weeks," sand-lot ball out in the sticks. The Australians were ruled by the sporting goods companies then, Dunlop and Slazengers, and could be a bit more businesslike in hustling for under-the-table deals. Everybody gets all bleary-eyed talking about Wimbledon and all its hallowed traditions, but a lot of people have already conveniently forgotten that in the years before 1968 Wimbledon was as important to the tennis world as a meat market as it was a championship. The players' lounge at Wimbledon was where all the promoters pitched the players for their tournaments. Of course, it was all nickel-dime deals. Roy Emerson was the number one in the amateurs then, and Emmo might have made $30,000 for his best year. Today, players you never heard of who can't get past the round of sixteen, have already made $30,000 for 1973, and it's not yet half over. Lamar Hunt with World Championship Tennis and Gladys Heldman with the Virginia Slims' tour are primarily responsible for this bonanza, and then ATP came into existence and gave the players a balance of power too.

I talked to Mr. David about the present situation. He's a pleasant man, and I think he's being used. "Why are you letting the ILTF hide behind Wimbledon's coattails?" I asked.

He ducked the question. "It's a matter of principle," Mr. David replied, and we went round and round from there, the way people always do when principle is invoked. To the side, Roger Taylor was also dressing, intently — and he never put one word into the conversation. Roger is really caught in the middle here because he is British and therefore Wimbledon is his national championship as well as the championship of the world. Finally, exasperated and getting nowhere, Nikki and Ismail El Shafei and I went out to practice. Izzy, who is from Egypt, is another board member of the ATP.

Just as we reached the courts, the manager of Wimbledon came hustling out and forbade us to step on the courts. "This is a private club and we cannot accommodate you." Understand, this is a week before Wimbledon begins, and we can't get to practice until Wednesday. Can you imagine the U.S. Open golf course turning Tom Weiskopf away just before the tournament begins?

About the only other place you can get practice on the grass is at Queen's Club, which we all hate. Queen's always holds a tournament as a warm-up before Wimbledon; it'll begin the day after tomorrow. Traditionally, it offers the least prizes and hospitality — even common courtesy — of any tournament in the world. In the old amateur days, they wouldn't even make expense payments; at least everywhere else there was an honor among thieves.

But Queen's knows that the players must come to England to work on the grass before Wimbledon, so they've got us. You've heard of captive audiences; at Queen's, we're captive performers.

Today, as is so often the case, it didn't suit the club to let us practice, so Nikki, Izzy and I were turned away from there too. Finally, with the help of a friend, we got a chance to work out on the grass courts of the New Zealand Club.

*Sunday, June 17 — London*

This afternoon, we had permission to practice at Queen's on Court #3 from 3:55 to 4:30 and then on Court #5 from 4:30 to 5. When no one came to take our place on #3 at 4:30, we just did the sensible, convenient thing and completed our workout there. When we came into the locker room, a club official berated us loudly for playing "without permission." He just patronized us, spoke down to us with contempt.

Of course, this is a country where seniority and antiquity count for a great deal — I could never imagine a young man in his forties, like Kennedy, being elected Prime Minister — and since we began to stand up against Nikki's banning, we can all sense this attitude that we are being looked upon as naughty little boys testing our wise elders. Just as all blacks have been *boys* to many whites in the U.S., so are all tennis players *kids* here.

*Monday, June 18 — London*

Nikki's hearing reconvened at 10:30 this morning, and several of us on the board spent most of the day in court or conferring with our Queen's Counsel, the British litigator who argues our case. His arguments certainly sounded good to me, and we all remain quite confident that the judge will declare for us.

*Tuesday, June 19 — London*

I went back to the Pilic hearings this morning, and I have to admit that the ILTF's Queen's Counsel was just super. He had a chipmunk face and talked all the time with his shoulders thrust back so that he always looked uncomfortable, but he had a great command of the language and was quite persuasive. I didn't leave quite so confidently as I did yesterday.

I've been attending so many bloody hearings and ATP meetings that I've had almost no chance to practice, even if I could find a court to practice on, so I was pretty relieved that I won my first match at Queen's this afternoon without too much difficulty — 7–5, 6–2 over the little Australian Ross Case.

He's a cute little guy, looks something like a koala bear, and maybe that's why the other Aussies let him get away with such murder. They call him "Snake" for his deviousness, but they tolerate what he does. It's really amazing; I've never seen the Aussies put up with such highhandedness from one of their young kids. Maybe they're mellowing. Snake is incredible. The other day a bunch of Aussies were waiting for a car. It pulls up, the driver opens the trunk, Snake throws all his luggage right in and then takes the best seat up front like he owns the car. They all laughed and called him Snake, but they took it.

On the court, Snake brings to mind the young Rosewall. Not so good, of course, but of the same size and type. Case has one of the best volleys in the world, for instance; for all the talk about Muscles Rosewall's ground strokes, he has the best volley of all. One of the great misconceptions about modern tennis is that it is the big game — serve and volley. But the truth is, it is more a big volley game than a big serve game, and the best volleyers are usually the small guys with the short arms — like Rosewall and Case — not the big tall guys with the sweeping serves.

A volley is a controlled punch shot, and it's simply easier to control a short arm than a long one. I always volley better when I have the time to choke up. Lew Hoad used to cut a half inch off the handle of all his rackets, and that's not a bad idea.

The big serve nowadays is mostly a lot of talk, but hell, there are hardly more than a half dozen in the world. I'd say the only legitimate cannonballers around now are John Newcombe, John Alexander and Paul Kronk of Australia; Vladimir Zednik of Czechoslovakia; and Stan Smith, Roscoe Tanner and myself of the U.S. I would say that the seven of us are the only guys in the world who can put in 40 to 50 percent or better of our big first serves and not have 20 percent returned. If you can do that, your serve is big. Colin Dibley of Australia may have the fastest serve of all, but he doesn't get a high enough percentage in. His toss is all wrong, way over his head. Colin double-faults too much too.

Rosewall, you know, is himself one of the worst double-faulters in the game. That always surprises people, but Muscles has only an adequate serve — despite the fact he has every other shot — and so he doesn't work at it. Fred Stolle, on the other hand, hits doubles a lot because he has such a hard second serve that he risks trying to attack with it. Dick Crealy, Brian Gottfried, El Shafei, Nailbags Carmichael and Brian Fairlie are other guys who hit double faults. My doubles partner, Roscoe Tanner, is also vulnerable to hitting doubles. (I may not hit that many doubles myself but my second serve leaves a lot to be desired.)

A serve is the most personal thing in tennis, because nobody else is involved, and if you play with a doubles partner for a long time, you get to recognize his serve like someone's voice you know well or the body of someone you love. When I'm standing at the net while Roscoe is serving, without looking, I can tell how he hit the ball from its sound and trajectory as it passes over me. If the trajectory is, say, too sloping and flat, I can turn around and say, "You're not following through," even if I haven't seen him serve a ball all day. When I played a lot with Dennis Ralston, I could hear how he was serving. I'd say something like: "The ball sounds too flat, Denny. Put a little more spin on it."

The seedings for Wimbledon were released today — I'm number four after Smith, Ilie Nastase and Rosewall — but they were pretty much rendered moot only a few hours later. Marty Riessen came up to me at Queen's around five this afternoon, just after my match with Snake, and told me that the judge had ruled that the matter of Nikki Pilic and Wimbledon was out of his jurisdiction. He didn't decide against us; he just said that he had no right to issue an injunction.

Immediately, we called an executive meeting of the ATP for tonight at the Westbury.

Present were Jack Kramer; Pierre Darmon, the tournament director of the French championships; John Barrett, who represents Slazengers and writes tennis for the *Financial Times*; and, among the players: El Shafei, Mark Cox, Nikki, Smith, Jim McManus and me, and the president, Cliff Drysdale. We talked and argued for hours, restrained, remarkably civil, but always on edge, for we realized that we were in the process of declaring war. The issue was simple: should an independent contractor have the right to decide when and where he is to play? If Nikki Pilic could be forced to play Davis Cup and denied entry to Wimbledon, then wouldn't a precedent be set where, say, I would be forced to play some rinky-dink tournament at the risk of being denied admittance to Forest Hills?

At last, sometime after one o'clock, Drysdale called for the vote. Pilic abstained, since he was the issue. So did Barrett, who felt his association with Slazengers, who makes the ball used at Wimbledon, caused him conflict of interest. Cox voted for England. The other seven of us — Drysdale, McManus, Smith, El Shafei, Kramer, Darmon and me — all voted to withdraw.

It was almost two o'clock when I got to bed, but I lay there for a long time thinking. As far as I knew, it was the first time any athletes in any sport had voted, on principle, to withdraw from their championship of the world. I could hardly believe what we had done.

# 2

## "It is not the championship of the world"

*Wednesday, June 20, 1973 — London*

First thing this morning we had a full membership meeting of the ATP at the Gloucester Hotel and presented them with the board's recommendation. They accepted it with hardly a dissent. We seem united to a man — even the poor British, whom everybody sympathizes with.

Coincidentally, my match at Queen's today was against Roger Taylor. He's really on the spot. The British tennis people found him up in Sheffield, where his father was a steelworker, and when he was seventeen, they brought Roger down to Wimbledon, and he lived there, at the YMCA, for two and a half years, learning the game. Recently he moved back to Wimbledon — in a $120,000 house in one of the most exclusive sections of the village. Now I hear that his wife is making it clear to Roger that she expects him to play.

Under the circumstances, Cox is better off. He has his vote on the record against the players' withdrawal, and he is so bright and articulate, a Cambridge man, among the very cleverest of all the players, that he will be able to fend for himself. Mark is not a leader — don't put him on the line — but he is a great staff man, and he was the guy we turned to to chair the first meeting that led to the formation of the ATP. We were in Quebec City then, the

12

April of '71, and the word had come out that the ILTF and World Championship Tennis had just made peace. The way they had done it was simply by divvying up the whole tennis world. Nobody had even consulted the players, of course; they just went ahead and acted as if tennis tournaments didn't need tennis players. That really bugged us, and so we got together, five of us: Drysdale, Newcombe, Charlie Pasarell, myself and Cox in charge, and out of that came the ATP.

In contrast to Mark, Roger is the silent, handsome type. He was quite a ladies' man before he married Frances MacLennan, who was a Scottish player and well-to-do, but he never had to work at the girls. Roger never had to *say* anything. He has to work a lot harder on the court, and maybe that is why he is a different personality out there. Roger is forever questioning line calls, which, of course, makes him aggravating to play against.

Playing Roger is not at all like going up against Nastase, however. Everybody knows that most of the time Nasty puts that crap on for effect. But nobody ever questions Roger's motives or his honesty. He really believes that the out-balls are in and that his luck is all bad. I guess if you aren't as handsome as Roger Taylor, you figure you get all the bad breaks with women. If you are as handsome as Roger Taylor, you take the women for granted and bitch about line calls.

Today, though, Roger didn't have much to complain about. It was raining, so we played inside on the boards at Queen's, and he beat me 6–3 in the third. I just didn't play that well; I never could get in charge of the match. Besides, Roger can be tenacious. He's fast and he has a weak backhand and he seldom even tries to go onto the attack, but he's a top counterpuncher. He'll lob you, dink you, run you around, and he's a very steady volleyer.

I tried to get away from things a little tonight by going over to gamble at the Playboy Club, and who should I meet at the blackjack table but Joe Frazier. He's in London to fight the British champion, Joe Bugner. Frazier had no idea who I was. Other black athletes often don't know me, although the tennis boom has made me much more visible outside the tennis world. Anyway, Frazier did recognize me when I introduced myself, so I sat down and we played

13

together for some time.  I won 50 pounds and was delighted; old Smokin' Joe took home something like 7000 pounds.

This is terribly embarrassing to admit, but money makes me happy.  I'm not as secure about money as people like Pasarell and Graebner who always had the damn stuff.  But I don't mean I just sit on it.  I'm a pretty good giver to the causes I'm really interested in, and I love to play with money to gamble — even though I'll never risk losing more than $100 or so, tops.  But maybe if you never had money you're more inclined to use it just to remind yourself that you've got some.  I really love to gamble, I'm crazy about it — and when I win, even the small sums, I feel fantastic.  It's not unlike the way I feel with my tennis.  If I win a tournament, everything is perfect.  I don't worry about a thing, and everybody is my friend.  Generally, my whole outlook on life is determined by how well (or badly) I'm playing tennis — which, I'm damn sure, is not a good way to be.

*Thursday, June 21 — London*

Most of the British newspapers are down to calling us names now.  Only Rex Bellamy of the *Times* and David Gray of the *Guardian* seem to be covering the dispute judiciously and without emotionalism.  One players' handicap is that two or three of the tennis writers are members of Wimbledon and most of the others pine desperately to be the next into the club.  This serves to keep any criticism of Wimbledon to a minimum.  Peter Wilson, a Pickwickian character, who is already in the club, has advised his readers these past few days that the players are "brash . . . ill-mannered . . . overpaid . . . spoiled."

Jack Kramer has taken the brunt of the personal abuse, and after all these years he has been canned as the BBC commentator.  His ex-colleague in the booth is a fellow named Dan Maskell, with whom I had a run-in yesterday at the bar at Queen's Club.  I'm afraid I finally ended the discussion by storming out of the room.

Today I had a televised encounter with Peter Wilson, the tennis writer.  He began most of his comments by saying, "The recognized administrators of the game say . . ."

"Well that's the whole point," I finally said. "We don't think they should be the recognized administrators. Look, you need four things to run a tennis tournament: the court, the players, a sponsor and management. What do you need with recognized administrators? What function does the ILTF perform? They don't do anything except sell indulgences so that the players, the sponsors and the managers can run a tournament."

Later, Drysdale and I hurried over to the Gloucester Hotel, where most of the players were staying, because we had to collect withdrawal signatures. Wimbledon has decreed that since we all entered as individuals, we must withdraw as individuals. Dust to dust. For us, though, some individuals are more individual than others. What has happened is that Taylor and Nastase look like they're going to deny the ATP and play anyway. Roger is a special case, the neighborhood kid, but Nastase could set a bad example. He claims his national organization is forcing him to play, and this argument might appeal to a few other players with strong national organizations. So, Cliff and I scurried around to get four key guys signed up — Jaime Fillol of Chile, the leading South American; Manuel Orantes of Spain; and Adriano Panatta and Paulo Bertolucci of Italy, who carry the most weight on the Continent. They signed, and that ended any thoughts of defection.

Finally, tonight, Cliff called a new meeting of the ATP board and even offered a new compromise proposal that would sacrifice Nikki for assurances that the players would get a voice in the game. I want nothing of it, but I like what Cliff is doing. He's the president, and he wants to be sure. I always knew he was the brightest man we had, and now I'm sure. The office has made the man even wiser.

We reconsidered at length, but at the end, after six hours, at 3:30 in the morning, the vote hardly changed. It is all over now. There is still a Wimbledon left for 1973, but it is not the championship of the world . . .

Earlier today, Owen Williams, who runs the South African Open, came over to the Westbury, and for the first time we talked about the possibility of my playing in the Open this fall in Johannesburg. I have been trying to play in South Africa since 1968, when it appeared that the United States Davis Cup team might meet the South Africans in an Interzone match.

We had choice of ground for such a match but were prepared to relinquish it in order to force South Africa's hand. The issue became moot when the West Germans beat South Africa in a match played in France, but it made me think more about the matter. Especially, I decided that it would not be best for me to first enter South Africa as a member of a national team; I wanted the privilege of going in as an individual. So I applied twice, in writing, for visas, in 1969 and again in 1970. The South Africans considered me too activist, a latent troublemaker. The fact that I had once made a flip offhand remark to the effect that an H-bomb should be dropped on Johannesburg may have caused the government to arrive at this conclusion.

South African teams have been barred from the Olympics since 1964, and such diverse sports as soccer, table tennis, weightlifting, rugby, cricket — even big-game fishing — ban the South Africans from international competition. The efforts of one British student, Peter Hain, have played a vital role in shutting the South Africans out of competition. Hain's various STOP movements — aimed at either stopping the South African teams from playing in another country or at stopping foreign teams from traveling to South Africa — were especially crucial in forcing at least token concessions. Beginning in 1970, the Nationalistic government began to permit a carefully audited handful of world-class black athletes to filter through: a New Zealand rugby team; a few track stars; Evonne Goolagong, the Australian aborigine; Bonnie Logan, an American black tennis player; Lee Elder, the professional golfer.

It was all strictly window dressing, since there was no comparable integration (if any at all) permitted at the lower levels of sport, but at least it was a start. Then, about a year or so ago, Owen quietly let on to my lawyer and good friend, Donald Dell, that if I could keep a low profile and not rattle too many sabers they might even let me in too. Since my views on S.A. were well known, I could not lose by shutting up for a while. Then I could get to see the place with my own eyes.

The key factor in the equation is Dr. Piet Koornhof, the Minister of Mines, Immigration, Sports and Recreation — and primarily

16

Sports; the rest of his crowded portfolio tends to take care of itself. Koornhof is widely considered to be the most intelligent member of the Cabinet and the comer in the National Party, heir apparent to Prime Minister Johannes Vorster. From everything I've learned about South Africa, I really believe that sports is its Achilles' heel, and if that sounds like an exaggerated claim on behalf of sports, well, just consider this: what other government at any time in history anywhere in the world has felt obliged to place the most promising member of the government in charge of its athletic program? Usually that area is a political backwater.

And it was Koornhof who opened the doors. "The more enlightened Nationalists believe that the white Afrikaners, the party's main constituency, are ready to accept Koornhof's policy," Owen explained. "If so, it becomes petty and foolish to let in a lot of other athletes and continue a vendetta against Arthur Ashe. But understand how tricky this is. Koornhof has embarked on a very ambitious new policy — it's real brinkmanship. It would have been easy for him to have sustained his predecessor's policy. The Nationalists have nothing much to gain except perhaps a few liberal votes that would otherwise go Progressive — and much more to lose. This is a significant part of an experiment to see how far the people of this country are prepared to go down a new road."

Owen is himself, like Cliff Drysdale, a Progressive. Amongst the three major South African parties, it is a distant third — the only one of the three that professes racial equality. For espousing this mad philosophy, the electorate has responded by awarding the Progressives a single seat in Parliament. Owen was a world-class amateur player twenty years ago, just off the top ten, a broad, friendly man who, as a promoter, has made the South African Open into one of the half-dozen top tournaments of the world — and one of the most successful too. He is a man as decent as he is capable, and I believe that he wants the same things for the people of South Africa that I do.

I feel empathy for Owen too. As a South African white, he suffers that glib, easy stereotyping that I, as a black in the U.S., must also always endure. Owen came to New York a few years ago to run the U.S. Open, and did such a magnificent job at Forest Hills that it is an open secret that he could have kept the job if only he

17

had agreed to make one little concession: give up his citizenship. He was guilty by association. People were uncomfortable that an evil, racist South African should be running America's top tennis tournament — and never mind that he wasn't in fact evil or racist.

I told Owen that I would consider playing in South Africa only if four conditions could be met: first, that I would come and go as I pleased, anywhere in the country. Second, that the stands where the Open was held, at Ellis Park, in Johannesburg, would be "totally integrated," with no special sections for racial groups. Third, that a conscientious effort would be made to try and arrange a meeting for me with Prime Minister Vorster. And fourth, that I would be accepted for what I happen to be — a black man. I would not permit the issue to be avoided by supplying me with any temporary "honorary white" status.

"I couldn't stomach that, Owen," I said. He nodded, wrote down the four stipulations, and replied that he didn't see why there would be any difficulty in granting them. This surprised me. Then he told me not to drop any more H-bombs on Johannesburg — and added, in effect, don't call us, we'll call you. Blacks are used to hearing that refrain. The call never comes. So it is my guess that nothing more will ever come of it.


*Monday, June 25 — London / New York*

I've been so harried by everything that I upgraded my ticket and treated myself to first class back to the States. And boy, it sure didn't take long to know that I was back in New York. The taxicab meter read $1.00 before I got out of the Pan Am terminal. Understand, I don't mean the airport, I mean the terminal . . .


*Monday, July 2 — New York / Toronto*

I couldn't get up here to see Kathy as quickly as I wanted to because I had a press conference scheduled this morning at the Doral Hotel on Park Avenue to talk about the ATP, and there was no way I could put that off. It went very well too. Dave Anderson of the *Times* came, and so did the AP and the UPI. I think they all understand more clearly now why we acted as we did at Wimble-

18

don. Athletes are notoriously poor at attracting public support to their side in these disputes with management, with the establishment, because the other side already has a PR apparatus cranked up. The baseball players got raked over the coals when they struck last year, and the football players also took it on the chin when they went out in 1970. One of the things we have to do is hire a full-time PR man for the ATP.

As soon as the press conference was finished, I got the next flight out to Toronto. I had been getting more and more anxious to be with Kathy again, and she was getting a little panicky too. I could tell that over the phone. I think we discovered from this absence how much we really do care for each other.

# 3

## Gladiators & Troubadours

*Tuesday, July 3, 1973 — Toronto / New York*

The life we lead in tennis is most unlike that in any other sport. Tennis knows no season now, and it is spectacularly international. I don't really live anywhere. Even some of the players who are married, and with young children, are on the road so much that it is merely a convention for them to call someplace *home*. We come from somewhere, but we have no real home.

I've spent a year of my life in Australia, almost as much time in England and probably several months in airplanes. There has never been anything in sports like tennis today. I am not boasting that we are special, although we may be; but we are surely unique. The players are the modern hybrid of gladiators and troubadours. We entertain by combating each other all over the world. You try to beat a man's brains out on the court, take money out of his pocket, and then you return to the locker room with him, take a shower next to him, eat with him, drink with him, practice with him, chase women with him, maybe even play doubles with him, and two weeks or two months later, you draw him again, in Barcelona or Manila or Chicago, and all of a sudden you look across the net and it occurs to you that this is the same sonuvabitch who beat you in Vancouver the last time, and you give him no quarter, and ignore him when you pass next to each other between odd games,

20

and then you shake his hand when you beat him or he beats you, and you have a beer together and share a cab back to the hotel.

To adjust to playing big-time tennis now, you must have some capacity for suspending time and place. You pretend that you are standing still, while it is the rest of the world that is moving. That's not so hard to do. After all, the same people I left in London will be in Boston when I get on to my next tournament. And we will play tennis and do the same things. The courts will be different, like the restaurants and the money and the spectators and the other incidentals, but the experience will be the same. It's like sitting in a room and changing TV channels.

Playing the tour is much different from being on a team. You must depend more on yourself, of course; and you must depend on the people you beat for friendship. This makes us a bit odd. Sociologists would have a field day with the tennis tour . . . if we would let them get close enough. We are, however, a closed, proud elite, and we draw ourselves up whenever strangers seem to intrude. If four tennis players are having a conversation and they are joined by an outside acquaintance, the players will be likely to change the subject even if the topic is rather innocuous.

At Wimbledon, there is what is called the Players' Tea Room. If you are not a player, but some peripheral member of the tennis establishment — a promoter or a writer or a coach or a pretty girl or even just some hanger-on, a friend of a friend — it is easy to get into the Players' Tea Room. Either you give the old guard at the bottom of the stairs a pound or two the first day or you can climb over a little fence from a press balcony. But I have had friends — even former players — tell me that they feel uncomfortable in the Tea Room. None of the players is rude to the visitors, no one even says anything, but the outsiders tell me that they can sense being unwanted. There is a special irony for me in hearing that reaction, because it sounds exactly the way I often feel in gatherings where I am the only black.

Actually, the business of my belonging so strongly to the tour, of flaunting its territorial imperative, is really very foreign to the rest of me. I'm a loner by nature, and able to get along quite happily by myself. That's probably why I travel so well. I don't have to depend upon special tourist attractions and scenic overlooks; I can be

21

quite happy anywhere with my books and my cassettes. I still want to do a lot more traveling in my life before I do what everybody always calls *settling down.*

I think of the Doral Country Club of Miami now as home more than anyplace else, but because of business I'm also forced to spend a lot of time in New York. I stay in an apartment on the East Side. But New York is mostly just a clearing-house for me, convenient to airports and the businesses I'm involved with. I almost feel like I'm on holiday when I'm in New York, because I seldom play any tennis there but mostly just go to nightclubs and good restaurants and the theater, just like all the people who really do come to New York on their vacation.

Anyway, the reason I rushed back to New York today is because I have a date to play golf with Manny Parker. I stay in apartment A–1706. Manny and Ruth live in A–1606, right below. They are a couple of terrific people who don't have any children and have made me their surrogate son. We met because one night Ruth suddenly heard somebody making too much noise on her ceiling — which was me walking around A–1706 in my clogs. She inquired and found out who the noisy intruder was, sought me out down in the basement in the communal laundry room and told me to get some quieter shoes.

The Parkers always know I'm in New York, because they can hear me, so Ruth immediately gets on the building intercom and demands that I come down for a drink. It sounds like a pilot for a situation comedy: young black bachelor and his Jewish foster parents . . .

### *Wednesday, July 4 — New York*

No symbolism in the date — just a coincidence. I'm not much of a holiday guy anyway. Most blacks aren't. But I suppose that there is at least a benign significance in the fact that Independence Day was when I sat down and dictated letters to several friends, black and white, asking them for their views on any possible trip of mine to South Africa. I sincerely want to go, if only from a selfish point of view, out of curiosity, but I also am deeply concerned with how other blacks might take such a trip. So I wrote Julian Bond, and Congressman Andy Young; Congresswoman Barbara Jordan; Nikki Giovanni, the black poetess; Vernon Jordan, the head of the Urban League; Sargent Shriver; J. D. Morgan, the athletic director at UCLA, who had been my tennis coach; Bob Kelleher, the former head of the United States Law Tennis Association, who is now a federal judge; and Joe Cullman, the chairman of the board at Philip Morris.

There are two basic avenues used to approach the South African question. One is more a roadblock than an avenue, a militant, all-or-nothing policy, which maintains that nobody should have anything to do with the dreadful place: boycott it, freeze it out, ignore it and wait for its millennium from a respectable distance. The United States wasted a generation on that philosophy toward China; it still operates its Cuban policy that way. The other avenue is a gradualist one — result-oriented. It assumes that progress can only come in small chunks, that you deal for your advances as you can. Surely, it is less emotionally satisfying this way, but, I'm certain, more realistic and more successful. It was the way Dr. King gained his advances — although it was hardly a new concept with him. Frederick Douglass wrote in the nineteenth century: "Power concedes nothing without a struggle — never has, never will."

So you must be prepared only to chip away at power and injustice. And let's face it: sometimes you can't stand on your pride. I am terribly embarrassed now by some of the goings-on taking place in what is supposed to be free Africa. Amin's policies in Uganda seem no less despicable than South Africa's. The warfare among tribes in Burundi (and Nigeria before) is as murderous as anything whites have done to blacks anywhere in the world. When I was in the Ivory Coast last year I perceived a repression of freedom of expression that, surely, is only slightly exceeded in South Africa. None of this excuses things there, but all of it is important to keep in mind for the sake of perspective. The South Africans have not the only racist government in the world. I know that. Also, like it or not, it is all part of the general worldwide phenomenon of the lighter hues vs. the darker ones — and right now the lighter ones are winning.

I don't know whether I'm getting more pragmatic or merely jaded. I used to believe in Toynbee, in an eventual complete amalgamation of the races, but now I'm sure there will always be groups. It just seems to be the natural order for people to stay together with members of their own cultural stock. Race doesn't have to be the distinguishing factor either. On the tour, it is language which most determines how we separate ourselves. Anyway, if it is a bad thing to be prejudiced, it is a normal thing to express a preference. So now, after fifteen years of world travel, I must say that I am not for a nonracial approach, only for a multiracial one. Nonracial seems to me to be a concept against the natural laws of evolution.

*Sunday, July 8 — New York / San Juan / Palmas del Mar /*
*San Juan / New York*

I went down to Puerto Rico to play an exhibition at a new resort I'm involved with. I was booked on the 10:00 Eastern flight Saturday night, but there were mechanical problems, and they kept setting the departure time back every few minutes. Finally, at 10:50, they stopped setting the departure time back. The reason they stopped setting the departure time back was because they canceled the whole flight.

Also, they only canceled in Spanish, so that just those who habla Espanol could then hustle over to Gate 16 and take up all the good remaining seats on the 11:30 flight. As an afterthought, they crammed me and the other poor English-speakers into the middle seats, and by 1:00 the 11:30 lifted off with the 10:00 passengers. I got to sleep in the Sheraton in San Juan around five, or as you are supposed to say: it was *only* 4:00 N.Y. time.

Palmas del Mar is about a forty-five minute drive from San Juan. I always think of it first as Charlie Pasarell's place, since he's the home boy. Naturally, he was my opponent in the exhibition. I was the bad guy — and I beat him 9–8, although that is no big deal since he has been down here helping put Palmas all together and is somewhat out of shape.

Charlie has never been the most mobile guy in the world to start with. It takes him about three weeks just to warm up for a practice match. A funny incident was at UCLA with Herbie Flam, who

24

had been ranked as high as second in the country (in 1950). Since he'd gone to UCLA he'd come over sometimes and practice with us. He had a great touch, was very gifted with the racket. Herbie also had a very clever mind — he was one of the contestants on "The $64,000 Question" — although it could go off in all directions at once. Herbie would arrive at the UCLA courts wearing an old pair of Bermuda shorts and a faded T-shirt, with a floppy pair of Pete Maravich socks long before Pete Maravich thought of them, and dragging an old racket without a cover on it. He had a high nasal pitch, and he'd get out on the court, hit one ball, one ball, and say, "Okay, serve 'em up." And here he is with Charlie, who needs a lifetime to get prepared to play.

So this one day, Herbie shows up, dressed in his usual outfit, and he hits one back to Charlie, and as always, he says, "Okay, serve 'em up," and just as Charlie tosses the first ball, Herbie calls over, "Wait a minute. I've got to put change in the parking meter." And he ran off the court and neither Charlie or I ever saw him again for about another five years. He was like the Judge Crater of tennis.

Anyway, Charlie really is a picture player. If he could have been just a bit quicker, I'm sure he could have been the best player in the world, because he does have the best strokes of anyone I've ever seen. If I had to teach someone to play tennis, the first thing I would do is, I would say, go watch Charlie Pasarell play and try to do what he does.

I first met Charlie when we played the fifteen-and-unders at the Orange Bowl in Miami. I'm eight months older than he is, so that would have been 1956 or '57. He beat me that day 2–6, 6–2, 6–2, but we saw each other all during the juniors and beat each other back and forth. He impressed me. He came from a lot of money, he was cultured and sure. And I was an insecure southern black kid out on my own. There were no blacks and no friends to speak of. And Charlie, I found out, was just always there. I don't know whether he did it out of sympathy, but when I did seek out his friendship, he never refused it.

It was at UCLA, where we played together and roomed together off campus for a year and a half, that we really learned to understand each other. We alternated the number one spot on the team

25

there, just as we did for the country in 1967 and '68. Pasarell might have won that top ranking ahead of me in '67 because he beat me head-to-head in the finals of the National Indoors. To show you how close Charlie and I are, we watched that match together afterward over a delayed television broadcast, and sat there, each of us trying to point out to the other where we had taken advantage and where he could improve.

Yet Charlie's a stubborn sonuvabitch. We used to argue religion constantly. He always give me the Catholic SOP, as if a never-ending barrage of Perpeturo Succuro will finally save me in the end. I happen to really like Charlie's wife too. When he and Shireen got married a couple of years ago, I made them a present of a hotel room on his wedding night. Charlie means a lot to me. He is as nice a guy and as loyal a friend as a man can know.

In 1968, when we won the Davis Cup back from Australia in Adelaide, I cost the U.S. a clean sweep by losing the last match to Bill Bowrey. Even though we had already clinched the Cup, the Aussies were thrilled to escape a whitewash, and the crowd stood up and cheered Bowrey all the way off the court, while I left in despair. I felt like I'd let everybody down.

Charlie was standing by the players' gate, and when I raised my head up, I saw that tears were rolling down his cheeks. "It's okay," he said, "you're still the greatest." Then he put his arm around me, and I couldn't stop the tears either.

Because our set at Palmas ran on, they had to bring in the company plane to get me back to the airport at San Juan so I could get the 6:30 back to New York. I had originally intended to go to Miami, where the weather is nice and hot, and where I could practice at the Doral with Eddie Dibbs, but at the last minute I found out I had to return to New York. The reason was that the pictures we shot in May at Las Vegas for a booklet that goes with a cassette instructional I am doing turned out badly and we have to reshoot the whole act.

*Monday, July 9 — New York / Miami*

They picked me up at my apartment at 9:15 to go out to Forest Hills to shoot the photographs, which everybody said looked fine, which is approximately what they had also said at Vegas in May.

Then I went directly to JFK, so that I could get to Miami and hit with Dibbs, but the plane got in at 5:30, and poor Eddie had been just sitting there all the time. By then, it was too late to practice anyway, and I was too tired to go out so I went over to Rod Mandelstam's. He's South African, Jewish and used to be the teaching pro here at Doral. Strangely enough, some of my best friends are South Africans. Rod, his wife, Carol, and I just sat around and got pleasantly stoned.

*Tuesday, July 10 — Miami*

It's my thirtieth birthday today. I was born in Richmond on July 10, 1943, the day General Patton's troops landed in Sicily. Actually, I don't feel too excited today; I don't get much worked up for birthdays.

It rained today too, so I called the office in Washington at Donald Dell's law firm and found out if they had any correspondence I had to catch up on. Unfortunately, they're predicting a 70 percent chance of rain tomorrow, so there's no sense staying around. The only reason I came down was to practice.

I really like Miami though. I've lived in a lot of places — Richmond, St. Louis, Los Angeles, New York — but I'm thinking about buying some property down here. I don't own any land. I'm a gypsy, downright un-American, since I don't even own a car.

Miami has a good smell to it. Torben Ulrich, our tour guru, the bearded tennis-playing philosopher from Denmark, pointed out to me once that we all place too much emphasis on the visual, that we should not reach judgments about a place simply from what we obtain from our sight. And he's right. Cities do smell quite different from one another. And they sound different too. Miami is especially nice because its so tourist-conscious that they don't permit any industry to speak of, so there's almost no smog. And it seems to me there's still space to move around in here. Los Angeles is just becoming a warm-weather New York, plus it's spread out to even more disadvantage.

I don't miss L.A. or New York. I don't need that kind of go-go stuff. I've never been the life of the party. I'm not Tom Okker. I

27

just don't crave the fast life that much anymore. Maybe I sensed that I was burning myself out.

### Wednesday, July 11 — Miami / New York / Toronto

This is ridiculous. I came all the way up from Miami to practice, and I wasn't here for a half-hour before it started pouring. It's probably the 30 percent blue skies in Miami.

I have all my damn luggage I'm dragging around because I'm supposed to have been gone for a month, and it took a couple hours getting back to my apartment because some guy was holding up traffic, threatening to jump off the 59th Street bridge, and when I finally got in and called up Kathy, she wanted me to come up, so I went back to the airport and flew to Toronto. That's where I am now.

### Thursday, July 12 — Toronto / New York / Cincinnati

I flew back to New York this morning and went directly to the West Side Tennis Club, where at last I got a practice in. Between the weather, the airplanes business and Kathy, I have just flown 6000 miles in the last four days trying to get a chance to practice.

This was my last day in New York for some time, and it was so lovely that I set off on a walk down Fifth Avenue. When I passed Berlitz I got this uncontrollable urge to go in. It embarrasses me terribly that I can only speak English. I consider that the great failing of my life. I go bananas when I'm with somebody like Ion Tiriac, the big Rumanian, or Helga Schulte Hosl, the pretty German — both of whom can speak six languages fluently, switching back and forth. Almost none of the English-speaking players ever even make an effort to get along in another language. Julie Heldman is our best linguist, and Nailbags Carmichael, who moved from Australia to Paris, is another. The rest of the English-speaking players just barrel on in English and make everybody adjust to them, which, of course, they invariably do.

A lot of the foreign players join the tour without any real comprehension of English, and they pretty much are forced to learn it if they want to get along outside their own language clique. Also,

28

since so much of the tour is in the U.S. now, it is a handicap if a player doesn't pick it up. They learn by watching cartoons on TV or reading comic books. The language there is obvious and relates easily to the pictures. It really shames me that there are several players who knew virtually no English at all when I first met them, but who are now at ease with it: Orantes, François Jauffret of France, Alex Metreveli of Russia, Patricio Cornejo of Chile. Hell, Cornejo is getting to be a downright comedian in English, and he didn't know how to ask for the bathroom when I first met him.

So anyway, bugged by all of this, I stormed into Berlitz and signed up for a course which will guarantee me a working knowledge of 2500 words in French. I took three years of French in high school, and I do make an effort to speak it every time I'm in the country, and I honestly believe I'm very close to the barrier. I think if I *had* to talk it, I could break through. Since the whole thing will cost me $1019, now I have a great incentive.

The Catalina representative met me at the Cincinnati airport at quarter of eleven. I have to make some store appearances out here in Ohio for them in the next few days. We're in the process of negotiating a new contract with Catalina for the Arthur Ashe clothes line that will expand into international sales.

*Sunday, July 15 — Washington / New York / Boston*

I caught this late flight from Columbus to Washington last night and was figuring spending the night there, but when I was at the baggage counter I heard them announcing an odd flight to New York — in from San Juan — so I made that, and I was so happy to be back to the apartment that I took a taxi and gave four stewardesses a ride into town with me.

This afternoon, Kathy came in from Toronto and met me at La Guardia and we flew up here for the U.S. Pro Championships. I got in a little practice tonight too, which I needed. I haven't played a whole lot of tennis lately, have I? I just looked at my schedule, and the last eleven days I've made twelve flights and I've only spent one full day in the same place. Here's what I've done: New York — Amherst — New York — San Juan — Palmas del Mar — San Juan — New York — Miami — New York — Toronto — New

29

York — Cincinnati — Dayton — Columbus — Washington — Newark — New York — Boston.

It'll be nice just to stay in one place for a few days and try to make a living playing tennis.

# 4

## Two Finals

*Monday, July 16, 1973 — Boston*

It's been well over a month since I played a tournament. I can't remember being away from competition so long in the summertime since I started playing. But it was a bad day for us. Bob Lutz, who won this tournament last year, was playing downtown in an exhibition for publicity, and he was going back for a lob and wrenched his right knee. It just collapsed on him, and he was in great pain. They took him to Massachusetts General.

Bob is stocky, very well-built — so he probably puts more pressure on his knee than most players. Billie Jean King, who is built something like Lutzie — a comparison bound to infuriate (a) Billie Jean and (b) Lutz — had a knee operation once too, and she'll tell you how one bad knee can lead to screwing up the other. When Bob comes back next year, he'll have a tendency to protect his right knee by favoring it, and in that process, he may put too much strain on the left knee.

*Tuesday, July 17 — Boston*

I went down to Mass General and saw Bob. He has the operation tomorrow, but he was in good spirits today because everybody was coming down and making a fuss over him. Well, he is one of the

31

most popular guys on the tour. Big party man. He and Stan Smith have played doubles together going back to when they were kids, but they were always the odd couple. Even at the junior tournaments, Stan would stay back at the dormitory and jump rope, and Lutz would round up a few guys and go out and drink beer.

Bob has been married a few months now. Sharon is really a sweet little thing, and I'll be damned if I know how she manages to live with him. He snores something fierce. We were on a Pacific tour during the Vietnam war, playing matches and visiting soldiers, and in Bangkok we stayed in the American ambassador's house. Lutz and Bud Collins, the writer and TV commentator, were roommates, but Lutz made so much noise that Collins had to go downstairs and sleep on a sofa right in the ambassador's living room. Another night there in Bangkok, we had to wake up the ambassador himself to get back in his house. You see, they have these so-called massage parlors in Bangkok — beautiful girls, with numbers on their backs, for fast, easy ordering. Just like Burger Chef. In Saigon, that same trip, we were at the Cercle Sportif one night when Lutz declared that he was horny again, so an aide to the ambassador drove us over to this house that was reserved, more or less, for the diplomatic community. It was, as a matter of fact, just across the alley from the U.S. ambassador's residence. You should have seen the girls — unbelievably good-looking. Lutz and Jimmy McManus and I went in. Stan passed — Mr. Clean, you know. Lutzie and I also whiled away some hours in the red-light district in Peitow, Formosa. And, just for the record, we have spent some time together in places other than whorehouses.

In the tournament today, I beat Harold Solomon 7–6, 3–6, 6–4. It was a tough match, but I was very much pleased by it. Solly is a tiny little retriever, strictly a clay-court guy, and the stuff we're playing on here is a very slow Uni-Turf, which really bites the ball and throws your timing off. You don't outplay a guy like Solomon on a court like this; you play with him and outlast him.

Obviously, my power game works better on a fast surface, but if you can play the fast courts, you should be able to accommodate to the slow ones a helluva lot easier than the other way around. Besides, I grew up on slow concrete, a base-line player; I was born and bred in that briar patch. If I'm in the top half dozen or so fast-court players in the world, I'm still in the top twenty on clay, which isn't bad.

My serve travels, obviously, at the same air speed regardless of the surface, but it is not as hard to handle off the clay or the artificial Uni-Turf as it is off concrete or grass. I have a fast serve — a cannonball — but I don't have what is known as a heavy ball. My ball has the speed, but that can be a double-edged sword because if the receiver can time a fast serve, he can hit it right back at me as fast as I hit it at him. It's like in baseball where, invariably, the best fast-ball pitchers are the ones who give up the most home runs. Dibley, Smith, Graebner, Zednik and Tanner probably have the purest fast serves in the world.

But if you ask me who has the best serve in the world, I would say Newcombe, and John really hasn't got a fast serve. He hits a *heavy* serve, which mixes spin with velocity. Neale Fraser had a great heavy serve when I first came up; Pasarell and Tony Roche are a couple of others who hit tough heavy balls. If you are returning a heavy serve, you need more than timing to get it back; you need strength too. A good heavy serve from somebody like Newcombe can turn the racket in your hand.

When I'm serving, I like to get 70 percent of my first balls in. As a rule of thumb, if I miss just two straight first serves, I'll ease up on the next point and concentrate on accuracy. This is especially the case against an outstanding return of service — somebody like Rosewall, who can get almost any ball back. Newcombe has a good return too, although he is seldom credited with it. Ray Moore of South Africa always returns service well, and Dennis Ralston does too. Snake Case has the best return among the up-and-coming kids I've seen, but the guys who have played Jimmy Connors too tell me he's better at it.

For a second serve, I can hit either a twist or a spin. In many ways, because of the action of your body, these softer serves are more difficult to hit than a blazing speed ball. I've never met a player who hits a twist as his primary ball who doesn't end up with back trouble. Tom Gorman is the classic case of that now, and Roger Taylor also has periodic back problems. Roscoe is still only twenty-two, but I've warned him that someday his back is bound to act up. The trouble with hitting a twist is that you have to arch your back so unnaturally to pull it off.

A twist will kick high, in the direction of the spin. Roscoe has the big left-hand motion which can bounce the serve way up, and sometimes when I'm playing doubles with him, I'll just tell him to stop being fancy and serve every ball to the receiver's backhand. For most people, there isn't a harder shot to hit than a high backhand; it's almost impossible to attack off it.

For myself, as a general rule (against right-handers), I'll use my twist to serve into the ad court, the left-hand court, to the backhand. On the other side, to the deuce court, I'm more liable to use my spin. Essentially, a spin is the reverse of a twist. But it isn't as active a shot, and it will skid on a fast surface rather than kick. As a consequence, since it's not coming in high, it's not as offensive a shot; an imperfect spin serve will skid a bit too high, right into a guy's forehand groove.

A lot of the most knowledgeable tennis experts don't understand the effect of a spin. You see, it is the one serve you want to hit shallow. I want to hit a spin serve that will land at least three or four feet in front of the service line. I hit it with a roundhouse trajectory that will skid the ball to the side of the court. The receiver has to come up to play the ball, sure, but he also has to reach way out into the doubles alley or even beyond to make the play, and that opens the whole court up for my return. A long spin serve will describe a gentle parabola that's a setup to return.

Whatever the type of serve, you've got to remember that it's part of a package. The weakest part of my serve is my forehand volley. Anybody returning my serve is always thinking, well, no matter how hard Ashe hits this thing at me, if I can just get it back to his forehand, he may hit it into the net. Conversely, a large reason why I say that Newcombe has the best first serve in the game is because John always plays such a great first volley.

To reach the top rank in the world, you cannot just be very good and very consistent. You must have at least one outstanding stroke. I have two very reliable shots — my serve and my backhand. Then, to reach the absolute top you also cannot have any significant failing. I have one: my forehand volley. I can work

34

with it, modify my stroke and my grip, but I'm too old to ever really change it.

Of course, I get a lot of practice with it because everybody hits to it.

*Wednesday, July 18 — Boston*

Kathy and I came by to see Bob after his operation. He was still groggy, but the doctor was there and had already assured him that things had gone well, and that he could be playing in another six months or so.

I mentioned to Bob that it was ironic, in a way, to see him there all laid up and hurting because I think that the last time I was in a hospital was when we toured Vietnam together. We paid a lot of visits to the guys who had been wounded. That wasn't an easy thing to do either. A lot of the soldiers didn't have a clue as to who any tennis player was.

But the army somehow figured that we were important. When we played some matches in Saigon, we got a briefing from General Abrams himself, and they gave us a real VIP tour. We went up in a helicopter for a little excursion, and though it is against all the rules, the pilot let Stan take the controls for a while. We were there, but we weren't part of the reality. We were even introduced to Vice President Ky, since he plays tennis and came by to see us. I chatted with him for a while and gave him a couple of rackets.

A couple of years later I was in Paris and I saw him window-shopping outside a store on the Champs-Elysées, so I walked up to him and said, "Hey, remember me?" and he did, and we had a pleasant little conversation there. It can all be so disjointed. Here I was standing on the Champs-Elysées talking about tennis or the weather or fashions or some damn thing with Nguyen Cao Ky, while halfway around the world, thousands of Americans, like my brother Johnny, who was shot twice over there, were fighting a war.

Sometimes, in the life I lead, it is very hard to get an honest perspective. Perhaps the only real difference in my life is that while most people only have wars and celebrities and wild animals

35

come into their homes on television, I meet celebrities and see wars and wild animals in person. But how much difference is there really in that? I wonder.

*Thursday, July 19 — Boston*

After I did my laundry in the hotel machines, I had a little talk with Jimmy Connors. He's a strange kid, although I don't really know him because he doesn't play the major circuit. He is not at all popular with most of the players. They think he goes a little heavy on the gamesmanship out on the court — the hand-blowing and the ball-bouncing (before he serves) is just a little too studied. But the major resentment derives from the fact that he is the only major American player — and very nearly the only major noncommunist player in the whole world — who won't join the ATP. Most of us who do belong don't want professional tennis to become a closed shop, but still, it is galling when somebody like Connors comes along and benefits without doing his part.

The last time I saw him, he agreed that he would listen to my side, and he certainly heard me out today, but I'm afraid that he was merely going through the motions. He said he would consider what I said to him and get back to me, but I doubt that he will. He is mesmerized by his concept of "independence," and I could not convince him that membership in the ATP did not compromise his freedom. On the contrary, if anything, a strong union makes for more options, more freedom.

"If we're not strong, the promoters will give us no choices," I said.

"I want to go my own way," he said.

"Yeah, Jimmy, so does Alex Metreveli. But in Russia, he doesn't have that luxury of choice."

Connors just shrugged at me.

Nevertheless, insofar as tennis is concerned, I must admit that he has been handled very well. He has a manager — some would say a Svengali — named Bill Riordan, who comes from the little town of Salisbury on the Eastern Shore of Maryland. Riordan is a helluva promoter. He took the National Indoors out of New York a decade ago and made it the biggest thing on the Eastern Shore. I'll never forget one of those early years in Salisbury when I did better than expected, and Bill came up to me and pulled out a big wad of bills and peeled off two hundreds and gave them to me. I just didn't get that kind of payoff then; nobody did.

Riordan still runs the Indoors, and now he's put together his own circuit that is a showcase for Connors. What Bill has done is, he has picked Jimmy's spots for him, so that the kid has developed a winning syndrome. He is like an up-and-coming boxer who only gets thrown a carefully selected diet of palookas and washed-outs. Everything has been decided only with consideration to Connors' career. He doesn't play Davis Cup for the country; he doesn't play World Championship Tennis. Every now and then, fresh and primed, Riordan lets him dip into the big time: Wimbledon last month, the U.S. Pro here. He had to cross our picket lines (figuratively) to play at Wimbledon, but he got to the quarters, and he's already in the quarters here too. He beat Stan in the first round. He's in the other half of the draw from me, though, so I won't play him unless we both win through to the finals. I never have played Connors yet.

I got to the quarters myself tonight by beating Charlie three and four. It wasn't much of a match because it started at seven, just when the sun was going down. It was like the first game of a twi-night double-header, when the hitters are just guessing at what the pitcher is throwing. I just played the sun better than Charlie; neither of us played the ball very well.


*Friday, July 20 — Boston*

I beat Roscoe tonight 4–6, 6–4, 7–5. It was really a good match — it must have been a *great* match to watch — and I had to survive three match points to win it. It must be driving Roscoe crazy because he has never beaten me. One time tonight he had me 15–40 for the match in the third set, and I still got through on my serve. I served very well whenever I was down, which is always especially satisfying. Each match point came when I was serving, and two of the three times he was in the right-hand court, and a left-hander in the right-hand deuce court is usually big trouble for me. That's where Laver kills me all the time, passing me with the backhand down the line

I'm always relieved to get past any lefty. If nothing else, they have an edge on you simply because they're different. And most all of them hit with sidespin, which makes the ball take unusual bounces. Maybe it comes from the way left-handers are taught to write, way out and around.

Pilic and El Shafei probably have the most sidespin of any of them, and Nikki also has a fairly big serve. Among all the lefties, though, Roscoe has the hardest service. Another thing about left-handers is that they're always in demand. If you're scheduled to play one you've got to scout around and find another one to spar with. I often work with Izzy, and sometimes with Nikki, and of course often with Roscoe.

I do have one distinct advantage against the left-handers. Their spin serves go to a right-hander's backhand, and since most players are weaker off that wing, any player gets into a pattern of serving to an expected weakness. But I've got a better backhand than forehand, though, so often players keep going unconsciously to my strength because they are in the habit of working to that side. When I get into the groove, hitting backhand returns of serve off a left-hander's spin, I can go all day because the return that way is the most natural backhand shot. It carries perfectly cross-court and is my favorite shot.

That didn't do me any good tonight because Roscoe's bread and butter is the big twist, not the spin. But anyway, now I've beaten my oldest friend in tennis and my doubles partner on successive days. It's a lot different than on the other tours too, say golf or bowling, where you compete against a score and not a man. It's also different than what it used to be in tennis. In the old amateur days, there was no real money on the line, and you had fewer tough matches; certainly, you weren't playing the same guys you traveled with week after week. And the old pro tour was just a barnstorming circus, with the money based on guarantees. You lose in New Haven, so what — get him in Hartford tomorrow. Nowadays, you lose anywhere, you're done for the week, and you may have to nurse revenge for months before you can get a rematch.

If anything, I think you want to beat a close friend like Charlie or

Roscoe, in my case, more than a stranger.  Perhaps it is just human nature.  You see, if I lose to Kodes, I don't like it, but because I'm not a friend of his I never see him.  If I ever lose to Roscoe I'll be reminded of it all the time because every time I'm out with Roscoe it will occur to me again.

It's probably even worse on the wives and the girl friends when their men play.  Like Kathy and Nancy Tanner sat together and watched Roscoe and me play.  At least we can take it out on each other out there on the court; the girls have to sit there and be sweet to one another.  Or anyway, fake it very well.

But we all have to get on with each other.  Cliff Richey used to go through this business of not talking to his opponent before a match in order to get himself psyched up.  I understand Pancho Gonzales was the same way when he was younger.  But Cliff doesn't carry on that way so much anymore.  If we all acted like that, hell, the whole thing would come apart at the seams.  I read stories about football, how they post clippings up on the wall and try consciously to build up a hatred for the opponents — God, that sounds very nearly barbaric to me.

*Saturday, July 21 — Boston*

Rainy day: I practiced with Mike Estep, had a run-of-the-mill fight with Kathy, visited Lutz and saw my foot doctor, Dr. Sidney Brass.  He shaved some corns and calluses off my feet.  He also wants to get an impression of my left foot so that he can handmake a foot pad that I can insert into any shoe.  My left heel has a growth on the back which hurts like hell for about ten minutes before and after a match.  That's why I limp sometimes.

Tonight I had dinner with some cousins on my mother's side who live in Roxbury.  I just about lead the world in cousins, since both my mother and father came from large families.  My father's mother is still alive and healthy down in South Hill, Virginia, in her eighties, and she has 109 grandchildren and great-grandchildren, most of whom seem to have assumed residence somewhere in America wherever I am playing tournaments.  Black families are supposed to be disintegrating, and all American families are supposed to be flying apart, but the social scientists have forgotten to

39

notify the Ashes and Cunninghams that they're going about it all wrong.

*Sunday, July 22 — Boston*

The rain was gone today, and it was just gorgeous. And guess what? Out of the blue a fan I've never met sent me a rose — a beautiful, long-stemmed red rose. Somebody named Emily Eisenberg. Isn't that a damned nice gesture?

I beat Graebner four and four to get to the finals. He has always seemed to be psyched by me. I don't know why, but he has — and tonight was no exception.

In the other half of the draw, Connors beat Dickie Stockton, so now I finally get to play him tomorrow.

*Monday, July 23 — Boston*

Although I've never played Connors, I've had a chance to watch him, and I've worked up something of a plan for him. He likes angles, so I'll keep the ball down the middle and take those angles away from him. His biggest weakness is his second serve, so I'll work on that. Izzy made the doubles final, and is still around, so he worked out with me this morning so that I could have practice against a lefty.

This was a Monday final tonight because we had lost the day to rain, but the stands at Brookline were packed just the same. Boston is always a good tennis town, and you play up to that. But it was an odd match tonight. We went three hours and ten minutes and five sets, and still, I hardly ever felt that I was playing well. Sometimes I thought that I was lucky just to be out there, but we were dead even for four sets (6–3, 4–6, 6–4, 3–6) and I had an ad on Connors' serve in the first game of the fifth set, and if I win that one point I'm up a break, and maybe I run the whole thing out. But I didn't win the point, and he came back and broke me, and then he ran it out: 6–2 for the championship.

This makes eight finals I've been in this year (including Las Vegas and the WCT — World Championship Tennis — championship), but I've only won one, in Chicago in March. Everybody all of a sudden wants to know why I can't win a final. Nobody pays much attention to me when I point out that making eight finals is a pretty damn good show of overall tennis strength, of playing with consistency against all kinds of players on all kinds of surfaces.

But also, tonight I have to give the devil his due too. I didn't underestimate Connors going into this, but I came out with an even greater respect for his ability. You seldom encounter anyone who can hit ground strokes as deep as he did as consistently as he did. He was pressing me all the time, and for someone who is as immature as Connors is, he is surprisingly court-smart. I think a lot of that comes from Pancho Segura, who has helped coach Jimmy for several years. "Sneaky" is a great analyst — not a conceptual thinker, but a very calculated one. Connors seems to be the same way.

While he has no intellectual pretensions whatsoever, he does have a sharp court mind, a sort of spatial sixth sense that some guys have that tells you: if I hit such-and-such a shot from this spot in such-and-such a way, the odds are $x$ that the ball will be returned to such-and-such. Segura probably heightened that awareness, but it is not the sort of thinking that can be drummed into someone; Connors must possess the instinct. As a consequence, and since he moves well, Connors always seemed perfectly placed and in just the right form to hit back any shot of mine. I can't imagine two players less alike personally than Rosewall and Connors, but it was Muscles that he most reminded me of. Rosewall is uncanny when it comes to anticipation, and the fact that Connors has that instinct so highly developed at age twenty is really amazing. And like Rosewall he also has an exceptional return of service.

Unquestionably, I'd say that Jimmy is in a class with Bjorn Borg and Vijay Amritraj as the best young players in the world, but right now I would say that Vijay has the most potential of the three. He's so smooth, he reeks with class — and effortlessly as well. Borg reminds me a lot of the young Tony Roche — the big topspin forehand, the slice backhand, the utter devotion of a young life to tennis (both quit high school to tour). But Borg is still so very young that it is difficult to read his future. Maybe someday he will wake up and realize that what he is doing at age sixteen is impossible, so he will have to stop doing it. Or maybe he will just keep getting better.

Connors is something else again, a much more mechanical player than either of the others. Jimmy's more like Smith or Emerson. You've got to gut it out when you're that way, and there is no question but that Connors will do it, just as Smith and Emmo have. And the kid is meaner too. He'll make all the necessary sacrifices to win. He'll chase everything down.

A guy like Amritraj, it comes so easy for him, you question whether he will work hard enough for it when he has to.

*Tuesday, July 24 — Boston / Washington*

Long day. I'm bushed. Up in Boston at 6:15, so I could do a clinic for American Express down here at 10. At noon I got a little nap, but I just wasn't ready for my match this afternoon against Graham Stilwell. This is what happens when you're flying all around and playing different surfaces. I was in and out. I lost the first set 5–7, then played pretty well to win 6–2, but I immediately fell behind 1–3 in the third and I was really lucky to win 7–5. Stilwell let me off the hook.

It's only 10:30 now, but I'm going right to bed.

*Wednesday, July 25 — Washington*

I met Congressman Andy Young from Georgia today for the first time. Simply because I respect his views, I had written him about the South African trip, and, like the others, he advised me to take it if I could. Curiously, the one person who has reservations against my traveling to South Africa is a white man: Sargent Shriver. He wants me to go only if I can obtain some concessions up front. But all the others have reinforced what I wanted to hear. Nikki Giovanni, the poetess, wrote me:

> To me, these small communications are necessary. One is reminded that Dvořák heard the slave songs and made a symphony . . . Mankind has captured the heavens and is attempting to unravel the oceans,

yet the spirit must also be unlocked.  Do take care of yourself.  Be strong . . .

So, if I get a visa, I'll go.

*Thursday, July 26 — Washington*

I was practicing with Haroon Rahim at the Hilton, where I'm staying.  The place is packed and jammed with black people because the Urban League is having a convention here, and the Hilton is the headquarters.  It's a very strange feeling to be in a hotel with so many black people.  Even in black African countries, the hotel population is predominantly white, so this is a real experience for me.

The hotel courts that we were practicing on are right next to the swimming pool, and the place was awash with little black kids all splashing each other and running around chasing after each other — and all calling each other "nigger."  That's a very acceptable term, almost endearing in some circumstances, if used the right way among blacks.  It broke me up, listening to the kids, because I could see that the white people around were listening to all this in complete confusion.

*Friday, July 27 — Washington*

Beat Pilic 6–4, 4–6, 6–3.  Now I get Tom Gorman in the semis.

*Saturday, July 28 — Washington*

My father came up from Richmond today with a couple of friends to watch me, and they couldn't have picked a better time.  All of a sudden, everything was there for me.  I beat Gorman four and love, and played unbelievably well.  I just didn't miss many balls.  I always enjoy playing Tom anyway, and not only because I usually beat him.  He's a great guy, highly principled, and you always get the most sportsmanlike of matches with him.

Last December, when his bad back (from the twist serve) started

43

bothering him in the semifinals of the Grand Prix, he defaulted to Smith with match point in his favor. He knew that he could win the one more point to qualify for the finals and the extra money, but he also knew that his back was bound to stiffen up on him before the match and make it immpossible for him to play. So, for the promoters and the game, he took it upon himself to default. How many gestures like that do you see in sports today?

Tom is a good athlete, well coordinated and quick — not unlike Tom Okker, whom I get tomorrow in the finals. And Okker, like Gorman, is usually easy for me. This is a good draw. Both are retrievers more than attackers, and when my serve is on reasonably well, as it was today, I am liable to wear them down. Gorman has one of the best twist serves among the right-handers and he hits an uncommonly good overhead, but he pushes the ball on his ground strokes — doesn't swing through.

Tonight, I took my father out to dinner and then we all went out to Hyattsville, in the Maryland suburbs, to see my cousin Thelma Dodswell. She is the family historian on my father's side and can trace the Ashes back to 1735, when my slave forebears from western Africa were off-loaded from a ship at Yorktown, five decades before Cornwallis surrendered to Washington there.

I showed Kathy the family tree, and our crest, with its tobacco leaves and a broken chain, in crimson, gold and black. The family is spread all over America now but is still largely concentrated in the Virginia–North Carolina piedmont; my grandfather came up to Virginia as a young man, and then my father moved on to Richmond.

I have a fairly typical racial history, with so much diverse blood in me — Wasp to Indian — as in most black Americans, that it is really semantic nonsense to call me "black." I am black only by society's convenient definition, the one governed by the "one-drop" theory. To whites, being black is like being pregnant — you can't be a little bit of either. Racially, I am mixed, but psychologically I, as my forefathers, have never been permitted to enjoy the variety of life that really flows in my veins.

My maternal grandmother was so light that she could be taken for a white. Her oldest son is as dark as the ace of spades, but he has a full brother who is light — even lighter than Big Mama. I am

44

darker than he is, but, if you could place the whole of mankind on a huge canvas, arrayed in order, darkest to lightest, I would stand almost square in the middle. I've checked, you know; I've been all around the world. I'd also say that my lips, nose, cheekbones, coloring, hair texture all seem to be just about average, in between.

I get suntanned when I play outdoors, although I've never been sunburned. The last time I was in London, a sweet girl named Jo Roberts, who is a friend of mine, was driving me in her car and she looked down at my clogs and suddenly shrieked: "Arthur, your ankles are white." She couldn't have sounded any more surprised if I had feathers down there. Well, whatever color, I'm not very hairy. Even now, at my most hirsute, I only have to shave three times a week, tops. I wear my hair fuller than I ever did, and increasingly find myself poking at it on the court. I used to spin my racket, like a gunfighter, as a nervous habit; now I poke at my hair. You know, blacks' hairs are flatter than whites'. Whites' hairs, in cross section, tend to be more oval shaped, while orientals hairs are round and tubular. Because our hair is so flat, it tends to curl up. You didn't know that, did you?

My waist has finally gone up from thirty inches to thirty-one, but I still weigh only 155, and I stand just under six feet one inch. I don't have any fat on me. Even my thumbs are exceptionally long and thin. Also, like most blacks, I have very small, thin joints. You know, you'll seldom find a black person with fat ankles.

*Sunday, July 29 — Washington*

Hey, I finally won another final — and easily too, four and two over Okker. What can I say? To win at that score I had to play just beautifully, the same way I did yesterday too, against Gorman. When I'm playing this well, I can be almost euphoric out on the court. I just feel terrific. The thing is, at any time, whoever is across the net, you are never really playing an opponent. You are playing yourself, your own highest standards, and when you reach your limits, that is the real joy. It does not take a whole tournament, even a whole match, to get that feeling. If you are playing

45

your best, you can obtain it with just one shot.  I remember one
time today when Tom drove me into the corner, and I returned with
a winner, a chip backhand cross-court deep.  Perfect.  I can still see
myself: moving over, planting the left foot just so, reaching back
with the racket, bringing it across, following through high and
away.  Perfect.  Unreal so perfect.  The ball sails right where it is
supposed to go.  Suddenly, the essence of everything you have
worked a lifetime for is distilled into one shot.

The strangest thing about today's match was that Tom and I had
to warm each other up because everybody else had already gone
ahead to the next tournament in Louisville.  We practice together a
lot as a rule, but for real, Okker doesn't like to play me — or Smith
or Newcombe, anyone who can overpower him.  We have become
better friends all the time.  He has often stayed as my guest at the
Doral, and in Europe I've gotten to know his family, even his in-
laws.

Tom probably has the coolest attitude in the game.  By nature he
is a nervous individual.  He's always twitching, and even when
he's sitting down, he's moving.  On the court, he is always angry,
walking around, cursing under his breath.  You'd be amazed what
that cute little fellow says out there — constantly.

Yet despite all this nervous energy, Okker has no nerves as we
know them.  He realizes that he is one of the best players in the
world and that this fact will prove itself out over a year's time, so
that there is no reason to get despondent or mad over any particular
match.  All Tom really cares about, as far as tennis is concerned, is
that, when his playing days are through, his family will be comfortable.  Since he has the one great shot, a crazy topspin forehand that
he hits off the wrong foot, Okker is going to win his share, and he
is going to retire as a comfortable Dutch squire.  So: why worry?
And he doesn't.  If we were all like Tom, the psychiatrists would go
out of business.

# 5

## The Fun Is All Gone

*Monday, July 30, 1973 — Washington / Louisville*

The Marriott in Boston, the Hilton in Washington, the Ramada Inn here.  Or maybe it's the other way around.  It's easier and easier to feel that you're really not going anywhere.  And guess what's right outside my window?  National headquarters for Kentucky Fried Chicken.  Big white mansion, and it looks just like the headquarters of Litton Industries in Beverly Hills.  I don't know what that tells us, what conclusions you can draw when Kentucky Fried and Litton all look the same, but it must be worth noting.

*Tuesday, July 31 — Louisville*

We were supposed to put on an ATP clinic this morning for American Express, but rain canceled it, so six of us settled into a poker game instead: Okker, El Shafei, Pilic, Ray Moore, Phil Dent and myself.  That's an Arab and a Jew (Tom's half Jewish, anyway), a white South African and a black American, plus a Yugoslav and an Aussie.  You couldn't put a group like that together at the United Nations, not peacefully anyway.

Actually, most tennis players are apolitical even when they're not playing poker.  It's hard to even drag an opinion out of Izzy on the Arab-Israeli dispute.  Patricio Cornejo told me the other day that he's against Allende, but that's hardly a political opinion: he just thinks he'll have a better chance of starting up a tennis club under a new government.  Most of them could care less about apartheid in South Africa; South Africa is just another tennis tournament, like Sweden or Tucson.

The South Africans themselves are politicized, at least on that one issue.  Ray Moore has always opposed his government.  Drysdale is just as radical, although he has gone through something of a transformation.  I can remember in 1968 when Cliff used to argue very vehemently in behalf of George Wallace.  What happened is that he moved his family out of South Africa — they now live in Texas.  Also, Cliff and I have spent a lot of time together working for the ATP.  I was the one who nominated him as first president.  Ticket-balancing on my part.

Of course I can't pretend that the group we had together for poker was altogether typical in its great variety.  We have our little cliques, just the same as any neighborhood.  Language, of course, is primarily crucial to determining friendships.  So is age and nationality, because if a couple of guys are about the same vintage from the same country, it probably means that they met in the juniors and have been close for a long time — Pasarell and myself, for example.  In most sports, the best players don't meet each other until college at the earliest, and in most cases, at the pro level.  In tennis, your best friends are your closest competitors from before you reach puberty.  You bet this is my life.

Emerson and Laver came up together after Hoad and Rosewall.  Newcombe, Roche and Owen Davidson have been a threesome for years.  Now Snake and Geoff Masters are inseparable in the same way.  Jaime Fillol and Cornejo from Chile.  Eddie Dibbs and Harold Solomon among the young Americans.  Great little pair.  I call them Mutt and Mutt.  Solomon is Jewish and everybody thinks Dibbs is too, but actually he's of Lebanese descent.  He's very teasable and a locker-room clown, and perhaps the most amazing thing about Dibbs is that he has no ass whatsoever; the thing is concave.  He's from Miami, too, and he loves the place, especially the Flagler dog track.  We could be in the best restaurant in Paris, the beach at Honolulu, the Taj Mahal, and Dibbs would start going on about the good times he was missing at Flagler.

48

Another thing you'll find is that, as a general rule, the players of the approximate same ability tend to stick together. I suppose there's a blunt classism to this, but a lot of it is practical too. The reason I came to Louisville yesterday with Okker, after all, was because he and I had made the finals in Washington.

By the way, I won $54 at poker. The bad news is that the rain ended, and I went out and lost to some obscure Aussie named John Bartlett. I was just flat; I couldn't get the ball in. I wipe Gorman and Okker off the court, and then I get whipped by John Bartlett. If I could tell you *how* I lost to him, I would not have lost.

*Wednesday, August 1 — Louisville*

Tonight there was a Meet The Players Party given by the First National Bank, which is sponsoring the tournament here in Louisville. The players hate these things, which is not necessarily surprising. What is, is that so damned few of them understand their obligation to the First National Bank of Louisville and to all the First National Banks on the tour. Everyone talks about the tennis boom, and pros making $200,000, but tennis (and golf) are subsidized in a way that other sports aren't. The football pros, and basketball, baseball and hockey players, have their salaries paid by fans buying tickets or by television rights payments. In tennis, the *only* tournament in the world that makes it that way — strictly with the gate and TV — is Wimbledon. Eighty percent of the money that tennis pros makes in tournaments comes from sponsors backing them.

But most players don't want to believe this. If somebody puts up 80 percent of the money you make, and they ask you to drop by for one hour a week and have a free drink — you've got to be dead crazy not to do it. All you have to do is stand there and sip a beer and tell them what Nastase is really like and commiserate with their husbands' tennis elbow, and then you can politely skip. An hour is all you have to give them. Because I'm an officer of the ATP I've sort of taken it on myself to be an enforcer in these matters, either ordering or cajoling guys to go. A lot of the players act like you're asking them to sign up for World War III.

And, as in any other community, it is invariably the same few guys who volunteer every time, and, in most cases, the guys who make the appearances, who go to the parties, are also the top players. Some of the guys who bitch the most are the biggest losers who wouldn't even be able to turn a living on the tour if the few big names weren't attracting the big purses.

Part of our problem is the confusion of identity. Tennis does not have the heritage of professionalism that other sports have. A lot of us still playing — capable of winning tens of thousands a week — grew up in that system where you scuffled for every buck you could get under the table. Our real payoff was in favors. Just look at me: at the same time that I got turned away from a public movie theater, I was treated royally at the most exclusive country clubs in the United States. We all learned to expect to be catered to. We were put up at a magnificent estate, somebody's teen-age daughter or friend drove us around at our beck and call, we ate at the house or signed checks at the club, played golf there and got invited to all the tennis-week parties. Wherever we went, it was tennis week.

We were called tennis bums, and I suppose, yes, that is an accurate description, so far as it goes. More to the point, we were like prostitutes or bookies, liable for prosecution ourselves (at least in the press) while the people who created the system and patronized us went free.

But to this day the system is ingrained in us. We're schizophrenic. We used to play for peanuts and get everything on the cuff. Now we play for $100,000 a week and a lot of guys still think they should be treated like houseguests. In the U.S. it is still a fringe benefit of the tour that players will be invited to stay in private homes. So, in the locker room, you'll hear some guy who's winning five grand that week complaining loudly that his accommodations were too small for his whole family or that the estate where he's staying free for the whole week is a fifteen-minute drive away from the practice courts. I have no sympathy for that kind of thing.

Of course, this anachronism exists because it still has some appeal to both sides. I'm more interested in my independence than in saving a couple hundred bucks by living with strangers, but a lot of players would rather save every nickel. You're never going to find Marty Riessen looking any gift horse in the mouth. On the other side, the people who open their homes up to players are themselves going on some kind of ego trip. Among the families, it's very competitive. If you've got Stan Smith staying at your house, you're the family of the week.

Truthfully, there's a little of the Mrs. Robinson stuff involved too. I don't mean that it's commonplace, but then it isn't extraordinary to hear about how the lady of the house paid a surprise nocturnal visit on the young tennis-playing guest.

But, slowly, that facet of tour life is going out. We are becoming professionals. I was driving somewhere with Ion Tiriac the other day, and suddenly he furrowed those bushy eyebrows of his, and he looked away and got very sentimental. I don't remember exactly what triggered such an unusually dreamy interlude from Tiriac, but he just looked off and said: "You know what is missing nowadays, Arthur? The fun. It is not fun anymore, tennis. That is all gone now."

And he's right, of course. We all traveled together then, one big happy family. A lot of it was brothers and sisters — the Aussie boys watching after the Aussie girls, for instance. And there was some pairing off too. I went out with a beautiful Swedish player named Ingrid Lofdahl for a long time; she still is the sweetest person I ever met in my life. And some people even got married. Lesley Turner and Bill Bowrey. Mary Ann Eisel and Peter Curtis. Cliff Drysdale and Jean Forbes. Carole Caldwell and Clark Graebner. And then some people got divorced too. There were always a lot of local girls wherever you went. Always lots of parties. Always lots of fun. What the hell — it didn't matter all that much. You were all amateurs. Or anyway, you didn't have any money to speak of. And everybody was twenty-two years old. If you were thirty, as I am now, and still playing tennis, you were barnstorming one-nighters in the midwest, while all the amateurs were playing the Caribbean circuit for some silverware and a suntan.

Hardly anything seemed really important. Tennis was an interim sort of thing, like going into the army for a couple of years. I can remember staying up with Tony Roche till two or three in the morning at the Saddle Room in London the night before he played a doubles final at Wimbledon. At Wimbledon! Another time, in Paris, I was with Charlie and John Konrads, the Australian swimmer, and Tiriac and Nastase and some dates till four in the morning just before Nastase had to play a mixed-doubles final with Rosie Casals. Tiriac was especially good company in those days. With a few drinks, he would eat glasses (preferably fine crystal) and bang foreheads with whoever dared take him on. And, as I remember, the only reason we bothered to call it quits at four that morning was because that was when Nastase threw up all over his date.

But nobody stays up till four anymore drinking before a big match, because it's not a big match anymore — it's big money. Also, everybody is married damn near.

So, what the hell: we gave up the fun for the money. The last of us who knew, who *lived* all those paleolithic shamateurism days will be phased out in another five or six years. By then, I guess the whole tour will be made up of guys like Brian Gottfried, practicing twelve hours a day and sleeping the other twelve.

*Saturday, August 4 — Louisville / New York*

We all sat around the pool this morning reading the paper about the World Team Tennis draft that was held yesterday. I was a rather low draft choice of the New York team, having earlier unburdened myself of a Shermanesque statement. The ATP is firmly on record opposing the WTT. We just don't approve of the principle of guaranteeing players' winnings. You give guys a salary to play tennis, why should they take a chance on tournaments?

Later, Roscoe and I lost to Orantes and Tiriac, and I got the first plane out afterward. It's been pretty much of a wasted week, and all my own fault.

*Sunday, August 5 — New York / Toronto*

I've got a week of business commitments ahead of me, starting in the midwest, so I flew here this morning to spend a day with Kathy. We've been going out for about a year and a half, and almost exclusively for the last seven/eight months. There's more to our relationship than meets the eye.

We also have a very volatile relationship, but I think that's rather predictable, because we are quite different from each other, in

52

background and in temperament. But I like girls I'm not familiar with. For that matter, I like people I'm not familiar with. They interest me more. An exotic girl can snow me because I don't know quite what to expect from her, and that intrigues me.

Generally nowadays, no matter where you are in the world, you find women more assertive than ever. The American girls are the most outgoing of all — no question — and more direct than ever. Occasionally, you'll even run across one who asks you out and then demands to pay the bill. One time, not so long ago in Paris, I was standing with a bunch of friends at the cashier's at Leroy Haynes Restaurant, and this absolutely gorgeous American black girl came up to me and said flat out: "I'd really like to make love to you. If you have some time while you're in town, would you please give me a call?"

But hey, you should have seen me. Cool. I was so cool. I was cooler than Walt Frazier. I said, well, I'd see if I could try and fit her into my schedule — something like that. Actually, I was so excited just at the thought of it that my heart was pounding a mile a minute.

From the other side of things, with the girls that have really mattered to me, Women's Lib has been very trying. People should understand that most men had no preparation for it. I grew up with a father as the head of the house. I don't know if, all of a sudden, I could psychologically handle a fifty-fifty split in my house. I mean: who breaks the tie? I do want to be up-to-date and fair and all that, but the truth is that I also don't want any woman telling me what to do with my life (and vice versa too).

So all right, if that sort of thinking makes me a male chauvinist, then I'm a male chauvinist. But I'm not a pig. I certainly would solicit the advice of a woman I respected, and I'd act on it. But in a marriage, I must have the fifty-one – forty-nine split.

After I got into Toronto, Kathy and I went out to a place called Centre Island, which is off the city, in Lake Ontario. It costs you thirty cents apiece to get out there on the ferry from downtown. It was a glorious, gorgeous day, but a kind of disjointed experience, because this happens to be Carabana Day in Toronto, which is when all the Canadian immigrants from the West Indies celebrate their heritage. Half the time, I don't know where I am anyway — Tucson or Stockholm or Tokyo, Marriott or Hilton or Ramada — but this had a special dreamy quality about it, since we were sitting out on the grass, idly watching speedboat races against the skyline of Toronto, Canada, while all around us there were Jamaicans and Trinidadians and Barbadians in their native dress, and the music was all calypso, "Yellow Bird" and "Jamaica Farewell" and the limbo. So faraway; it was all so faraway. So we talked about those kind of things.

We talked about what our kids might look like if we did get married. And what kind of a flap that would make. *If,* everything was if. We decided that her family would have to adjust more than mine. Not so long ago, few Jewish families would permit a daughter to go out with a gentile, much less with a *schwarze.* My family could care less, though — and the same goes for our real friends.

I told Kathy a funny thing. In some old black families it was vital that a daughter marry a guy lighter than she was. Some mothers were really hung up on this, and a lot of fathers too. Right up until a very few years ago, one of the top black fraternities and one of the top black sororities based their selection more upon the color of the candidates' skin and the straightness of their hair. Some sophomore could possess the talent of Marian Anderson, the brains of Barbara Jordan, the looks of Cicely Tyson, but if she were just a shade too dark, she was, as they say, blackballed. Any girl who married a darker man was, simply, marrying down. Lightness was the ideal. I even heard that in my own family, although, mercifully, this sort of thinking is definitely on the way out nowadays.

"You know," I told Kathy, "what a catch you would have been for me twenty-five years ago." Of course, twenty-five years ago, I couldn't have pulled this off. I couldn't have gotten close to her.

*Monday, August 6 — Toronto / Detroit /*
*Minneapolis*

Appearances for Catalina. I used to loathe them, but I've come to rather enjoy them. Really. Started today at 6:15, flying things like North Central Airlines. I'm staying at the Marquette Inn, which must be about the most beautiful new hotel I've seen recently. The

54

rooms are sort of like a hospital, they have so many gadgets. Also, a sunken bathtub.

*Tuesday, August 7 — Minneapolis / Boston*

Two more store appearances. Not bad: we ran out of glossy photographs.

*Wednesday, August 8 — Boston / Amherst*

Back to my tennis camp. What a hassle. I honestly think these people get good coaching and their money's worth all around, but I'm just not cut out to be a teacher.

*Thursday, August 9 — Amherst / New York*

Got back to the apartment and made just enough noise here in 1706 to be heard in 1606. *Hello, Ruth, I'll be right down.*

*Friday, August 10 — New York / Denver*

Full day of working at the Philip Morris office. Plane to Denver. Staying at the airport Holiday Inn. Dinner at the Colorado Mining Company, which is not only a restaurant, the name notwithstanding, but about my favorite restaurant in all the world. A man who can have a drink with Manny and Ruth Parker one night and eat at the Colorado Mining Company the next obviously has the world as his mistress and would be mad to get married.

*Saturday, August 11 — Denver /*
*Pagosa Springs, Colorado*

I'm involved with a large resort here — it's an hour by air from Denver — and I like the place so much I'm thinking of buying some land. The air is so clear here it cracks. They tell me it gets to 50° below in the winter, but of course then everybody hastens to assure me that that is just a dry cold, and that a dry 50° below is downright

55

balmy. It's the kind of place where people tell you that you'll sleep well, and you do.

*Sunday, August 12 — Pagosa Springs /*
*Denver / Washington / Richmond*

Slept well last night. Traveled all day. Besides my own luggage, this whole time, all over the country, I've been dragging around the golf clubs that belong to Frank Craighill. Frank is Donald's law partner, and we're going to meet in a couple of days down in Miami and play golf.

I got a lot of letters and work done on the plane. One of the best things about airplanes is that they don't have any telephones.

*Monday, August 13 — Richmond*

I'm back home now — and funny how easily I still say that, although I haven't lived here for years. Maybe it is mostly just because I had such a happy childhood here. If you have a happy childhood somewhere, I guess that is always your home.

My mother died when I was six, but perhaps because I was so young I was able to accept her loss relatively easily. And I loved my father very much. I had no real problems learning to accept my new stepmother when she came into our home a few years later. We had such a good family, and I was totally absorbed in books and athletics.

Of course, I can remember segregation, the hard, legal segregation of that time in Richmond. I suppose I was always *aware* of it, but it was not a concern to me. I can clearly recall the white line on the floor of the bus — it was just to the front of the rear door — and I understood that I was required to stay behind it. I don't ever remember discussing it; it was just understood. I used to ride the buses a lot with my stepmother. We'd get on at Chamberlayne Avenue and ride over to Broad Street, and then transfer to the Number 6 line to go over and see my grandmother.

The first time segregation really got to me was the summer I was ten, when I first went up to Lynchburg to practice my tennis under Dr. Walter Johnson, a black physician who took prospects on for the

56

summer. Anyone who's ever sat in a Greyhound knows that the best seat is the one right across the aisle from the driver, the first seat on the right-hand side. You've got a clear vista looking out the front window. I sat there because I wanted to see the country. It was not just going the same old places on the old Number 6. I wanted a good view, so I sat there because it was the best one. The driver just looked over at me, and very nicely, he said: "Now son, you know you can't sit there." And so I got up and went to the back.

You've got to remember that people my age — I'm in the last batch — still have a certain tolerance of segregation conditioned into us that the black kids today can't understand. And also keep in mind that it may have been easier to grow up in the segregated south in the forties and fifties than in the north, which was integrated more in name than in fact. At least in the south, things were explicit, and so you knew where you stood. Also, I'm sure that we had a higher quality of life. We weren't jammed into the ghetto tenements. Me, I even lived on what seemed to me to be an estate. My father was a maintenance man and special policeman for a black park named Brook Field, and we lived right there, by the pool and the courts. Sure, I knew the pool was for blacks only. I knew that; at some point it occurred to me that it was always just us "colored" swimming at Brook Field. But no one could have convinced me that any whites' pool could be better than Brook Field. Do you understand? How could any place else possibly be any better — because everybody was always having such a good time.

Do you see how happy I was? I didn't know any difference.

Since my brother, who's a lifer in the marines, and I have moved away, my father has built his own house about thirty miles outside of Richmond at a place called Gum Spring, up in Louisa County. My stepmother still goes into town and works as a domestic. God knows she doesn't have to, and I wish she wouldn't, but she enjoys the work, so she goes.

This afternoon, my father and his good friend Wesley Carter and myself went fishing, and we caught some perch and spot for tomorrow's breakfast. Hunting and fishing are my father's great loves, and I've always enjoyed going along with him. People always ask me how I manage to shift back and forth between black and white societies, but in many ways they miss the main point.  It is just as much a change for me to move between my Manhattan apartment and my parents' house out in the Virginia woods as it is for me to move between the black and white worlds.  The Louisa County me is quite a different fellow from the East 72nd Street me, and I adjust automatically, even though I appreciate exactly what I am doing.  And it has nothing much at all to do with race.

Of course, I suffer frustrations because I don't live in one community, as most people do.  Perhaps that's one reason why I get depressed so easily.  Now, my most comfortable world is the tennis tour, where there are so many races and nationalities thrown together that the natural shape and color of things is blurred.  It will be a real emotional letdown for me when I must finally leave that society.  The largest part of me is part of it.

*Tuesday, August 14 — Richmond / Miami*

We had the fish we caught yesterday for breakfast, and then I just cleaned away the dining room table and caught up on some work because it was raining outside.

There are few people outside the family for me to see anymore when I come to Richmond.  My main point in coming here is to be with my family.  Of course, in time I've been separated from many of my old friends.  Circumstances have given them and me such different outlooks on life that it would, too, be especially interesting to see them again, and I should make the effort.  It is not me that is different, after all, just my unique black experience.  I'm sure that the thinking of my old schoolmates would be very similar to mine if they had shared my experience.

I am a black, an American black, but I am a Have and, essentially, I am a capitalist.  That is a strange mixture for any one person to be.  It is very easy to feel guilty being a Have — especially when so many blacks are Have-Nots.  Part of my problem may be that, even though it does not appear this way, I am an incurable romantic deep down inside.

My father drove me to the airport this evening, and on the way we stopped in downtown Richmond.  Daddy has a custodial service, which supplies the maintenance for two or three banks and some office buildings. It's really interesting to see the expressions on people's faces when they recognize that the skinny black guy emptying the trash cans is Arthur Ashe. I get a kick out of that.

My father is an Arthur too. In fact, both to him and to me, he is Arthur Ashe; I am "Arthur Junior." I take a great pride in being a Jr. I always sign everything, even autographs, with the Jr.

*Wednesday, August 15 — Miami*

The juxtapositions in my life may be what distinguishes it most. Suddenly, and regularly, I am shifted from one environment to a totally different one, from a rural black home to the Doral Country Club. I keep an apartment here; I represent Doral on tour and oversee the tennis program at the club.

I played twenty-seven holes of golf today with Frank Craighill. We really had a lot of fun today — bets coming and going. I like Frank; he's becoming a good friend.

The whites I met in tennis tended to be more upper class, a different kind of white people than what most blacks meet. It seems impossible to say (I'm getting old), but I've known Clark Graebner for almost twenty years now, since I was twelve. The kids in my school would tell each other how awful the whites were, and they were surely right — the white people they encountered in passing probably were awful. I knew some awful whites myself, but I knew whites who were decent people too; I knew Clark Graebner was a good kid; I knew he was no racist. I knew white people who were just like us. But how can you convince other kids of that if they've never seen it?

At UCLA I joined a black fraternity, Kappa Alpha Psi, in my junior year. Walt Hazzard, the basketball All-American (who is now known as Mahdi Abdul-Rahman), was my big brother. Truthfully, however, joining a fraternity was somewhat forced on my part at this time. The one common thread that had already begun to run through my life was that tennis players would be my best friends. It was simply the natural order of things, the line of least resistance.

So I joined Kappa Alpha Psi in order to cultivate more black friends on campus, and the kicker is that I eventually caught hell for that from blacks.  If you'll remember, it was not until right after I got out of college in '66 that the black power movement started on the campuses, and it was a couple of years after that when I first met Stokely Carmichael.  We were chatting casually at the Reverend Jefferson Rogers' house in Washington when the subject of college came up, and I mentioned that I had been in a fraternity.

"That's Greek," Stokely said.  "How could you do a thing like that?  Greeks are whites."

Well, I had to admit that I had never thought of it in those terms.  But Stokely had worked the whole thing out.  As painful as his attack on me may have been at the time, I must admit that it's good to have people like that around to prick your conscience.  They keep you thinking, even in a matter like this when I still disagree with him.

*Friday, August 17 — Toronto*

What a gorgeous day this was — a fantastic moment to be on the face of the earth.  I'm not here just to see Kathy though.  The Canadian Open starts Monday, and for me there's always something special just in getting back to the tour — even though it's barely been a couple of weeks that I've been away.  You walk into the locker room for the first time again, and you feel good and warm and comfortable.  At times like these I actually stop and wonder: why can't the whole bloody world be just like our locker room, with all these races and nationalities and cultures getting along?

But, of course, we're all young and healthy and making good money and playing games, and the world is none of these things.

60

# 6

# The Level of Expectations

*Saturday, August 18, 1973 — Toronto*

This was Guess-Who's-Coming-To-Dinner-Tonight, north-of-the-border division. Actually, I've met Kathy's parents before, several times, but this was the first time we had ever really planned a long, extended evening. I thought about it all day. I practiced with Okker, but my mind was all over the place worrying about tonight. It just has so many ramifications — racial, social, religious.

But, like so many things in life, it wasn't worth worrying about at all. I mean, it went off without a hitch — a very nice dinner and conversation. One thing that helps me in a situation like this is that I am very good at cocktail-party conversation. I've had to do it so much for so long in tennis that I have not only become very good at it, but now I even rather enjoy it. Kathy is completely different from me in this regard. She likes to get down to the heavy one-on-one confrontations.

*Monday, August 20 — Toronto*

I beat Antonio Munoz four and one today. Munoz is the number four Spaniard, one of those little Europeans who retrieves everything; good backhand too. Naturally, his game is clay, and I'm not advertised as any kind of clay-court player, so it will be conveniently forgotten that I swamped him today on clay. If I — or any big hitter — had lost today to Munoz, everybody would have said: *Well, what'd you expect, Ashe can't win on clay.*

To be truthful, I could not always speak so easily about clay. I used to be downright afraid to expose myself on clay. In '65, I won two singles against Mexico in the Davis Cup at Dallas, on fairly fast courts. The next matches were in Barcelona, on the real slow clay there. Bubble-gum surface. I was playing well that summer — in fact, even after we got to Spain I was still handling Frank Froehling, who was supposed to be our top slow-court specialist — but I didn't want any part of risking myself out there. As soon as I won at Dallas, I said: "All right, Frank, it's your turn." I was just going to pick my spots, play only the fast-surface Davis Cup matches.

Well, Spain bombed us. Ralston and Froehling lost the opening singles, and they clinched it in the doubles, and Froehling lost again, for good measure, in the first match the third day. So we were down 4–0, with a meaningless match coming up between Dennis and Manuel Santana. The Spanish asked to withdraw Santana, so as not to aggravate an injury he had, so Dennis wanted out too.

The captain, George MacCall, asked me to play for Dennis, and I begged off. I just didn't want to put my neck on the line. Everybody in the locker room could sense that I was afraid, and I knew it, but I just wasn't going out there on the clay. I couldn't handle it. I'm sure that was when I began to make the mistake of confusing defeat with embarrassment, as so many people do. I thought I would embarrass myself by losing. Actually, as I've finally learned, if you play your best, it doesn't make any difference.

So I gained something from the experience in Barcelona. I was ashamed of myself, I sincerely regret it to this day, and I won't ever duck anything again in my life.

One of the strangest things in tennis is that for all the fuss always made over the difference among court surfaces, virtually nothing is ever said or written about the differences in balls — and let me tell you that the change in balls is a great deal more difficult to cope with than the change in surfaces. Here this week we're playing on clay, but with high-pressure American balls. The clay will help some players, but if we played a European brand of ball here, that would improve the chances of the Continental players by as much as a third, even a half. There's that much difference between balls.

Europeans as a rule have long, fluid strokes — they hit through the ball — because the player must do the work and apply the muscle to the heavy European balls. Americans and Australians tend to be slashers, with shorter strokes, because our balls jump. It's very simple. The American balls — Wilson and Spalding and all the others — get their resilience from the air pumped into them. But European balls obtain their resilience from the rubber itself.

The fastest balls are the Wilson and Spalding. Then comes the Slazenger, the Wimbledon choice, then the Dunlop, and finally the Italian Pirelli and the Swedish Tretorn. The last two are the really slow balls. Hell, you can stick an ice pick through a Tretorn and it won't make any difference. If you did that to a ball that depends on air pressure for its bounce, you'd virtually deflate it.

The American balls, in baseball terminology, are much livelier. You hit one right and it goes *bing*. You can wrist them around, flick them, and they get easier to handle the longer you play with one. A Wilson loses its fuzz and gets noticeably smaller. Really. On the other hand, the European balls are heavy and get deader the longer you play with one. You hit a Pirelli or a Tretorn, even a Dunlop, it goes *thump*. You try to wrist one of them, it will just die on your racket. European balls are just not flickable. Not at all.

Because the Europeans grow up with the slower balls, they tend to build an entirely different game than what we incline to in America. I think it is possible to postulate that Bjorn Borg may become a great player only because he is so extraordinarily precocious. If he had developed more normally, he would have spent another four or five years in Sweden, learning the game by playing almost exclusively with the Tretorns. Then perhaps it would have been too late for him to adjust to the livelier balls that he would find in the other parts of the world.

The balls you grow up with really influence your whole approach to the game. Take the Europeans. Because of the heavy balls, so many of them opt for a loosely strung racket for even more control. A typical Continental player will string his racket with about fifty pounds of tension; hell, that's like a lacrosse stick to me. I string

63

my Heads with at least sixty pounds. And your style — from the ball, to the racket, to your whole game. The cannonball serve, the sharp, angle volley are not so much strokes of a fast surface as they are lively ball strokes. You just won't ever find me hitting a drop volley unless I *know* I can't miss. The damndest thing of all about Chris Evert is that she learned to hit those drop shots of hers from the base line with American balls.

*Tuesday, August 21 — Toronto*

I played tennis with Kathy at her club this afternoon, and then afterward we went downtown to the Canadian National Exposition, which is like a country county fair. And hey, I won two prizes for her too. One time I broke two dishes with one ball. How about that? Now I'm an all-around athlete.

*Thursday, August 23 — Toronto*

This afternoon I beat Patrice Dominguez in three sets. Afterward, I took Kathy and a couple of her friends out to dinner at a soul-food restaurant named the Underground Railway. Toronto has a very small black population, to be sure, but the Underground Railway is among the first of the soul-food places aimed at the population at large. The Boondocks in New York is another one. I suppose in a few years that soul food will be like Italian food or Chinese food, a *variety*. Before long they'll probably be serving the stuff from plastic containers on airplanes.

Anyway, here was our cast of characters tonight: Arthur R. Ashe, Jr., black American; Kathy Benn, Jewish; her friend Rubin Trissman, also Jewish; and his fiancée, Susan Johnson, Wasp. We had such a good time taking off after one another that we ended up staying another two hours after dinner.

Mainly, we directed our fire at poor Susan, since she just happened to be the only Wasp. What bugs me, and what I told her, was how lucky she was that she wasn't in the minority so that she didn't have to waste a lot of her time thinking about minority problems. Because I'm not a Wasp but I live in Waspdom, I have to spend a significant part of my life trying to figure Wasps out. Right away they have a big edge over me because they're not obliged to spend a lot of their time trying to figure me out. They can just go about the business of living their lives.

I love evenings like this. I really do. I don't think there's anything I enjoy more than getting into conversations with people of diverse backgrounds. Unfortunately, too many blacks my age and younger tend to feign a certain nonchalance around whites that destroys the hope for communication. The country suffers, because, as a rule, young blacks and whites just plain clam up around each other.

*Friday, August 24 — Toronto*

Can you believe it? I lost to Ivan Molina in the quarters. Guy from Colombia. He certainly has more of a reputation than John Bartlett, but still, it is just inexcusable on my part — especially since he took me rather easily, four and three. He just passed me all through the match. Molina barely made this tournament without having to qualify, and he only did make the draw because he has some reputation on clay. So he comes in, and beats Laver yesterday — which is more than I can say in my whole bloody life — and today he beats me and gets to the semis.

Was I overconfident? Yes, all right, I was. And, obviously, Molina's win over Laver gave him just the right amount of confidence. You often see that happen to a player when he gets a big win. That raises his appreciation of himself so that he is automatically a better player the next time out. Last week or two days ago, if I had played Ivan Molina, he may have been delighted to have won the first set from me and then he would have rolled over and played dead. But today, I let the guy take one set from me, and you can see him thinking: hey, I can take another set from Ashe, because, what the hell, I'm the guy that beat Laver yesterday.

This is not, however, necessarily a universal reaction. Many times (and I think especially where Americans are involved), a lesser player who upsets a star will relax his next time out. With that one upset, he has already exceeded his level of expectations in the tournament, so he is satisfied. If he loses, he can say, so what if Ashe beat me — I beat Laver to get to the quarters and I wasn't even expected to do that. If you do catch a player who has done better then he expected and already passed his level of expectation, you have a great advantage.

*Sunday, August 26 — New York*

I went out to the Greenwich Field Club today to practice with Ralston, Gorman and Smith, the first time I'd been back on the grass since Queen's two months ago. A ball skids coming off the grass and wings in low, and that takes some getting used to. But it is not simply the speed itself that upsets you. There's a good analogy here between me and clay. I grew up and learned the game on very slow concrete, so a dead surface itself has never offered me any problem of adjustment. But what is so difficult for me about clay is that you slide a little bit on it. Just a little — but that is enough to throw you off. No matter how long I play on clay, I always feel like I'm out there on roller skates.

The similarity with grass is that it is the one surface that is uneven. The quickness, having to stay low — any good athlete could learn, in time, to make these adjustments. But the real trick to switching to grass is mental because the ball takes so many bad bounces. You can never get grooved on grass, as you can on all other surfaces.

It is not the speed of grass that does a guy in, but the unpredictability. A couple of guys can hit for four hours on clay, but you will come off a two-hour grass match more fatigued because you are so much more mentally spent. This is especially true at Forest Hills where the courts are significantly more uneven than at Wimbledon. You can never stop concentrating at Forest Hills, or you're dead.

# 7

## The Worst Day of the Year

*Monday, August 27, 1973 — New York*

El Shafei and Drysdale and I went out to Greenwich again to practice and came back to town for an ATP board meeting. All the players are talking World Team Tennis, and it's getting very sticky, particularly among the Europeans, because the WTT season is scheduled to begin in the spring, in conflict with their big championships.

I'm not being cynical here, merely obvious: WTT does not first serve the fans or the players. I believe that its foremost devotion is to the arenas — which is okay, that's American business; only I would like them to admit this. WTT is being scheduled at a time — the spring and summer — when the arenas are empty. It wasn't created to fill a need or a demand, merely dates. The priorities are all upside-down. None of this would really concern me except that WTT's waves may swamp much more of tennis. Philippe Chartier of France spoke to me last night, and he honestly believes that WTT will spell the end of the European tournaments.

*Tuesday, August 28 — New York*

We had a bear of a meeting of the ATP today. There were sixty-seven members on hand, and they agreed with the board not to sanction or support World Team Tennis. WTT is making a lot of noises, talking lawsuits, but we are standing firm. I think WTT is finished once and for all.

I take no pleasure in any of this though. None of this is personally easy, because tennis is so damned incestuous that you always must end up taking sides against people you know well and like. The commissioner of WTT is George MacCall, whom I've known for a decade. He's been a friend, my Davis Cup captain, even a business associate. George and I have been extremely close, in good times and bad.

The first time I really got to know MacCall was early in 1965, when I took a semester off from UCLA and toured Australia with a U.S. team that George was the sort of tour leader of. He's a fine senior player, but he was never of championship caliber, and he got that position — and subsequently was made Davis Cup captain as well — because he'd made a great deal of money in insurance and could afford taking the time off to handle the post. Those were the days when the Davis Cup captain was almost purely a political choice. If a guy was rich enough and had the time and came from the section of the country that had the votes or was due favors, he was the selection.

I won four tournaments down in Australia that tour, and later that year, George gave me my first singles assignment in an important Davis Cup tie when he played me against Mexico, and I won them both. There were some good times together. And we suffered too. The lowest point in my career, the absolute nadir, came in 1967 when I lost the deciding point to Ecuador in what is generally considered to be the greatest upset in Davis Cup history.

This was at Guayaquil, on the clay, of course. But what the hell: earlier I'd taken both my singles against Mexico on the slow courts in Mexico City, and the very next week after the Ecuador fiasco, I went to Milwaukee and won the United States Clay Court championship. But this time, I lost my opening match to somebody named Miguel Olvera and then Riessen and Graebner managed to lose the doubles too after being ahead two sets to one, so I came into the fourth match against Pancho Guzman with the U.S. down 2–1. I promptly wiped him out in the first set at love, but that

68

probably made me cocky and he began to settle down and hit everything back, and he won the next two sets 6–4, 7–5.

I came into the locker room for the break in shock, and George started raging at me. Even at that point, though, as mixed up as I was, I knew the poor guy was acting out of frustration, not anger. That was the sad thing about it all: George was the captain; for three years, he was the captain, but he could never lead us, he could never tell us what to do — because he didn't know. He wasn't a good enough player to know. The frustration would drive him bananas. At the crossovers, I'd sit down next to him, and he'd wipe my racket and say, "Concentrate" or "Get your first serve in" or "Keep the ball in play," things like that, that 90 percent of the people in the stands could tell me just as well.

But Ecuador was the rock bottom for us both. Our first team, in '65, had lost in Spain, the next year in Brazil; now he could see his last chance fading in Ecuador. In the locker room, he kept banging the metal lockers and talking off the top of his head. Finally, a couple of the guys kind of walked him away from me and Cliff Richey came over to me and said, "Look, don't try to hit any winners. Just keep the ball in play. Get it back. Once you prove to this guy that you can match his patience, you got him." Cliff had the next match to play — the decisive one if I won — but he was the one who had to become my coach now. It wasn't George's fault; it was the USLTA's — an archaic system of indulgences that was bringing us our just desserts.

Cliff calmed me. I went out and won the fourth set 6–0. And immediately, I had my confidence back and I started to get offensive and go for winners, and I got down, and risked some more to catch up, and all of a sudden he had the set 6–3 and we were beaten by Ecuador. Their captain was so damned happy, he tried to jump over the net and broke his leg. I can't measure how deep was the hurt for MacCall. I had never felt worse in my life.

George is an incredible salesman. He could make an easy fortune every year selling insurance, but like all those people who buy their own sports franchises or bid to get players to stay at their houses, George must need the satisfaction of making it in sports. After the three Davis Cup failures, he went into pro tennis and ran what he called the National Tennis League — but he lost out in the pro war to Lamar Hunt and WCT. So George needs WTT to succeed. I know damn well he'd rather have that league make it than he would sell a million, a hundred million dollars' worth of insurance. And here I am fighting him tooth and nail, trying to stop his dream, and he's talking about suing my organization, me and all the things I have fought for in tennis.

Nothing personal, George, nothing personal.

*Wednesday, August 29 — New York*

We have had a heat wave building for the last couple days, and today, in honor of the opening of Forest Hills, it peaked. What can I say — it was unbearable, agonizing hell. I drew Colin Dibley, too, which is an extremely tough opening match, especially on grass. Colin is a big lantern-jawed Australian with a great match temperament, magnificent enthusiasm and a very unpredictable serve that has been timed by some PR man at a million miles an hour or something. As inconsistent as he is in getting the thing in, it probably is the fastest in the world, and at one time or another, Colin has been the top-ranked Aussie amateur and twice a quarter-finalist at Wimbledon.

Naturally, we beat each other to a pulp too, and we took four long sets. I'd seen Colin get cramps in long, hot matches before though — he cramped up at Las Vegas, when he *beat* Newcombe — so I always had the feeling that if I could hang on, I would win in the end. For one thing, he serves so damn hard that it takes a lot out of his body. And that was the way it went too; he had very little left. I was so exhausted by it all, though, that it hardly feels like a victory. I'm certainly not any kind of drinker, but after this match I went back to the locker room and just quaffed three beers in nothing flat — just chug-a-lugged them as if I was an Aussie my-self. I'm enervated.

Still, I suppose it's an improvement from my first appearance here, in the Nationals of 1959, when I was sixteen and drew Rod Laver on the same grandstand court where I played Colin today. I was so scared then I threw up, although I did have the grace and just enough time to do it into a towel. I didn't play too badly either.  I had one set point against Rocket and lost 6–2, 7–5, 6–2 — and it's fourteen years later, and I still haven't beaten him.

Even more nerve-racking is when you have to make your first appearance in the Stadium at Forest Hills.  Remember, tennis players aren't used to playing in stadiums before thousands of people.  Roscoe tells the greatest story about that experience on himself — about his own debut in the Stadium (and it was against me too).  First, he won the toss of the racket, but he was so nervous he couldn't remember what to say.  I don't mean he couldn't make up his mind whether to serve or receive, I mean he couldn't remember what the choice was.  So then he casually poured himself a cup of water at the umpires' stand, but his hand was shaking so that he spilled all the water out.  So that no one would take notice, he just went ahead and pretended to drink a cup of water that wasn't there.

When you play in a tournament like Forest Hills, one that means so much to you — and it's my national championship, so I value it even higher than Wimbledon — your every impression is magnified.  The second year I played here, when I was seventeen, I faced a guy named Eduardo Zuleta in the second round.  I was staying with a family, the Glasses, during the tournament, and that morning they had served me pancakes, which I love.  Well, when Zuleta creamed me in straight sets, it stuck in my mind that the pancakes must have been responsible — made me logy and all that.  I've never had pancakes or French toast on the day of a match since that morning thirteen years ago.

And here's the kicker.  About five years ago, I was talking to Jim Ryun, the mile record holder, and the subject of training methods came up.  Jim mentioned that he always ate a big pile of pancakes before a race.  Naturally, I asked him to explain.  It seems that pancakes are almost completely carbohydrates, which are capable of getting into the system faster than any other substance.  They contain glycogen, a simple sugar, which is a great muscle food.  A steak, on the other hand, cannot be used by the muscles as quickly or for as long.

Nonetheless, despite having Ryun explain this to me — and many other athletes since then — I'm still so hung up on the Zuleta loss in the Nationals of 1960 that I can't yet bring myself to eat pancakes on the day of a match.

71

*Thursday, August 30 — New York*

ABC was around today, taping players' responses to the Billie Jean–Bobby match. Riggs is on the cover of *Time* this week. Can you believe that? Among some of the players, there is grousing that the whole thing is a detriment to the game of tennis, but myself, I love it. I don't see how it can fail to generate more publicity for the whole sport — and besides, how can anyone not favor the one thing in the whole big bad world that is just good clean fun?

*Friday, August 31 — New York*

I beat Sherwood Stewart today in three straight uneventful sets, which is just what I needed. It was slightly cooler, but something approximating reasonable weather is still a day or so away. The foreigners, of course, have all been having a field day at our expense, but I suppose that's typical of all travelers — tennis players, tourists, businessmen; I imagine even spies bitch about some other country's weather.

As a rule, the foreign players learn pretty quickly to take the U.S. for granted. It's a place where you come and take money home from. A lot of them never really catch on to what we're really all about here, though, so that a bright guy like Tiriac always has a covey of young foreign players hanging around him, seeking guidance. I don't mean Ion just knows where to catch the subways and how to work the Magic Fingers on motel beds, he's clever enough to find and pull the levers of power that relate to him in any country. Guys like Okker or Pilic or many of the English-speaking players also have it all down to fun and games over here too. Many of the other Europeans, like many American players in Europe, never feel comfortable here, though, and are anxious to get back to the Continent as quickly as possible.

However simplistic this may sound, I am always struck with the impression that the European players (taken as a group) do reflect a much more set, stable, socialistic view than do the Americans. Corny as it sounds, Europe does come off as fixed, America as the frontier. The Europeans are forever grumbling about how low the amounts guaranteed to first-round *losers* in our tournaments are. They say, hell, why should I fly all the way over here when I might not even make my expenses. They are conditioned to expecting a little, and not shooting for a lot.

I honestly believe that if the big-money tournaments were in Europe, that is, if the situation were reversed, that our guys would risk going over there, gambling for the big kill, and not just worrying about making expenses with first-round appearance money. It's interesting that the U.S. golf tour, which was strictly a domestic creation, has always had an incentive-type purse scale which doesn't even pay players a nickel unless they qualify for the last two rounds. Maybe that's why so relatively few foreign golfers have ever been able to cut it over here.

*Saturday, September 1 — New York*

Roscoe and I lost to Dickie Stockton and Brian Gottfried in straights. We played late in the afternoon, and we might as well have stayed home. We just didn't click, individually or as partners. It was strictly a team effort.

It's unusual for me to be out of the doubles so early, but for once I'm also playing mixed, as Althea Gibson and I have paired up here. Althea is married now, teaching as a pro in New Jersey. She was, of course, the only black woman ever to win Forest Hills — plus Wimbledon, the French and Italian. I'd love to be able to see Althea and Margaret Court meet, both on their best days. I'm not so sure Althea wouldn't give Margaret her toughest match.

I'm not too keen on Margaret's views — she has commented that South Africa has an agreeable situation that works rather well — and I also think that Billie Jean is gutsier and has done a great deal more for the women's game, *but* — look at the records and there can be no doubt that Margaret Court is the best female tennis player of all time. No doubt.

*Sunday, September 2 — New York*

I'll tell you what this was. This was the worst day of the year. I don't want to think about it. I lost to Borg in four sets and then

Althea and I went down in straights. The kid beat me solidly. I'd love to say that I underestimated him, but I didn't. He just out-played me. I made far too many errors.

Jesus, I feel like an old man. I'm thirty years old and teeny-bop-pers are upsetting me. It takes something like this to make you aware of how really short an athlete's life is. It seems like the day before yesterday that I was the kid, beating the old man.

Technically that was 1965. The old man was Emerson, who was the defending champion at Forest Hills, and at Wimbledon too. It was the quarters here, and of all the matches I've ever played, I think I'll always remember that one on top. It was my first big win: 13–11, 6–4, 10–12, 6–2, on the Marquee Court. I can still see the blacks, what few there were, watching me beat the champ. I had arrived. Wherever Bjorn Borg is tonight, I know how he feels.

Myself, I feel frustrated. Somehow it is worse to go out at Forest Hills, because it is the last big one of the year. I know I am good enough to win it, as I have, and am good enough to win Wimble-don or any other tournament in the world — but here it is, another year gone without a major title. I'm not deluded, you understand. I know how good I am. I cannot expect to win every time, but I can win, and when I don't, it hurts.

Rosewall is a better player than me — even at his age, and surely for one match. Laver is still better, and so are Nastase and New-combe. But I am just this tiny bit away from them. Just this much. Newcombe is just a little steadier than I am, for example. But that's all. I'm just off that top rank, and ahead of all the rest. Oh, Smith and Okker probably rate with me, although Tom has never won one of the Big 4 and Stanley and I have each won a couple. But the three of us are not yet in the class of Laver, Natase, Newcombe or Rosewall. I'm not complaining, you understand, but it's times like these, when I have just lost, that I think about how close I am to being the very best in the world, and that is so very, very frustrat-ing.

There is no man in my life, except, of course, for my father, who meant so much to my development as Dr. Johnson. He was one of the few blacks in the country qualified to coach tennis. Dr. John-son also had intermittent charge of Althea when she was coming up, and along with his son Bobby, who did the bulk of the actual

74

on-court coaching, Dr. Johnson really guided me from the time I was ten years old until I went away to college. It was under Dr. Johnson that I learned to play tennis. But he never taught me serve and volley. It wasn't his own style, the net game, and he said that I could get it in time. And the serve I did get. But I never could get the volley, not enough. It's a touch shot, and I guess I was too old to pick it up naturally by the time I started trying, around age sixteen or so.

Understand now, I don't feel sorry for myself — I'm not apologizing — and I'm certainly not blaming Dr. Johnson. This man made me a tennis player, for God's sake. But the fact is that if mine had been a typical situation there would have been twenty other coaches around me, and I would have learned the volley at age twelve. I think I would have. Of course, you can't rationally isolate these points either. If I had been white maybe I wouldn't have had the drive and discipline I have, and I would have given up serious tennis as soon as I learned the volley. But this is no time to be rational. It is a time to be emotional, which is what people want me to be anyway. They see me so cool, and give me all that crap about putting on cool and not caring and all that. Well, let me tell you, when you are this close to being the greatest in the world, in being supreme in this one skill that you have devoted your life to, when you are that close but know you will never be closer because of this one thing, this fluke, well you think about it over and over at a time like this, however pointless that is.

After all the losing, I also had to hurry back into town for an ATP meeting, and it turned out to take three and a half hours. I had no idea it would last that long, and I had Kathy waiting outside the meeting room, and then we got going and I just forgot about her being there. I just forgot. You can imagine how that went over.

# 8

# *Wives and Strange Bedfellows*

*Monday, September 3, 1973 — New York*

Well, every cloud has a silver lining.  Since I've been completely eliminated from Forest Hills, singles, doubles, mixed, the works, I don't even have to go out there.  So, Kathy and I just went strolling down Fifth Avenue and saw a movie, and tried to forget all the bad things of yesterday.  I told the answering service to take all the calls — to hell with it.  Kathy loved that.  She likes it best in Europe where I am not so accessible, and where nobody can catch me on the phone all day.  She relishes that existence: I practice, play matches and eat three meals a day with her.  I live a much more ordered life in Europe away from the telephone.

Tonight we had dinner with the Riessens at Trader Vic's, and then we all went over to Hippopotamus.  Kathy said that I was looking too closely at some of the girls on the dance floor.  I was, I'm sure.  But —

*Tuesday, September 4 — New York*

I went back out to Forest Hills today and worked out, but on the clay courts.  I'm getting ready for an ABC television tape tournament — one of those things they always call a "classic" — down at Hilton Head, South Carolina, so I needed the work on clay.  I won the Eastern Clay Courts at Forest Hills when I was seventeen, and the year before, when I first played the clay there, that was the first time I met Richard Gonzales.

He is known as Pancho, but I have always called him Richard, as most people do who know him personally. I practiced with him at Forest Hills today.

I always like to play with Richard because he never fails to show me something. Especially, he has been the best person to analyze my serve — particularly when I go off with my toss. That first time I met him, when I was sixteen, all of us kids were given a chance to hit a ball or two with him. Right away he growled that I was hitting the forehand too close to my body. Maybe he took a special interest in me because I was black, and he had suffered a lot of discrimination for being a Mexican American. I know that made him easier for me to identify with. He's always been my idol, and, after a fashion, always will be.

My favorite Gonzales story took place when we played Brazil in the 1966 Davis Cup. The matches were at Pôrto Alegre and there was a tournament also being played nearby, so one night Ingrid Lofdahl came over for a visit. MacCall had taken out an extra room, sort of a community suite, where we could all relax together. Well, Richard happened to run into Ingrid in the lobby right after she arrived, and he invited her to come up to the suite to see if anybody else was around.

Brazil is very proper about this sort of thing, and a house dick tailed Gonzales and confronted him just as he and Ingrid were about to go into the room. The detective said that since Richard was not married to this woman, he could not permit them to enter a room together. The way Richard responded to this was to reach back all of a sudden and slug the guy square on the chin. Absolutely cold-cocked him. Then he put the key in the door, Ingrid and he stepped around the fallen form and went into the suite.

Tonight Kathy and I had a quiet dinner and watched TV. We both remembered that it is exactly a year since we began dating seriously. Still, I'm very conscious of not wanting to get married till I'm through playing. I've seen too many of the guys on the tour get married and get really changed by it. Tennis doesn't come first anymore. And if the wife is mad at you, she's not going to hold back being mad until tomorrow just because you're trying to get prepared to play John Newcombe today. Hell, I have that problem with Kathy and I'm not even married.

But it's even tougher on the wives — especially the better educated ones. Being married to a tennis player can be very demeaning, and there's really nothing a wife can do about that. Kathy appreciates this. I'm a name, a celebrity, and if she ever married me, she would always be Arthur Ashe's wife. She couldn't get away from that. I think that Nancy Tanner is going through that sort of identity crisis now. She is trying to understand that she is no longer Nancy Cook, but she is not even Nancy Tanner; primarily, she is just Roscoe Tanner's wife. In the tennis world, nobody really bothers to sort out the wives as people; they are just tolerated as appendages. It's not right, but that's the way it is. It will change in time.

Marriage seems to work best only at the extremes. There is, for example, Sally Riessen, who is a designer in Chicago. She is extremely independent and rarely travels with Marty; they have no children, just their two disparate careers. Shireen Pasarell is very much her own person too. But so were Wylita McKinley and Fran Froehling, and they could not accept the competition with tennis and got divorces. I wouldn't even dare speculate on how many conflicts Chrissie Evert and Jimmy Connors will find if they go ahead and get married. There are enough with one player per marriage.

John Alexander is married to a Canadian; Michelle doesn't want to live in Australia, John does. Rod Laver married an American girl who was older than he was and settled in California, but Ken Rosewall hops back to Australia, to Wilma and the kids, like he was taking the shuttle from New York to Washington. Roger Taylor got caught in that crossfire between his wife and his father this past Wimbledon. I heard that Frances said that since he was British, he should play. His father is an old steelworker, a loyal union man, and he said that it was Roger's duty to stick with his union, the ATP, even if he didn't agree with them on every issue. Frances, of course, won, and Roger has been treated pretty roughly since then by a lot of guys.

Maybe the best marriage on the tour belongs to Frew and Sally

McMillan. They are never apart; she and the two little kids go everywhere with him, and Frew devotes himself exclusively to being with his family. You rarely see him hanging around with the boys, much less playing around. Others of the most successful marriages on tour are made up of women who have pretty much submerged themselves to their men. Mickie and Cliff Richey seem to have an idyllic marriage, and her life is his. Barry and Margaret Court seem to have come to the same kind of accommodation — with the sexes switched, and with Barry managing to maintain his masculinity in the bargain. Annemarie Okker is content to stay in Tom's shadow, although she will pick her spots and speak up on occasion — and he'll listen to her then too. On the other hand, Nikki Pilic has made it plain to Mia where she stands. Before they were married he told the other players: "She must gif up everythink for me. Everythink!"

Kathy could never be that way of course, and, for that matter, I could never marry anyone like that. Kathy and I have our own special problems of course, but the interracial and interreligious things are not issues. They never even come up with the people we care about.

*Wednesday, September 5 — New York*

Kathy left for Toronto today, and I went out to Forest Hills to work out with Horace Reid, a black kid from Atlanta whom I help send to UCLA. He's playing much better.

Then I had my teeth cleaned and tonight I went to the movies with the Dells, Donald and Carole.

Having Donald around is very comforting to me. He's knocking himself out working too hard, but you can't make him stop. Carole understands by now: if he says forty-five minutes, expect him in three hours. He has, himself, also adapted to his own position in tennis. He is right in the middle of a game that is controversial and in a state of flux, so that Donald is going to attract a lot of fire. Can't help it. He used to be terribly sensitive to any criticism, and took it too personally, but he has finally learned to roll with the punches.

He takes a lot of heat — as do all the people in the front lines of the tennis war. They call him Donald Deal and whisper that he is trying to take over tennis for himself. Crap like that. Part of the problem is that Donald is so active he appears nearly ubiquitous. He is the ATP counsel, he represents a number of top players, he runs tournaments in Washington, he even appears as a color announcer on some televised tournaments.

Of course, this sort of thing is generic to the whole game. It seems that everybody in tennis wears two hats. Gladys Heldman runs *World Tennis* magazine, one of the strongest voices in the game, and she also started the Virginia Slims women's tour. Jack Kramer is a sectional delegate to the USLTA and director of ATP. For a long time, Bob Malaga ran the USLTA and awarded tournaments to Cleveland, where Bob Malaga promoted them. Although I am a life member of the USLTA and am its official players' representative for the men, they have not permitted me to represent the U.S. in the Davis Cup for several years now. Tennis is a very Byzantine world. You get some strange bedfellows. At the same time the ATP was fighting the ILTF tooth and nail at Wimbledon a few months ago, we were siding with the ILTF against WTT. Class dismissed.

I know how much Donald must take because I suffer in a reflected way, with people calling me one of "Dell's boys." That is doubly hard for me to take because of the *boy* connotation, but that aside, the implication I hate is that all of Donald's tennis clients are some kind of a numb monolith, stumbling about blindly following his orders. Several of us are in a few businesses together — an insurance agency, the Palmas del Mar resort, some tennis camps. It's fun, and as a group — Smith, Ralston, Lutz, Pasarell, Riessen, Tanner, Gorman and myself — we have an excuse to get together. But the idea that Donald has us all walking around in lock step is just idiocy — and it burns the hell out of me.

Aside from the group ventures, I'm also involved in a lot of independent deals. I put on clinics for Coca-Cola and American Express; I have a regular schedule of appearances at Doral; I have varied responsibilities for Philip Morris (especially in the nontobacco product areas); I make a lot of appearances for Catalina for the Arthur Ashe clothes line; and I help promote the Head Competition Racket that carries my name and that I helped to design. (Ev-

80

erybody thinks first of Head *Ski,* since that came first, but in fact, the company now makes more from tennis than skiing.)

It's ironic, but a number of these business associations date back to my "amateur" days and were arranged by amateur officials to keep me above the subsistence level so that I could continue to play as an amateur for $28 a day in expense money (a figure arrived at, for whatever it matters, on the basis of ten British pounds — back when a pound was worth $2.80).

The reason that I am so closely identified with Donald is not so much because he represents me or because we work together with ATP, but because we are such close friends. Only Charlie in my whole life has been as good a friend as Donald, and I know that only Frank Craighill and Lee Fentress, his partners, are as close to Donald as I am. I am even a godfather to one of his little twin daughters, Alexandra. And he knows very well how highly I think of him. A couple of years ago I made a speech at the National Press Club, and I pointed down to Donald and my father, and I said: "It's really nice to be standing here today with the two people in my life whom I would trust with my life — my father and Donald Dell." I think it surprised all hell out of him that I would say that in public, but I'm glad it's on the record.

Friendship aside, Donald is a helluva lawyer too — utterly scrupulous and thorough. Once he represents you, he dogs you to make certain you live up to every commitment. I just don't understand how so many of these athletes go about demanding that their contracts be renegotiated. What is the sense of signing a contract if it is always open to new terms? There are too damn many exceptions made to athletes. Too many otherwise sensible men kowtow to athletes and let them break contracts ("renegotiate" in the euphemistic vernacular) when they would never tolerate such behavior with their own business associates.

I saw Henry Hines, the long jumper, not long ago, and he was telling me about the new pro track organization that he had signed with. He started complaining that he wasn't making enough, that the glamor boys were getting an unfair, disproportionate cut. I just said, "Henry, did you sign? Did you sign?" Once you have put your name on a contract, don't complain.

Of course, Donald and I are not always in agreement, and since he is a lawyer, we can have some spectacular disputes when we do argue. Invariably then, at some point, Donald will get a very serious look on his face, stare solemnly at me and say: "Arthur, I really don't believe that you mean that, and here are two reasons why you don't." Then, he will tick off the two reasons and, *every time*, make up a third reason just for good measure.

I first met Donald at the Westerns in Milwaukee in the summer of 1962. He was out of Yale then, going to Virginia Law, helping with the Kennedy campaigns. Donald has always been something of a contradiction: a flaming liberal with southern friends. He was also ranked number five in the country at that time and was top-seeded in the tournament, the hard cheese, just back from Wimbledon. All that impressed me much more, I'm sure, than his budding political affiliations.

We did not get to know each other really well until 1968, at the time when he succeeded George MacCall as the Davis Cup captain. In the three years just preceding, we had lost to Spain, Brazil and Ecuador, and Donald turned our effort into nothing short of a *quest* to get the Cup back to America. He established a certain esprit even before we played a match: we wore turtlenecks and double-breasted blazers (far-out fashion at the time) and we let our hair grow (also very daring then) and called ourselves The Mod Squad.

Nine of us played together almost the whole year. We played the West Indies, Mexico, Ecuador, Spain, India and Australia, March to December. Clark Graebner and I played all the singles, Smith and Lutz all the doubles, with Charlie and Jim Osborne rounding out the squad, with Donald, the captain, Ralston, the coach, and Gene O'Connor, the trainer. *We* were the original world team tennis.

I look back on the whole experience with a special fondness because it was also the year I won Forest Hills. I won thirty straight singles matches over a space of two months; I won every Davis Cup match except the very last one, when Bowrey beat me. It was all so perfect, so dreamy. One day in Adelaide, Graebner came up to me and very casually said, "Oh, Art, can you come downstairs for a minute?" And when I got to the lobby, my father was standing there. Oh, it was the end of innocence that year. Sixty-eight was when modern tennis was born.

In January, while I was finishing up my two years in the army, a promoter named Dave Dixon opened up a pro round robin tour with what he called "The Handsome Eight" — and what the players called "The Handsome Seven and Roche." Dixon had raided the amateurs for Tony and Newcombe and some others, he bought up Ralston's contract and obtained some backing from Lamar Hunt; this turned out to be the forerunner of WCT. At the same time MacCall was operating the National Tennis League, which had much the better players — Laver, Rosewall, Andres Gimeno, Emerson, Stolle — but only Gonzales among the Americans, and Richard was well past his prime by then. The pro game was legitimized in the spring when Wimbledon announced that it would go open. Like that, it was a whole new ball game. In August, just before Forest Hills, MacCall invited me out to lunch. He took me to Schrafft's, and over sandwiches and Cokes, he offered me $400,000 for five years. At Schrafft's: four hundred thousand dollars!

I'd never heard of that kind of money before. Still, I certainly wasn't going to sign anything until after the Davis Cup was over in December, so I had the opportunity to sound out a lot of opinions. My favorite response came from one of the officers of the USLTA. His considered advice was: "Now, Arthur, don't do anything rash." I remember Donald saying: "You only sign once." That was his starting point; and keep in mind that 1968 was still a time when athletes really did only sign once. The Koufax-Drysdale package deal was fresh in our minds too, and Donald was really the first one to suggest that maybe, just maybe, $80,000 a year wasn't so much after all. Compared to $28 a day it looked fantastic, but should we compare it to what had been or what might lie ahead? I began to think: if I were worth $80,000 in August, I had to be worth much, much more if I did well at Forest Hills or if we won the Davis Cup.

So, at last, I turned the $400,000 down and settled for $280 for winning the U.S. Open — ten days at $28 apiece. And I was right. In the end, as Donald had suggested, the $80,000 a year really did turn out to be just a piece of cake.

# 9

## *Choking*

Laver and I got in here together and practiced on the Tartan surface. It's hot as hell, if not quite as bad as it was a week or so ago in New York.

I drew Stan in the first round tomorrow. This is one of those TV deals, where they tape all the matches and play them back once a week next summer.

*Monday, September 10 — Hilton Head*

Stan beat me 4–6, 6–4, 6–4, but it was not the kind of friendly match between dear old pals that we usually have. In fact, he really pissed me off, if you want to know the truth.

The rules are that you are allowed one minute at the crossover, and there were a number of times when Stan was taking ninety seconds. Hell, once I looked back and he was changing shirts, and very leisurely. I think I'm in better condition than he is to start with, and also, he lost to Kodes in the semis at Forest Hills two days ago, so he's tired and upset too.

If this were any other sport but tennis, Stan couldn't get away with that crap. If a player isn't ready to play in the time allowed, then he should be docked a point. If Stan came out there a couple of times to serve, down love–15 before he hit a ball, the hanky-panky would end. We need professional officiating in tennis. You can really get away with murder in a thing like this too, because it's a canned TV series. There's no way the umpire can say, "You're defaulted, Smith," because that would mean that we would be having an hour of test patterns on the network some Sunday afternoon next summer, and I just don't think the sponsors will buy that.

Of course, unfortunately, in any situation you're at the mercy of the referee. I've always felt that a referee's decision could have cost me the 1971 U.S. Open. I was up two sets to one and a break on Kodes in the semis and playing extremely well, but it started to rain, and Vic Seixas, who was the referee at Forest Hills that year, was reluctant to call the match. The thing was that I was getting the worst of the rain because I wore eyeglasses then, and the rain was filling up my glasses and making it impossible for me to see. Kodes turned the whole thing around and beat me in five sets.

After that match, I knew I had to give up the glasses. I've worn soft-lens contacts ever since.

Anyway, after the match with Stanley today, we went out and played nine holes, and he took me there too. He's a good guy, Stan, my present pique notwithstanding. We're good friends, if we're not exceptionally close, because I think both of us are too independent; also we have many dissimilar tastes. But Stan gets a bum rap when people call him stuffy. He's a little square, sure, but he's got a good sense of humor, he likes to go out and have a couple of beers and some laughs, and he never tries to force his views on anybody. If Stan were not as understanding as he is upright, he never could have played doubles all those years with Lutz. (And for that matter, you can say the same thing about Lutz.)

Stan has a habit of smiling after he wins a point. It's just a reflex with him, but it often appears smug and condescending, and it really burns a lot of guys up. It drives Newcombe crazy. But I know Stan doesn't mean anything by it, so it doesn't bother me. I always have to wish him well. He made himself a player and he deserves all the success he has gained.

*Tuesday, September 11 — Hilton Head*

In the mixed doubles here, they've paired me with Billie Jean, which must be somebody's idea of a joke. The odd couple — and I see where she's really been coming down on my case lately. Here's a recent published quote from Mrs. King: "Don't tell me about Arthur Ashe. Christ, I'm blacker than Arthur Ashe." Hmmmm.

I let it pass today, mostly because I suspect that she's really not personally mad at me, only in dispute because I've been opposed to World Team Tennis. Billie Jean's the star of the Philadelphia franchise, and her husband owns another team in the league. Also, I've been against her contention that the women should get prize money equal to the men at tournaments where they both play. Of course, now, I don't go quite as far as Tiriac, who got up at the last meeting of the ATP and shouted: "Iss perfectly hokay to let them haff equal prize money — iss hokay if dey play three out of fife sets, just like us, and if dey play us!" That brought the house down.

I do believe that women's tennis has one distinct advantage over men's. It is the matter of identity. The average fan, of whatever sex, can relate better to the girls' level of play. Even a great natural athlete like, say, O. J. Simpson, is intimidated when he comes out to watch men play, because when he sees us slugging the ball around, he knows that it is far beyond his capabilities. The girls' game is, by contrast, so nice and leisurely, though, that anyone can identify with it.

In any event, Billie Jean — "The Old Lady" the girls call her — and I kept our differences to ourselves, and we made a pretty good team. I enjoyed playing with her, and we beat Chrissie and Stan 7–5 in the third today, so tomorrow we play Newcombe and Margaret in the finals. I'll tell you one thing I've learned playing with Billie Jean: she is a much better player than I imagined, and now I honestly believe that she has an excellent chance to beat Bobby Riggs.

*Wednesday, September 12 — Hilton Head / Atlanta / Chicago*

The Old Lady and I lost to Newcombe and Margaret 6–3 in the third. No excuses. We won the first set 6–2 and should have walked away with it, but we let them down, blew some shots and let them back into the match. Then we never could turn it around again ourselves.

Now it's two A.M. in Seattle, five o'clock my time. As soon as I finished the match, a private plane took Rocket and me to Atlanta, and then I got a flight to O'Hare, and we had to sit on the runway there for an hour before I finally got the connection into here. I'm exhausted and have two matches tomorrow, or today, whatever it is.

*Friday, September 14 — Seattle*

This was disaster. I've never lost to John Alexander before in my life, and this afternoon he kills me, one and two. I'm not prepared and I'm not in the right frame of mind, but still, under any circumstances, I should get more than three games from J.A. He's got the big hammer serve, but he doesn't have enough flexibility in his game to dominate someone like me as he did.

But then, I'm just not going well. I haven't really played a top match since I beat Okker six/seven weeks ago in Washington. Of course, everything bad about my game is magnified by a performance like this, but my forehand was especially bad. You know, even when we're playing at our best, there are certain shots we're all scared to hit. I will do damn near anything to avoid hitting a forehand cross-court from the base line. I don't cross my left leg over so I hit the shot with too open a stance.

The odd thing is, like tonight, in warm-up, I hit a couple of forehand cross-courts right on the button. That's often the case. But as soon as I get one to hit in the match, I screw it up, as I did tonight, and that reinforces my fears, and I spend the rest of the match trying to run away from the shot.

*Saturday, September 15 — Seattle / Los Angeles*

I caught an early plane; I wanted out of Seattle. When you get in a bad streak, you are inclined to run like this, as if your game was merely something you misplaced, like a toothbrush or something. I went right to the L. A. Tennis Club and hit for a solid hour and a

half with Jaime Fillol.  Jaime's my pigeon.  I've never lost to him.
And today, if we had been playing a match, I would have been
lucky to have won a few games from him.  I could not hit the ball at
all.  I had zero feel.  And no movement.

What do I do?  Pull a Gottfried and practice more?  Or lay off?
I'm trying to convince myself that it must be the different court surface here — very fast concrete after clay — but who am I kidding?  I
haven't played well on anything lately.


*Sunday, September 16 — Los Angeles*

Kathy got in.  Her luggage didn't.  Lost somewhere.

I practiced again with Jaime and was hardly better.  I need
another pair of shoes.  On concrete, you can literally go through
a pair of shoes in one week.  I don't wear out shoes as fast as a
lot of players, though, because I run on top.  I don't dig in, the way
Riessen does, or Richey, Orantes, Guillermo Vilas, Harold Solomon.  Take a look at one of those guys after they've played a
match on clay.  Not only will their shoes be filthy dirty, but so will
their socks.  But someone like myself, or Nastase or Okker or Gorman — when we play on clay we'll come off with our shoes still
bright white and our socks spotless.  It's really funny when you see
a match between a driver and a floater — say, Orantes and Okker.
Afterward, you can't believe that the two guys played on the same
court.

There's the same type of difference with rackets.  A guy like Frew
McMillan, who plays a touch game, will use the same racket — his
is a Dunlop wood — for a whole year or more.  Riessen's the same
way; Marty can go almost a year with one tournament racket.  I'm
not especially hard on rackets either.  One gets soft on me every now
and then, but for everything — matches, practice, reserve — I'll
never need more than a ten a year.  I've learned how to get double
duty too.  After some time, the fiber glass in the head of the racket
will go a little weak.  When that happens, the racket gets wobbly,
and I'll put it aside for a fresh one — but I'll come back and use the
wobbly racket on the clay courts, where I'm looking for more give.

It's the heavy twist game that ruins rackets.  Laver signed with
Chemold a few years ago, but he broke so many he had to give it

88

up. It's the spin, not power, that also breaks strings, and guys like Okker better get used to using a lot of rackets because suddenly there's a scarcity of good gut around. Even the balls are breaking now too. In this tennis boom, the quality of tennis balls has dropped off markedly as the demand has risen. The Spaldings at this tournament are breaking right and left. I mean that 5 or 10 percent of them are busting up, literally flying apart at the seams.

*Monday, September 17 — Los Angeles*

Airline found Kathy's luggage.

*Tuesday, September 18 — Los Angeles*

Kathy and I went over to Beverly Hills and had dinner at The Luau. She lived out here for about a year some time ago, and some old boyfriend spotted her and came over to our table to say hello. It was quite a surprise for her, and I must say that I had strange reactions about it myself, but . . . oh well —

*Wednesday, September 19 — Los Angeles*

Roscoe and I beat Milan Holecek and Patrick Proisy in straights. Proisy was twenty minutes late, and he should be fined. On the other hand, I'm always amazed when Holecek even shows up. He's the player without a country. He left Czechoslovakia and lists West Berlin as his residence, but he doesn't have any passport at all and just sort of floats around the world. Each country passes him on to the next.

Afterward, Kathy and I went out to Marina Del Rey to have dinner at a place named The Randy Tar. And — oh, I suppose it's all part of getting to know each other well, but — You can just about guess what happened. I don't want to get into it. I'm recording this in the bathroom.

*Thursday, September 20 — Los Angeles*

Beaten again. This time by Raul Ramirez, the Mexican, who's only twenty years old, but another very promising kid. They're

89

coming out of the woodwork. This match turned on one stroke: I was volleying extremely poorly, and he was volleying well — his topspin was just dipping over the net. He saw what he could do early, and since he had nothing to lose, he started to take chances, and his level of expectation rose very quickly. He tightened up in the third set when it occurred to him that he really could win, but I'm just not playing well enough to take advantage of a situation like that. I'm tight out there now too.

Of course, I never *look* like I'm choking. I'm a slasher, a free swinger, so I always appear loose — but that can be very misleading. Like right now, when I'm nervous on the court, I have an actual difficulty in breathing. And that problem is compounded when I try to run. My legs move stiffly, and soon my whole body offers only the most deliberate movements. It's as if I've lost all instincts for playing tennis, so that my mind must try to explain repeatedly to my body what it already knows how to do.

Well, I did win one match tonight. We were all up in the bar, packed in, and as soon as I saw Billie Jean play that first game I knew she had it. There was no choke there. She was moving so easily, and Riggs looked so slow, and there was no way he could overcome that with con, because she just wasn't scared the way Margaret had been. And I knew Billie Jean could hit the ball, from playing with her at Hilton Head. So, I called out for a bet, and got the prevailing odds, 5 to 2, $50 to $20. Then, after the first set, I got 3 to 2, $30 to $20, that she would take him in straights.

When you've got one player who can't move and the other can hit the ball and isn't nervous, you have got a sure thing in tennis. So I won $80 on The Old Lady . . .

# 10

## *Cool*

*Monday, September 24, 1973 — Concord, California*

The tournament is in Alamo, which is about twelve miles from where we're staying in Concord, but for publicity purposes, they scheduled a match across the Bay, in San Francisco, at Golden Gate Park, and I beat John Lloyd of England three and three. We played at lunchtime, and since the rest of the tournament didn't start until late in the afternoon and there is only a thirty-two-man draw, I am in the round of sixteen before the tournament starts.

Kathy has gone back to Toronto, so I played golf this afternoon — and what a glorious day — with Stan, Nailbags and Ray Moore.

*Friday, September 28 — Concord*

I'm playing better. I beat Alexander 7–6 in the third to get to the semis — a good match under the lights, even though I'm afraid that I always had that awful Seattle loss to him in the back of my mind. Now, tomorrow I play Emerson. Roscoe had him a set and was serving at 5–4 in the second for the match, but he lost that game at love, and the set, and the match, and so he was feeling pretty badly when we had to go right back out and play Roy Moore and Onny Parun.

We've switched sides in this tournament. Previously, I was playing the left court or the ad court, and that is my best side. Unfortunately, it is Roscoe's best side too, and we decided that I would be a better right-court, deuce-court, player. Usually you want a very reliable, solid guy on that side, but if I'm not that, at least I'm more experienced than Roscoe. The new arrangement is working pretty well, although it took us three sets tonight. It was 12:30 when we left the court.

*Saturday, September 29 — Concord*

I can't believe today. I beat Emmo 7–5 in the first and then began to fall apart, and by the third set, he just ran through me: 6–1. I don't know how to describe a match like this because I came into it with a good frame of mind, no excuses. But then I just wasn't there after a while, I disappeared physically, emotionally, mentally. I felt like playing, but I couldn't get my body to do what my mind wanted it to.

There are matches like this when I wish I wasn't so damn cool out there. Everybody thinks I put the cool on, but it's natural for me not to get rattled. I don't try to look cool or to act cool, as people believe. The only time in my life that I ever had a bad case of nerves for any sustained period had nothing to do with playing tennis. It was last year, when I was trying to put the tennis program together at the Doral. That gave me an ulcer for about ten days.

But all things considered, I probably envy guys who have a more normal personality on the court. I wish to hell sometimes that I could be like Emerson, or Newcombe or Richey, any of those type of guys who can salvage a bad match with exuberance. I'd see Emmo hit a good shot tonight and get all fired up, and that could carry him right along. If I hit a good shot, it doesn't establish any emotional momentum in my game, the way it works with most people.

You've got to understand that whereas my coolness is altogether real now, it is an adopted shield. I think I can trace it back directly to Dr. Johnson's reminder about being the only black kid, to always have to be on guard, to be in command. It's not normal at all for a player to keep in check as I do.

92

*Monday, October 1 — Dallas / Jackson*

Got to my Holiday Inn room at Love Field at 2:30 this morning just in time to get up to make a 6:30 flight into darkest Mississippi. I'm giving a speech before an Urban League luncheon; my appearance was arranged by my Aunt Lola Baker, my father's sister who lives in Gulfport, Mississippi.

After I spoke we went for a clinic and then over to Jackson State, the college where the police murdered several of the students in that terrible disturbance a few years ago. I played an exhibition match there, and James Meredith was on hand. He told me that he is starting a voter registration project, but he said that it is tough sledding because the blacks in Mississippi are still scared and economically too insecure to take chances.

Jackson must be one of the toughest places in America for black franchise — it really takes you back in time when you hear about blacks being *afraid* to vote in the 1970s — but then, everywhere I go in the U.S. I find that we are still politically unsophisticated, just now coming into our own. Suddenly, we're a significant part of the establishment we are talking about destroying a few years ago — and we're still a little tentative. Blacks will not really have arrived in politics until we start publicly disagreeing with each other.

*Wednesday, October 3 — New York*

Here's a breakthrough: I'm doing a commercial for Simmons Beautyrest. Imagine a black guy doing a commercial for sleeping. A lot of white people always figured we weren't good for anything else. Because of an FCC regulation, I had to sign a statement that I really did sleep on a Beautyrest — which I have, for years — and then I had to pose, so they could cut out a model of my back to use in the commercial.

*Thursday, October 4 — New York*

For a forty-five-second commercial, we shot from 8:15 this morning until 5:00. I did have a pretty cute line to say: "Beautyrest supports my back, which supports my backhand, which supports me."

93

*Friday, October 5 — New York*

I spent most of the day at a board meeting of the Educational Pol-·icy Center. The EPC, headed by a young Ph.D. from Berkeley named Bill Boyd, is devoted to bettering the goals, aims and achievements of blacks in higher education — especially the role of blacks in those colleges that remain predominantly black. A lot of those places are really hurting nowadays.

*Saturday, October 6 — New York / St. Louis / New York*

This morning I flew out to see Richard Hudlin. I lived with the Hudlins when I was seventeen, my last year in high school. Rich-mond was still pretty much segregated then, so there was no place I could play indoors in the winter, and Dr. Johnson arranged for me to live with the Hudlins. Mr. Hudlin was an old friend. Actually, St. Louis was de facto virtually as segregated as Richmond — Sumner High, which I attended, was all black — but I did have an opportunity to play, and with good competition. Chuck McKinley and the Buchholz brothers were all around St. Louis then.

That was where my game really developed. Before St. Louis, I just stayed in the backcourt and pushed the ball around, but out there, on the fast boards, my serve began to come, and I first learned to volley. Maybe it would have happened anyway, since I was just finishing maturing and gaining full control of my body, but, whatever, it was in St. Louis that year that I became the kind of player I still am. I had a great year there. I was at the top of my class at Sumner and got the scholarship offer to UCLA.

Now the Hudlins have another young black prospect staying with them, just as I did thirteen years ago. His name is Juan Farrow, and he was one of the last of Dr. Johnson's protégés. Juan has a real chance. He won the U.S. twelve-year-old title in 1970 and the fourteen-year-olds' last year. I never did anything like that at that age. I was seventeen before I won a national USLTA title. But Mr. Hudlin called me the other day and asked me to come out because Juan is having some problems of adjustment. He is very precocious in tennis and life is rushing at him. Everything seemed reasonably

94

well, though, so after a couple of hours I got back on a plane to New York.

*Tuesday, October 9 — Toronto / Los Angeles*

I've just arrived, Room 639 at the Beverly Wilshire — very plush, even if the phone doesn't work.  But I can sit here and watch the Arab-Israeli war on TV.  It's freaky.  I've never seen a war from Beverly Hills before, and when I checked in I also saw Warren Beatty and Goldie Hawn in the lobby.  Or maybe I saw them on TV and war in the lobby.  You can't be too sure these days.

Notwithstanding this dispute, if you travel at all, you need only one eye half open to see that population is the *only* real major issue in the world today.  I come back to the States and hear some black people tell me that birth control is some kind of white conspiracy.  The Catholic Church says it is a sin, and some blacks say it is cultural genocide.  Here are millions of people, *millions* — black mostly, but that is incidental — starving to death in sub-Sahara Africa, and black Americans and Catholics are telling me they have a *right* to make more babies.

Dick Gregory, whom I greatly admire, is perhaps the best-known black who supports the genocide theory.  As I understand it, he believes that we must keep on producing at a higher birthrate to help ourselves politically.  But surely, there must be easier ways of stuffing the ballot box.  What does it profit blacks if we gain a bigger share of the agony?  Is it really an accomplishment if we are the ones who are presiding at the end of the world?

*Wednesday, October 10 — Los Angeles*

What an incredible day.  The Vice President of the United States of America copped a plea and resigned, I got a cable from Owen Williams that the cabinet in Pretoria will rule on my visa application at a meeting next Tuesday, and Sidney Poitier offered me a part in his next movie.

I was working all day filming for Catalina, and Ward Wilson, who is in charge of men's national sales, told me this afternoon that there were still some stores in the south that would not take the Arthur Ashe line. I said, "Well, you're either pretty brave or pretty dumb to stick with me. You could get somebody like Stan instead and avoid all that trouble."

He said: "No, we're quite satisfied with you, Arthur." And I believe him too. Which is always nice.

### Thursday, October 11 — Los Angeles

After some more Catalina appearances, I had dinner out in Marina Del Rey at a place called The Warehouse with an old army buddy. His name is Hank Friedman, and I used to share a BOQ with him when we were both lieutenants stationed at West Point. He didn't tell me at the time, but before they assigned us to the same quarters, they asked him if he wanted to live with a black man. Of course, nobody bothered to ask me if I minded living with a Jew.

### Friday, October 12 — Los Angeles / Palm Springs

Got into Palm Springs late, but played golf with Jack Watte, who is the president of Catalina. We're both down here for a clothes convention, and I've got to finish up making a commercial at the Racquet Club.

Anyway, we played for a $2 Nassau, plus dollar a birdie and dollar a greenie, and after a horrendous start, I took a couple of bucks off him. It's always nice to beat the president, especially since I made him give me two strokes a side.

# 11

## *Nasty Times*

*Monday, October 15, 1973 — Madrid*

I'm now in the Hotel Melia Madrid, Room 1125. It's October 15. There was no October 14, due to lack of interest. I got up in Palm Springs and went to bed here, with intermediate stops in Los Angeles and New York, where I watched the Mets win the second game of the World Series. We also had an unscheduled stop in Lisbon. The airlines are getting more and more tricky about that sort of thing. "Nonstop" used to mean, curiously enough, that there would be no stops; now, apparently, it only means that the airline will not try to stop you from getting there. "Direct flight" has come to mean, it seems, that they promise not to go backward.

I practiced forty-five minutes with Okker after I got in and took a hot bath. I never really slept on the flight, and all I could manage all day were sort of intermittent cat naps. This has been, so far, a thirty-two-hour day for me, and when you get in the middle of a switch like this, you never really know what your chances of sleep are. It's about 11:00 P.M. now, California time. Or April 4, 1967, California time. Or something. *Buenas noches.*

*Tuesday, October 16 — Madrid*

I slept eleven and a half hours.

It's an old wives' tale that the second day out after a long flight is the worst day. And let me tell you: those old wives were right this time. I lost to Edison Mandarino of Brazil three and three tonight. I felt fine, really, but I had no touch. It was the trip, I'm sure. But understand, this is no alibi, because this sort of routine is sheer stupidity and I get what I deserve.

We fly halfway round the world and meet some top-ranked player at noon the next day. It's crazy, sheer madness, and we're cheating ourselves and the fans.

### Wednesday, October 17 — Madrid

No word from South Africa. If the cabinet met last night, they either tabled me or aren't prepared to let me know their answer yet. I spent much of the day on the phone to the ATP offices in Paris, talking with Pierre Darmon and Kramer. Nastase says he won't pay his fine from Wimbledon, so, as of tomorrow, he's out of the ATP.

### Thursday, October 18 — Madrid

Things are still screwed up. I couldn't get to sleep till 3:30 this morning, and today the weather turned rotten again. It was freezing out there, but we beat Andy Pattison and Jaime Pinto-Bravo four and four. The racket felt odd in my hand, which is often the case in cold weather. When it's cold, there is a homeostatic response as the heart starts pumping extra hard to get the blood out — especially to the extremities. Your hands puff up a little so that the racket handle feels larger.

It's surprising how few players bother much about their hands. Gonzales was the most thorough about hands. He would tape the tips of his fingers and some joints, especially in hot weather, in order to trap the moisture in, to keep the skin soft. He would use Chap Stick, or any of those lip balms, to put on the places on his racket hand which most tended to crack — usually the knuckles of the forefinger and thumb. If they get too brittle and crack wide open, it can be bad trouble for a long while.

*Saturday, October 20 — Madrid*

I watched Nastase play Okker today. If you notice, whenever you see a pro watching other pros play, he will almost never applaud, no matter who is on the court. Well, when players see Nastase do things, they applaud. I was watching him with Laver and Ray Keldie tonight, and we all three just marveled at him. One time he made a drop shot that was so perfect Okker couldn't reach it even though he was standing at the service line and is about as fast as anyone in the game. Nastase had him 5–2, 40–love in the third — and he lost. He just started fooling around, and it got away from him.

I've known him for seven years now, and he has never really changed. By our American standards, he is utterly tactless. In the middle of the match tonight, he saw me standing there and called out, "Hey, Negroni." That's Rumanian for black. Actually, I get off easy. He calls Smith "Godzilla," which is a derisive allusion to his size; he calls Kodes, the Czech, "Russian," and all the South Africans he calls "racist." You know, very amiably: "Hi, racist." But he can go over the line too. After a match they played in Los Angeles a couple years ago, Nasty flat out called Okker "a dirty Jew." Tom jumped him and everyone in the locker room had to rush in and break it up.

Nastase does not take it nearly so well as he dishes it out. He left the court, shaking, when Graebner came to the court and threatened him at Albert Hall a few years ago. When the crowd at the Foro Italico in Rome got on him in one match, he just quit — walked right off the court in the middle of a game. This past February, at the National Indoors in Maryland, which his friend Bill Riordan runs, Nastase tanked to Brian Gottfried because he suffered a couple of bad calls. He is much worse with the officials than with the players, and, of course, it is significant that in tennis officials have little recourse to retaliation.

But as much of an ass as he is on the court, Nasty is a totally different person once a match is finished. You cannot berate him, as you would an American or, say, an Aussie. He'll merely turn it around and reply: "Of course I'm not perfect. Are you perfect?

99

Ahh, all you Americans are the same. You all think you're perfect." He has company in that respect too. Many foreigners — particularly those from Southern Europe — think that
we're the ones out of step.

It is a cultural gap that cuts all the way across society. Our businessmen will knock themselves out working 12/14 hours a day. The
Southern Europeans will break from one to four and spend most of
that time with their mistresses. Same way on the court. Some accept cheating as the natural order of things and really cannot comprehend how that philosophy either surprises or offends us. Whitney Reed once told me a story about a time in Rome when a little
linesman robbed him blind, eventually costing him the match with
his outrageous calls. A few months passed, and at Wimbledon a
stranger came up to Whitney and gave him a warm greeting. Whitney had to admit that he didn't recognize the man, whereupon the
stranger replied: "Don't you remember me, Mr. Reed? I'm the
linesman from Rome who made all those bad calls that cost you the
match." And he said it just like that, altogether sprightly and
amiably — and he was quite dismayed when his old pal didn't
respond in kind.

But once you understand this arrangement and realize that the
Southern Europeans forget everything that happens on the court,
then they are pretty easy to take. I get along well with all of them,
except possibly for Kodes, who is generally unpopular with all the
players.

I never took Nastase's wife out before he married her, but I knew
Dominique before he did and I more or less introduced them one
night at Hippopotamus. I was showing Nasty around New York
and Dominique was out with Nailbags. Since then I've had dinner
with her family in Sweden, and not long ago, when he was playing
in New York, I took her sister and her mother and Nasty all out to
dinner at Elaine's. But you see, if we had played a match the next
day, he would have taunted me and harassed me and used every
dirty trick in the book.

At times on the court, he is downright arrogant, for he can marvel
at his own prowess. When he makes fun of an opponent — the
most un-American thing of all — he is only being childish, not
malicious as it appears to us. He is so vain he doesn't realize what

he is doing to his opponent.  Besides, he is so gifted *and* entertaining that he can get away with more abuses.  He is so good that I actually can get inspired watching him play.

I think that only another professional player can really appreciate how good Nastase is.  He just floats across the court.  Floats.  And he possesses such mechanical efficiency, such near technical perfection, that he commands a certain professional reverence.  Nothing interests him but tennis.  He has told me that he is totally unconcerned about the world around him, and he does not want to involve himself in any way off the court.

And yet, given this incredibly gifted and devoted athlete, we have someone who can lose from 5–2, 40–love.  It is impossible to fathom him.  Nastase is a walking paradox, a before and after, a beginning and end.  If Hegel could study Nastase, he would have the answers to all his questions.

*Sunday, October 21 — Madrid*

Right now, I just want to kiss off the rest of the year.  I want to resign all my obligations and go back to Miami and work on my weaknesses.  I have been playing worse and worse, but I am simply ashamed at how I played in the doubles today.  Roscoe and I were playing Frew and Nailbags, and we won the first eight games, 6–0, 2–0.  I thought we were going to double-bagel them.  Then I fell apart.  I kept losing my serve.  They beat us 8–6 in the third.  It was awful.

I used to cry when I lost as a kid, and maybe I'd be better off doing that now.  Maybe we'd all be better for that.  In the U.S. now, so many kids grow up, as I did, confusing embarrassment with losing.  We have such an insatiable desire to win that one is shamed by defeat.  Is it our outlook on sports which affects the rest of our lives or is it our determination to succeed in all areas — and sports is just one of them?  Which came first: Green Bay or Vietnam?

Of course, when I start talking to myself this way, I have to be very careful that I'm not copping out.  I tell myself that there can be only one winner, and that I've won often enough.  I tell myself that it is crap about how you're only as good as your last game.  I tell

101

myself that my record stands. I tell myself there is too much emphasis on winning. But I must watch that I am not just telling myself these things to explain my losing lately or to excuse myself from not trying hard enough.

*Monday, October 22 — Frankfurt / Madrid / Wiesbaden*

I arrived in Germany this evening after Nailbags and I got in eighteen holes.

In my assignments for Philip Morris, I do sort of institutional advertising. I'm going to have a press conference at the base here and do some interviews with *The Stars and Stripes,* and besides, with so many black GIs over here, I think the air force itself welcomes the presence of a visible black civilian. Of course, it's rather an ironic feeling being with the military at this particular *point in time* because I just learned today in the Madrid airport that Nixon had fired Cox and Richardson and Ruckelshaus. I read it over a guy's shoulder in his Paris *Herald-Tribune.* "I think we got a dictator on our hands," he said.

*Tuesday, October 23 — Wiesbaden / Ramstein*

I was picked up this morning by Colonel Henry, who happens to be a fraternity brother, and Lieutenant Jones, the race-relations officer, and they took me over to the 17th Air Force where I met — look out, world — a black general named Clifford. Boy, was I impressed, and I am not easily impressed. But this dude could go all the way. He's a brigadier now, but you could visualize him with four stars.

Then we drove for an hour over to our European Headquarters in Ramstein. It is the harvest season here now, and the farmers, with their women in babushkas, were out working in the countryside. The landscape was thrilling, gloriously bright with the changing leaves. For an American, Germany is very reminiscent of New England this time of year.

Of all the places I've been and all the things I've seen, nothing in nature has ever affected me like the autumn of Germany today, and as we passed through the countryside, the hills rushing at us with their colors, I had some kind of mystical communion. I remembered that Beethoven had come from this part of the land, and suddenly, feelings for him washed over me. I could somehow comprehend, in that instant, how a man who had seen these autumn hills, as I, could be inspired to do what he did. It was like sitting in Abraham Lincoln's chair. I could hear Beethoven's Ninth. I could hear it and see the flags waving against the sky. And then the Sixth: I could sense the passion he must have felt. Oh, it was eerie. The passage with the violins was so clear that I'll see the trees waving back and forth in the wind whenever I hear it.

At Ramstein, I gave a press conference, and then was permitted to join in a race-relations seminar. They bring both officers and enlisted men in for several days of concentrated study about race. It is a serious problem because the black soldiers in Germany suffer much of the same discrimination as they do back in the States. It has been a decade or more since I was denied entrance to any establishment in the States, but four years ago, in Berlin, I was refused admittance to a bar. I was just looking to have a nice mug of good German beer, but, apparently, I was in the section of town where the white GIs congregate, so the Germans who ran the place barred my way.

At the panel discussion, I was amazed at how brutally frank the exchanges were. When there was a real need for candor, the black officers were not afraid to speak harshly to white superiors — and the blacks were backed up by their white sergeants. "The horrible thing we see here," one black captain in the seminar cadre told me, "is that when we bring officers in for five solid days of race relations, the bigot in them eventually comes out — and some of these bigots are bird colonels."

That evening I had dinner with General Jones, a four-star commanding the whole U.S. Air Force in Europe. We were joined by General Ellis, a three-star, plus a lieutenant general, a major general and a brigadier. So I dined with the crème de la crème of the whole U.S. Air Force in Europe — and not to mention General Jones's daughter, who is very cute indeed.

I had met General Jones several months before, and almost immediately tonight he asked me if I had any comments to offer on what I had seen or heard. Perhaps he was merely being polite, and I didn't want to sound like a one-day know-it-all, but I spoke right up, about housing abuses, about some gaps in the race-relations program. Even though I am a civilian, a lot of black officers and NCOs had briefed me carefully because they realized that I at least would get the general's ear for one night, that they could reach him much faster through me than through the normal institutionalized channels.

General Jones listened quite attentively. He was probably using me to gain information and scuttlebutt as much as the young officers were in passing it along. I'm a conduit, which is a rare position to be in our society. I can see both sides of the fence. In this case, I was myself an officer in the army for two years, so I know how it works (and doesn't work), and, as always, I'm a black man who lives in a white world, and can communicate in both societies.

I slept in the BOQ tonight.

*Thursday, October 25 — Toulouse*

I slept late, ten hours — very unusual for me. Kathy's meeting me in Paris in a few days. And hey, I finally got a *Herald-Tribune* so that I could find out if we still have that old form of constitutional democracy that I had grown so attached to over the years. Somehow it's worse to be away from your country when a crisis arises. I'm finding out what it's like for those players who come from South American countries when they're on the road somewhere and they read there's a coup or a revolution back home.

*Friday, October 26 — Toulouse*

This is just a little four-man tournament — Pierre Barthes and François Jauffret for the home country, Tiriac and me for the road team. Unfortunately, Ion got sick and went down one and love to François tonight, so the promoters asked Pierre and me to play best of five, and I beat him in four.

*Saturday, October 27 — Toulouse*

I beat Jauffret to win 8000 francs, the little tournament was a success and on to Paris . . .

*Monday, October 29 — Paris*

Kathy is in and we had a wonderful time last night on the Left Bank at a place called La Coupole, which is sort of the in freak spot — transvestites, beggars, guys with earrings, people in tuxedos, tennis players, everybody looking at everybody else. Great fun. I'm in Paris, I like the hotel, we went up to Notre Dame, the whole bit — and then I picked up a copy of *The Guardian* this morning, and now I'm depressed.

The story says that the U.S. has struck a deal with the Portuguese. We'll back their control of their African colonies, and in return they'll let us keep on using their Azores bases, so that we can supply Israel. The U.S. is trading African support to support Israel. Couldn't we have found another way to both continue our commitment to Israel and also show Black Africa that, at least morally, we support it too?

Although I support Israel the saddest thing is that most of the black population in America will not blink an eye at this. There are many more blacks than Jews in the U.S., yet the Jews look out for their brothers overseas and affect our international policies — and we blacks don't, or perhaps can't. I suppose I should be realistic. The U.S. is not an African country. Its priorities are in Europe, and then in Japan and the Mideast. I even think that blacks have been placed at some traditional disadvantage because there is no black language that binds us to Africa. The United States stays closest of all to England because of the linguistic bond. Blacks don't have anything like that. It is the most obvious way that we have been separated from our heritage.

*Tuesday, October 30 — Paris*

I've been in France for a week now, and the maddening thing is that I'm no more comfortable with the language than I was when I

105

arrived. Oh, I manage the *bon soirs* and *merci beaucoups* well enough, but hell, I can do that sort of thing in Italian and Spanish too. The agonizing thing here is that I can read the language — I really have a nice vocabulary. I am just fine until somebody starts *talking* to me.

But I escaped two disasters. I went shopping with Kathy and still came back financially liquid, and then I played tennis with Patrick Proisy and snuck by 7–5 in the third. We're playing with Tretorn balls on a slow surface known as Mate-Flex, which really fluffs the balls up, so I can't hit many serves at all. I'll take any win I can get over a home boy playing Tretorns.

*Wednesday, October 31 — Paris*

Let the record state that it was on Halloween when they finally agreed to let Arthur Ashe into South Africa. Owen Williams called me at nine this morning with the official word, and it was on the radio this afternoon. Even before then, I had a call from the South African embassy. They told me I could pop around and pick up my visa any time.

I played Borg tonight, the first time since Forest Hills, and I beat him two straight, 7–5 and 6–3.

*Friday, November 2 — Paris*

I lost to Okker 6–3 in the third, and it is especially irritating because I was a service break up early in the set. If there is one place Tom is going to beat me, it is on a court like this with these balls — but this is no sour grapes. Not now.

Only about two or three dozen people in the world know it when it happens, and it only seems to happen for a month or so at a time, but in almost any year, at some point, Tom Okker becomes the best player in the world. This is the case right now. He could beat anybody in the world at a game of tennis. Earlier this year, he was in a slump and didn't even make the WCT finals, but as I mentioned earlier, he always figures it will even out, and with him, with his temperament and talent, it always does.

106

Gee, what a complete coincidence: the International Lawn Tennis Federation allowed South Africa back into the Davis Cup in 1973 to play in '74. A more cynical man than I might think that I was a quid pro quo.

It so happens that a white South African named Blen Franklin, who is the president of the South African Lawn Tennis Association, came to see me the other day, just to say how pleased he was that I was coming. Just a pleasant little chat. Then it turned out at the ILTF meeting that he used me as one of the "eight points" explaining why South Africa should be allowed back in the Davis Cup. So they're ahead; they've already hooked something very big with me as part of the bait. I'm not surprised, though, because I assumed they would use me in some way.

It can work both ways though. There is a concept in international trade called comparative advantage. Two nations will trade with each other if each believes it can gain. My going to South Africa is a trade. They've already gained something out of me, and I'll gain something too. If nothing else, my presence signals a pause in apartheid. In the sweep of history, a pause maybe for only five minutes — but maybe next time ten. I am banking on a trait of human nature that concessions are won with great cost, that, indeed, small concessions incline toward larger ones.

People who do not want me to go point out to me that I will be a tool of an illegal government, one chosen by a minority electorate. Unfortunately, this is true; also unfortunately, it is the only government South Africa has got. People take pains too to point out to me that I will only be window dressing. This is no revelation either. But I look at it this way: a woman who uses a cosmetic to touch herself up invariably finds that eventually she depends upon cosmetics.

But there are a lot of reasons why I'm going. The South African Open is the sixth most prestigious in the world. I want to play in it, and I want to win it. And I'm curious. I probably know as much about South Africa as any person in the world who has never been there, but I wonder how secondhand impressions will square with reality. I'm human: I just want to see the damn place with my own eyes and my own mind.

But those are selfish, personal reasons.  Others are more important, more cosmic, and whereas I don't see myself as Jackie Robinson or even as Rosa Parks, neither trailblazer nor pawn of history, I do think I'm just a little bit of progress.  Ellis Park will be integrated, and I will be a free black man on display.  There is also always the chance that the trip will show an immediate athletic profit, that I will spot a black kid who has potential.  Probably that is expecting too much — but then, three years ago Stan Smith and I stumbled upon a teen-ager in Tanzania who was good enough to earn a tennis scholarship to Southern Methodist.

In his book *Soul On Ice,* Eldridge Cleaver has pointed out that in the States, the white man makes the rules about who can play with whom, in sexual and athletic participation.  In the U.S., the white man supposedly puts restrictions on sex, while permitting the black to show his masculinity through athletics.  In South Africa, the black is denied even this compensatory freedom.  He is only allowed athletic prowess in his own little sphere and is forced to conclude that a black would lose to the white.  South African blacks have never had one of theirs become a national sports hero; their idols are restricted to neighborhood status, and when you must limit your idols, surely you must limit all the dreams and aspirations, and you remain, perforce, a limited man.

Sometimes, perhaps, I lose sight of the fact that it is important for me to do well in the Open.  If I lose in the first or second round, I have no platform; I'm just an interested tourist — who happens to be black — gallivanting around South Africa.  Donald reminded me the other day on the phone: "Remember, nobody listens to losing quarter-finalists."  And the way I've been playing lately it's all the more discouraging.

*Saturday, November 3 — Paris*

Incredible.  Roscoe and I just hammered Okker and Riessen, four and two.  Our best match of the year.  It was never in doubt, and they really played extremely well to win six games.  Afterward, they told us that they had been wondering for months when we would catch on and switch sides, with me taking the right court.

108

*Sunday, November 4 — Paris*

We lost to Nastase and Juan Gisbert 7–5 in the third, and they broke my serve to win it at 6–5 — with me up 40–15. Nastase was impossible. All the usual crap — stalling, complaining. At one point in the second set he was acting so badly — or maybe I should just say he was acting badly more often — that I finally got fed up and asked for the tournament referee. He's a little fellow named Mister Osterag that everybody knows, and he came over and wagged his finger at Nasty and watched the rest of the way. And Nastase was a little better thereafter. Damn, he can be aggravating — and Mr. Charm right afterward. He was all giggles and pals in the locker room. He's also agreed to pay his ATP fine for bucking us on Wimbledon, so he is, officially speaking, back in our good graces.

I took Kathy to the airport. I won't see her for three weeks and five days. Can you imagine if I showed up in Johannesburg traveling with a white woman? They'd probably like it better if I dropped that H-bomb.

*Monday, November 5 — Paris / Stockholm*

The good news is that I arrived here at five o'clock in the afternoon with plenty of time to practice. The bad news is that it was already pitch black dark. I mean we're playing indoors, but still . . . The sunlight hours, so-called, are from 9:30 to 3:30. It's very depressing and the Swedes combat this by drinking like crazy.

I'm in Room 202 of the Strand Hotel, which is as austere as you might expect: no drawer space, just a closet and just myself. And a note of some confusion: I picked up a copy of the *Herald-Tribune* today, and the headlines were small and nice and calm.

*Tuesday, November 6 — Stockholm*

Sunup: 9:30. Sundown: 3:30.

*Wednesday, November 7 — Stockholm*

I've developed some strange rash on the back of my right arm and elbow, so I went to a skin doctor today, and he told me I had something called utecoria. It's no big deal, but it's annoying. Turns out Nastase had the same thing last May.

We had a four-hour ATP meeting this morning. Jack and Donald both came in, and we had twenty-three players present. We're trying to stand firm against the WTT, against the principle of *guaranteeing* players prize money, win or lose. The whole thing is coming to a head. I had a very interesting chat with some WTT people, one of whom is a nice guy named Joe Zingale who runs the Cleveland franchise, which owns the league rights to Borg. These people are talking a lot of money. They've come all the way across the Atlantic just to try to sign the kid.

I said, "Joe, there is no way Sweden is going to let Cleveland, Ohio, take Bjorn Borg from them. He's a national treasure."

"Bet me, Arthur," he said. So I took him up on it. If he signs Borg, I've got to buy him a no-holds-barred dinner for four at a first-class restaurant. If he doesn't, Joe buys me the dinner.

Sweden is going bananas over Borg. It's like Wimbledon fortnight, but with all of the attention focused on one player. He meets Nastase tomorrow night, and I don't think there's ever been a hotter ticket in Scandinavia than for that match. And it's really gratifying to me to see this sort of enthusiasm in my sport.

I beat Frew McMillan three and four tonight. He is, of course, the most unorthodox player in a game that is increasingly peopled by unorthodox players. First of all, Frew wears a cap on the court at all times, outdoors or in, and on top of that, he hits two-handed from both sides. Connors and Chrissie have gotten all the attention for their two-handed backhands, and several others also use that stroke — Drysdale, El Shafei, Jim McManus, the kid Billy Martin — but Frew swings it like a baseball bat from both sides. This reduces his reach and mobility, which explains why he is so much more superior as a doubles player, where he has only half a court to cover.

But like the Borg mania and the Bobby Riggs nonsense, I like the

110

two-handed stuff, or more accurately, I like what it represents. We've been so damned hidebound in tennis that I think it's beneficial any time the game gets some variety. For years, tennis instructional books have read like military how-to manuals.

Perhaps it's a reflection of our times, but I believe that this is a period when experimentation is accepted with more grace than before. The luckiest thing that ever happened to Borg is that he came along at a time when nobody was determined to make him play by the book. His excellence is largely founded on his difference. And he's like all the great topspin players — Laver, Santana, Okker — you can't hit the ball as well as they do if you do it the "right" way.

All I know is, whenever I hear the purists carry on, I just remember what Gonzales has told me so many times, that the best one stroke he has ever seen in his life is Sneaky Segura's two-handed forehand.

And finally today, for whatever it is worth, this agonizing piece of nostalgia: Roscoe has gone back to the States, so Tiriac and I are playing as a doubles team here, and tonight we drew two guys from Hungary. One of them turned out to be a nineteen-year-old kid named Balazs Taroczy, who was a ballboy for me in Budapest ten years ago. Not only that, but he and his father had personally met me at the airport when I arrived that time and had escorted me to the Grand Hotel. He knew all the people I played, all the scores, everything. He was nine years old then — and he and his partner beat me and Tiriac tonight. Boy, do I feel old.

*Thursday, November 8 — Stockholm*

Borg vs. Nastase. It was a circus. Outside, they were scalping tickets for $200 apiece, and inside the crowd was going berserk. The kid won eight of the first eleven games, and the place started coming apart at the seams. Nastase won the second set, but Bjorn came back and took the match, and it all exploded again. I just can't believe that the Swedes will let Joe Zingale take this joy from them.

The only other time I ever saw anything else like this was in Barcelona in 1965, when Spain beat us in the Davis Cup, and they threw cushions in the air and poured down out of the stands and hoisted Santana up on their shoulders and carried him around like a king. I remember what awful mixed emotions I had at that time, because even though we had lost, I was happy for Manolo, so glad that he had done well amongst his own people. And I felt the same for Bjorn tonight. But we're "too big" to have that sort of thing happen in the U.S.

*Friday, November 9 — Stockholm*

Okker beat me again. He's just playing too well now, and I'm not. I'm already starting to worry that I'll go down to South Africa next week to make history and get wiped out in the first round. Also, I'd really like to have had the chance to play Borg here.

*Thursday, November 15 — London*

You'll notice that there's been a gap of nearly a week here. You may wonder where it went. Well, more or less I called it off. On the one hand I'm preoccupied with South Africa ahead, and on the other I'm disenchanted with myself. It's easy to keep a daily diary if a lot of interesting things are happening all around you, and it's even easier if you are pleased with yourself. But if things are dull and you get bored or mad at yourself, then it's an entirely different situation.

I started off back in June keeping the diary in longhand, but I soon switched to tape, which is easier and more natural for me. Sometimes, it's nothing to do it every night, like brushing your teeth. Other times, it's like pulling them. And sometimes, a few times, you go to work in the middle of the day on the tape — either dutifully, because you should; or apologetically, because you've been lax; or enthusiastically, because you have something you really want to say. It's a great luxury I have that somebody will listen to me — for a year, anyway. Two weeks or a month from now or sometime, this disembodied voice of mine will appear in a room in Connecticut, logging the long-ago, faraway events of London or Stockholm or wherever — recorded, then transcribed, edited, *preserved*.

112

I offer this slight intrusion about the diary process here only because there should be at least a token word made in passing. At some point in the keeping of a diary, the fact of it becomes, necessarily, a part of the life and, therefore, a part of the diary. Because I must recapitulate my day, I think about it more. Sometimes I don't want to say the things I have to. But then, twenty years from now, or fifteen or thirty, I will surely look back on this year as the year I kept the diary, more than I will remember many of the things that I kept the diary for.

I did make an effort to restore my few days' lapse on one occasion this week. I went from Stockholm to London last Saturday, and then up to Nottingham two days later. The tournament has a split venue — London and Nottingham. The time I figured when I could catch up on the diary was as I watched TV as Princess Anne was married. But sorry — playing back the tape, I find cheers and flourishes from the television and these two sole comments from myself:

(1) "There's no doubt in my mind that if the monarchy were to be abolished, England would disintegrate. This wedding just encapsulizes all my feelings on that subject." And,

(2) "Hey, Mark Phillips wears a Rolex watch just like mine."

These two revelations aside, I'll also note now from the scoreboard that I beat Patrice Dominguez in the first round and lost to Tiriac in the second. As far as I can recall, that's the first time ever that Ion beat me — which is certainly a first-class confidence builder for playing in South Africa on the world stage.

Of course, I must say that everybody has been most considerate of my feelings, and they have all done their best to bolster my confidence for the experience ahead. So, late this afternoon, as I was standing in the lobby of the Westbury waiting with Nailbags to get a cab to the airport for the flight to Johannesburg, Nastase came by on the way to play his match. He moved across the lobby, stood by the front door for best effect, waved gaily at me and yelled: "Hey, Brown Sugar, don't let 'em put you in jail."

# 12

## *Part of a Gradual Harvest*

*Friday, November 16, 1973 — London*

We fly out tonight on BOAC, a through-flight to Johannesburg, with a stopover in Nairobi, but even as late as this afternoon, in my room at the Westbury Hotel, members of SANROC — the South African Non-Racial Olympic Committee — tried to convince me not to go. We argued for several hours, going round and round the same points, but I remain convinced that my way is the one that can best serve the purpose of eventual equality. Economic sanctions have been tried against South Africa, legal appeals to domestic courts and world courts, political pressure and the force of international public opinion, and all of them have proved unsuccessful at breaking apartheid. On the other hand, the country bends a little for sports. South Africa seems more upset when people won't play with it, than when they won't trade with it.

The country is, after all, ideally situated and structured for playing games. It has a subtropical climate which encourages year-round outdoor activity, and it has a year-round subservient population to do the dirty work and allow whites leisure time. Not surprisingly, South Africa also has among the very highest indices of divorce, suicide and alcoholism in the world. You see, idle hands are the devil's workshop.

Spectator sports have no competition with television either, since South Africa holds back the tide of human communications from its blacks by denying television to everyone.  Thus, the whole land focuses heavily on major sporting events.  Bob Foster, the American black who is light heavyweight champion of the world, arrived in Johannesburg earlier this week to start training for a title fight on December 1 with a white South African challenger.  This is the first interracial fight in history in South Africa, but once the appetite for the best boxing is whetted how can it be the last?  Same with tennis, or any sport.

*Saturday, November 17 — Nairobi / Johannesburg*

The flight was crowded, and I was jammed into an inside seat, next to Nailbags.  He slept better than I did.  Our traveling party included Donald, who has the flu, and his wife, Carole; Richard Evans, a British journalist who is also the press officer for ATP; Frank Deford, who is covering for *Sports Illustrated;* and Bud Collins of the Boston *Globe,* who is to join us in Johannesburg from Australia.  I wish *Jet* or *Ebony* had sent a black reporter along too.

At quarter to four, London time, when the morning sky was just beginning to color over Africa, Donald and Richard took me upstairs to the first-class lounge to try and prep me for the press conference I would have to face when I arrived.  One of the more curious inconsistencies of South Africa is that it still has a relatively free press.  There is a certain oblique censorship and a greater implied censorship (if you go too far), but the papers do enjoy a surprisingly large degree of freedom.  The Afrikaans-language dailies seldom exercise the right.  The government of South Africa has long been run by the Afrikaners, the Boers, descendants of the Dutch, who were the first Europeans to settle southern Africa.  The British came later and now dominate the cities and the business of the country, although they are a white minority.  The English-speaking dailies, notably the *Star* and the Rand *Daily Mail,* can be quite outspoken, even altogether critical of the Afrikaner government.  As long as the government has the Afrikaners in the bag though, it seems content to let the English-language newspapers lurch and snap to no real avail, all the while making the country appear freer than it really is.  So I could face some tough questions from the English-speaking press.

115

I had agreed as part of the deal that I would keep my counsel and hold any substantive opinions for my departure. This would also serve to keep the press from hounding me, so that I would be able to concentrate on playing tennis. I decided to start my statement this way: "I'm here in a spirit of cooperation. I've come as a man, nothing more, nothing less, and I look forward to a fascinating twelve days . . ." Pretty pat stuff — but, as it turned out at the conference, everybody was being so polite to me that my remarks were accepted with a ponderous courtesy.

It was, all things considered, a mellow welcome to the land. Shortly before the plane landed, a little man came up to me, and said: "Mr. Ashe, I'm one of those horrible South Africans" — and he paused — "and I just want to wish you the best of success. I promise you we're not all as bad as we're supposed to be, and you mark my words: three fourths of the people will be pulling for you." When we landed, this gentleman came down the ramp right after me, and another white South African who had also wished me luck came up on the other side, and together they sort of convoyed me into the terminal.

There were a few black people waving and snapping photographs from the balcony, but it was a quiet reception, and of course deceptive, too, because the international building, where we came in, offers a sort of diplomatic immunity to blacks. There are no separate facilities there, no physical evidence of apartheid. It was just like landing in Sydney or Rio or Brussels or any damn place. It was very disconcerting that way.

And, like a lot of places, the customs line was long. When my turn came, the official took my passport without offering me any special recognition and flipped through it till he came to the visa stamp. He glanced at it for a moment and then abruptly turned and took it back to a uniformed officer, who seemed to be in charge. This guy looked like he just came in from the Boer War: starched, short-pants, long-socks uniform; swagger stick; bushy mustache. He exchanged a word or two with the customs man, who turned, walked back to his cubicle and stamped the passport with no more to-do. As I passed, the officer with the swagger stick said, "Welcome to our country, Mr. Ashe."

116

I had flown for more than half a day and missed most of a night's sleep, but I felt fine physically. Emotionally, however, I was shot. But I put on my mask, the one I must keep on for the next couple of weeks. I have this ability to take it all in and never to let on how I am feeling. Nobody can tell the difference.

Owen Williams and his wife, Jennifer, drove us from the airport through the city to the house where we were going to stay, in Sandton, the best section of town. My first impression was that apartheid was a much more subtle proposition than I had anticipated. If you were white, I doubt if you would even have seen anything out of the ordinary. It is what you *don't* see. During the entire trip from the airport, nearly an hour's drive, I saw only two blacks driving cars. All you see are the Africans walking — and walking slowly, as if they really have no place to go.

We are staying in the house of a wealthy insurance/real estate man named Brian Young. He is Jewish, recently divorced, and lives alone in this huge, opulent place — alone with the usual complement of servants, of course. He is away this weekend, on a trip to Swaziland. One wing of the house is turned over to four of us: Frank Deford and I each in a private room, Donald and Carole in a suite. Richard Evans and Bud Collins (when he arrives) are staying in private houses nearby. While Brian is away, our host is Gordon Forbes, a contemporary of Owen's and once a world-class player himself, whose sister, Jean, is married to Cliff Drysdale. Forbesy is divorced too, so he has moved into other of Brian's guest quarters to look after us.

The place is very Spanish, sprawling, with the obligatory trappings of the neighborhood: a Mercedes or two in every garage, a swimming pool, tennis court, gardens, the majestic purple jacaranda trees and a burglar alarm system. There is a cook, a maid, a gardener. Forbesy orders steaks all around for our luncheon as soon as we arrive. Steaks, apparently, are the everyday staple of the cuisine and are served like hot dogs. And when I ask for a cold drink, the maid, Anna, drops her eyes and says: "Yes, master." *For God's sake.*

So here is little Artie Ashe, the skinny black kid from the capital

117

of the old Confederacy, all set up in a mansion, carrying on jes' like the white folks, and gettin' hisself called Master. I knew in advance that a lot of people would call me a hypocrite for living in a white man's house — and the matter was discussed, very carefully, at length. But the only other alternative would have been to stay in a first-class hotel, such as Bob Foster and several of the white tennis players did. When we were invited to use Brian Young's house, we were assured that our host genuinely wanted our company, and it provided me with a privacy and a convenience that was bound to help my tennis. Staying in Soweto, that grim black "city" that serves Johannesburg, was really impossible. I did not come to South Africa in sackcloth and ashes to serve penance. I know damn well how badly the Africans in this country live, but I cannot see how it would serve any useful purpose for me to live like one my-self. I know I'll catch a lot of heat for this, but I think it's best this way.

This night we went to a cocktail party that was given by the various South African breweries which had joined together to spon-sor the Open. It was the very essence of brotherhood: whites, blacks, Coloreds, Asians all eating and drinking together. Of course, it was all illegal too, because whites are not permitted to provide drinks for persons of any other race. (And what do I call these persons? You can't just say blacks, because there are also cat-egories of Coloreds and Asians too. And you can't say minorities, because the minorities are the majority here. I hate to say "non-white," which is the accepted term, because that means that a race is defined foremost by the absence of what it is. To be devilish, I'd like to call the whites "nonblacks." Anyway, I use nonwhites under protest. After the breweries' illegal party, Owen called ahead to a little restaurant, and we all went out to dinner. Every-body was just lovely to me. If I had been a native nonwhite, I would not have been permitted in the place. Hell, if I had been a native nonwhite, I wouldn't even have been permitted to be up that late in Johannesburg. There's a curfew for all nonwhites at 10 P.M.

Somebody told me today that the only way to understand South Africa is to assume that it is either run by madmen or evil men. I'm catching on.

*Sunday, November 18 — Johannesburg*

Went out to Ellis Park today for a hit, and saw my first WHITES ONLY signs. You know, since every visitor who takes a picture in South Africa finds it easiest to portray the fact of apartheid with restroom signs, most people who have never been here think, I'm sure, that the whole country is nothing but a land of public toilets. I was almost relieved at last to see some segregated restrooms; otherwise, it would be like going to Paris the first time and not seeing the Eiffel Tower or visiting Egypt and missing the pyramids. And right away, somebody wanted to take my picture in front of the HERE BLANKES or DAMAS BLANKES Africkaans signs. It does freak you out to see those things though. It wakes you up.

I had a hit with some of the country's best black players. I'm afraid that none of them is very good, though, which, considering the tennis facilities and coaching, is not very surprising. You can't just bring a handful of them into the Open, beat them love and love in the first round and then send them back to nowhere till the next year's Open. We've got to obtain the right for the best players to compete on the Sugar Circuit — a series of top domestic tournaments — and at all levels of competition.

Luckily, I don't have to play my own first-round match until Tuesday, which should give me enough time to get acclimated to the altitude here. Jo'burg (everybody calls it Jo'burg) is 500 feet higher than Denver. This is surely the reason that almost all South African players have the same, limited style: short, blocky swings. The ball moves fast in the light air, but inversely, the Dunlops they use here fluff all up and get very heavy on your arm. The South Africans could always handle everybody else's case when they got them down here in their own air. They even won the women's Federation Cup when that was played down here a couple years ago — and there isn't a single outstanding South African woman player.

I'm going to get an oxygen tank tomorrow for courtside. You've got to limit yourself. Forget about angles. Just try to hit the ball in the middle of the racket. If you hit it off center, it's liable to soar on

119

you. I mean, balls you hit out won't just go a little long — they'll hit the backstop.

Luckily for me, as badly as I'm playing, I've drawn a first-round opponent who's coming in from New Zealand tomorrow, so he's bound to be less acclimated to the altitude than me. It's Sherwood Stewart, ranked thirty-sixth in the U.S., from Goose Creek, Texas. I go halfway around the world, and finally get into South Africa, and how do I make history: I play a guy from Goose Creek, Texas.

*Monday, November 19 — Johannesburg*

I saw my first reference book today, the odious pass that all non-whites must carry, signed by their employer. The blacks call it, I learned, "my stinker."

Still, apartheid is handled with such sophistication that it is sometimes easy to forget that South Africa is nothing less than a police state. The injustices here go far beyond the seminal matter of racial inequality. Informers of all races are everywhere. The secret police — Bureau of State Security, or BOSS (isn't that magnificent? — straight out of Ian Fleming) are ubiquitous. Arrest is arbitrary, incarceration capricious, and there is an execution, on the average, every nine or ten days. Without any trial, you can be imprisoned for three months at a clip — and they can repeat that each and every three months, ad infinitum. There is something especially unsettling about hearing the expression "go inside" being tossed about in any conversation, in the most respectable company. Jail is an everyday fact of life here.

House arrest, or something known as "banning," is virtually as effective though. Banning is an insidious device which permits you to exist but not really to live. If the government bans you, you cannot publish, attend a university, visit a library, travel or even meet with more than one person at a time. You could not, for example, even play a game of doubles. Seventy persons have already been banned this year. They just banned a swimming administrator who was too outspoken on the subject of multiracial swimming competition.

There is, in fact, increased repression in South Africa, belying the well-publicized "liberal" breakthroughs which have permitted me to play here and Foster to fight.  The universities and churches are being pressured by the government to conform, and, for the first time, the newspapers are genuinely concerned about the full threat of censorship.  Today, out of the blue, the government declared that blacks and Coloreds could not compete against each other in amateur sports.  It is as if they have unscrewed the top off one bottle of apartheid and given the rest of the world a good heady whiff of that but then screwed the lid even tighter on all the other bottles — and tightest of all on those that are concerned with men's minds: the schools, the press, the churches.

I had met some black journalists at Ellis Park and was chatting with them near the courts, when, suddenly, one of them said: "Please, Arthur, we cannot talk here, this is a public place."  So some of us moved on to the privacy of the players' lounge (presumably it's not bugged), and they emphasized to me what I already knew — that many blacks do not want me here, that they feel my being here legitimizes the government and lends it some credence.  As Cliff Drysdale explains it: "If you accept the hypothesis that all this must end in violence, then any visit from an outsider — Arthur's, Foster's, anyone's — any dealings with the government only prolongs that agony."

After the other writers had left, a reporter named Don Mattera, of the Johannesburg *Star,* stayed and we talked by ourselves for a while.

"Do you think I should have come?" I asked.

"Oh, I'm glad you're here," he said.  "We need some contact, we need to be periodically assured that people in the rest of the world still understand and care.  Committed black Americans should visit South Africa."  He paused; he spoke softly, evenly.  "But someone like Foster only hurts us.  That kind of person should stay away."  Foster had already spent a week in Jo'burg without making any contact with the black community.  Moreover, he had declared that he "loved" South Africa and might like to build a vacation home here.

"Will you write that about Foster?" I asked.

"No," Don said.  "I wouldn't criticize another brother.  There'll come a day when we'll have the luxury to criticize, to disagree with each other in public, but right now we need solidarity above all."

121

Mattera, who is classified as a Colored, is a poet as well as a journalist, and Nikki Giovanni saw his work when she visited South
Africa and was much impressed with it.  Don has his first collection
of poems at the printer right now.  That stuns me: how anyone
could perform any serious creative effort in this atmosphere.  Everyone must be so careful politically not to offend the government
that I would think that this fear would inhibit the spontaneity of
life that results in the creation of any art.

Not long after Don left, I met the President of South Africa, Jim
Fouche.  He is an old man, the ceremonial head of the nation, the
best equivalent for royalty in a land without royalty.  "How do you
like South Africa?" he asked me.

"How are you enjoying the tennis?" I answered.

*Tuesday, November 20 — Johannesburg*

Bud Collins, the Boston writer, arrived last night and came over
to Brian's for breakfast with us this morning.  "I flew in with Sherwood Stewart," Bud said.  "You know why he's here?  He thought
he would come because he wanted to see something historic.  He
thought it would be interesting to be here to see you break through
in South Africa.  Now he flies ten thousand miles and finds out he's
the poor sonuvabitch you've got to break through."

Sherwood and I came out to play just after noon.  There was no
wind to speak of, and in the warm stillness, a few small clouds
spotted about a high blue sky.  The courts at Ellis are cement, and
the center court is surrounded on all sides by a dandy little covered
grandstand, which seats several thousand.  The roof is aluminum,
topped by several light towers and embroidered with a few billboards, one of which, for Scotch, actually says: "Time to serve Black
& White."  The stands were not quite filled, but for a weekday the
crowd was quite large, and I could see blacks scattered all about the
place, including one whole boxful at courtside.  I learned later that
an usher had run up to Owen about this time, and, distraught,
cried: "Are you Mr. Williams?  You must do something.  The
blacks and the Coloreds are sitting in all the white seats."

Owen said: "I'll take care of it."

For the record, I won the first point that a black who had been

122

persona non grata ever played on the center court at Ellis Park, in Johannesburg, Republic of South Africa. It was a forehand, down the line. I won that game, a service break, and the set, and the match: 6–1, 7–6, 6–4.

Afterward, I decided to go out to Soweto. I had an informal agreement with Owen that I would keep him posted at all times as to my whereabouts. He wasn't going to stop me from going anywhere, he just was concerned. On his part, it was superfluous, because by now I was convinced that I was being tailed wherever I went anyway. I'm not paranoid to think that anybody was out to get me; I imagine it was just to make sure that nobody killed me or kidnaped me and brought South Africa a lot of bad publicity.

But it was eerie, anyway. I've never been tailed before — and for cops and robbers writers, I have some friendly little advice: if the gasoline crisis remains with us, tailing is going to be an increasingly difficult operation. The Arabs are pretty tough on South Africa because of its Israeli sympathies, and already there are tough gasoline restrictions here. Among other things, there is no gas sold anywhere on Sunday, so there are virtually no cars on the road on Sunday. And Sunday was when I became positive I was being tailed, because the only car around was the one always back of me. Believe me, it is going to be very difficult turning a good dollar in the tailing business from here on, on Sundays anyway.

Owen's car is at my disposal, along with his driver, Solomon. He is a perceptive black man from Mozambique, friendly, shrewd, indispensable to Owen, with such a broad knowledge of the events and the people of Jo'burg that I thought initially that Sol must be an informer. But he is not, I am sure. For one thing, aside from his Man Fridaying for Owen, he runs a large dance troupe, which performs the indigenous tribal dances of southern Africa. The ensemble has received several offers to perform in the U.S., but the government has forbidden them passports. Presumably, informers get better treatment.

Soweto sounds like some quaint old African name, while actually it is just a bureaucratic abbreviation for Southwest Township. And I always visualized it in terms of the usual suburb, hard by the city. But suddenly Solomon and I were buzzing along an open road, passing nothing but gold mines. "Hey, where's Soweto?" I asked.

123

It was seventeen miles from Jo'burg.  And not only do the blacks have to train and bus in and back every day for work, but they must buy most of their goods from the white man.  Soweto has a population upward of a million, but it is not a city so much as it is an urban reservation.  The government owns all the houses.  No public transportation within the city.  One fire brigade, one hospital, one switchboard for 500 phones.  Plumbing is rare, and perhaps a tenth of Soweto has electricity.  Unlike the whites, who have free education, the blacks, who can least afford it, must pay tuition, so that thousands of kids never go to school, and roam the streets, idly passing all the formative hours of their lives.

All of it sprawls.  The best of it is endless rows of tiny little cottages; the worst, shacks of paper, of wood, of tin.  The last tableau remains the most vivid, and the most heartless somehow.  It was late in the afternoon now, and the thousands of workers were coming home from the long day in Jo'burg.  Many had risen before dawn, and many were burdened with food and other items they had to buy in the city.  There was the train station, and before it, a great field, maybe half a mile wide, which they had to cross before they even got to the houses of Soweto.  We watched as they came, hundreds, thousands of them, filing toward us as the sun fell across their backs.  Suddenly it occurred to me that I had seen something very much like this once before, and then I remembered that that scene was in Africa too, a time in Kenya when I saw hordes of wildebeest crossing a broad savanna.

"Let's go back, Sol," I said.  The servants cooked a steak for me as soon as I came into the house.

### Wednesday, November 21 — Johannesburg

The paper was waiting for me with breakfast, and the story on the front page: they had banned Don Mattera.  The banning order must have been in process, even as I sat talking with him Monday.

I beat Barry Phillips-Moore in straight sets this afternoon, four/four/ and one, and then this evening several of us went downtown to the headquarters of the United States Information Service to attend a reception for black journalists.  Foster had also been invited, but declined.

It was dusk when we arrived, and the lobby of the building was dark, but there, standing at the bottom of the stairs, was Mattera. He was alone, except for an agent from BOSS. Don greeted me warmly, so calmly, and seemed mostly only apologetic that he could not attend the meeting upstairs — the one he had personally organized. "I don't want to do anything to jeopardize your visit, Arthur," he said. I shook his hand and commiserated with his fate. He only shrugged. "They have banned me, but they cannot stop me," he said. "If they put me in jail, they put me in jail. But they cannot stop me." He shrugged again.

He is thirty-seven years old. His livelihood is journalism, or was, till this morning. That is denied him now. He has six children and lives surrounded by squalor and violence. He has no electricity, just as he has no plumbing, so he writes his poetry by candle, or gaslight. I did not know it then, but he was writing a poem about me at this time. It reads:

> I listened deeply when you spoke
> About the step-by-step evolution
> Of a gradual harvest,
> Tendered by the rains of tolerance
> And patience.
>
> Your youthful face,
> A mask,
> Hiding a pining, anguished spirit, and
> I loved you brother —
> Not for your quiet philosophy
> But for the rage in your soul,
> Trained to be rebuked or summoned.
>
> As for me,
> When I asked them for bread,
> They gave the wheatfield,
> And I thought they loved me.
> When I asked for water,
> They gave the well,
> And I thought they cared.
>
> When I asked for freedom
> They took back the wheatfield
> And the well,

125

Tightened the chains
And told me, I asked too much.
Now, I no longer wait for
The wheat and water, but fight
For freedom  . . .

Mattera is a unique person, which, of course, is why they banned
him.  When he was a teen-ager, he was recognized as the toughest
kid in a community that features the casual violence of a doomed
people.  Don headed a gang called "The Vultures," and he even
killed, but they only put him in jail, because he merely killed other
Coloreds or blacks, and the government is really not to be bothered
with that kind of intramural mayhem.  But inexplicably Mattera
was somehow mystically transformed in jail, he came out for the
last time at eighteen, went back to school, educated himself, married and began to write his poetry by candlelight.  Even now, they
say he is something of a legend where he lives.  It is said that he,
the gentle poet, is permitted to walk the dark streets unmolested.
The thugs, penniless and hopeless, understand that they must not
attack Don Mattera.

And so, as he watched us go, we climbed the stairs to attend his
meeting.  I agreed to speak in the auditorium, so long as I could ask
questions as well as answer them.  There were about seventy-five
of us jammed into this small, windowless room — counting the
man from BOSS and a predictable number of informers.  The atmosphere was charged with fear and passion, and the place was as hot
from the tension as from the crush of people.  I did not really understand how scared the people were, though, until I looked over at
one of the group's officers and saw that his hands were trem-
bling — and that he could not stop them.

He stood first, and talked of Don Mattera: "He has spoken out for
the common brotherhood.  So our time must be short too, for so do
we.  We may be called on very soon to say no more."

"Power, power!" some of the people said, and others: "Shame,
shame!"

But they did not spare me.  I heard one man mutter "Uncle Tom"
at me, and others were no less opposed to my being there.  "You
come here, our people play in a tournament once, and the situation

126

remains unchanged. The black man still has his place — cleaning toilets. You stay away, all of you. All right, Arthur?"

"You mean you want me to stand on the outside and just watch you suffer?" I said. "That makes me very sad."

"If we isolate them, they're forced to change," another said. "Cut off South Africa, boycott it. Don't you see: we blacks wouldn't suffer any more than we already do. We are used to suffering. Only the whites would suffer more."

"Power, power!"

"Your presence delays our struggle. You go back to New York. Stay away, stay away. You come here and save their tennis. Soccer is dying here because of the sanctions placed on it."

"Sanctions won't work," I said. "When there's a choice, money over morality, it's always money that wins out. There's ten southern African nations trading with this country today. If the blacks cannot keep up a boycott, what makes you think the whites will?"

"We don't just want equality, as you do," a young woman said. "We were dispossessed. We want our land back."

"Look, I'm not saying that the United States is a proper analogy here," I said. "I'm not telling you how to live your lives. But I am saying that history shows that progress does not come in huge chunks. It comes bit by bit. There was the lady named Rosa Parks on the bus in Montgomery, and she was tired, and she said, *No, I'm not moving,* and the whole thing for us started from there."

"She would have been banned here," a man shouted, "and Martin Luther King would have been put on Robben Island."

"Please, I know these things," I went on. "Of course I know it's infinitely harder here than it was in the States. But I still see my being here as a start. You've got integrated seating out at Ellis Park. It was never there before. And we're trying to get black players on the Sugar Circuit. There will be something left when I'm gone. I'm always thinking of the guy behind me, so I tell my head to hold my tongue.

"Maybe I'm naive, but I think, when you're mapping out a plan for progress, emotion cannot be allowed to play a large role, except for drumming up support. I had a very wise man who taught me to play tennis, to play against whites, and in places no black man had

127

ever been before. His name was Dr. Walter Johnson, and he used to say: 'Those whom the gods wish to destroy, they first make mad.' "

I don't know if I convinced anyone. It was a time for declaring oneself, not for swaying others. I gave them an excuse to air all the things bottled up inside, even though they realized that everything they said would probably be in a report at BOSS the next morning. And there were many who supported my views. I don't know, maybe the crowd was split fifty-fifty. "You know," a funny little guy named Patsy said, "they tell me I can't sleep on the white man's sheets because I'm black, but they let you come and they find you the best beds, and if you're black and good enough to sleep on sheets, well so am I. Everytime they do something like this, they kick their own policies in the backside."

"Somebody like you comes," another man said, "it shows us an inspiration, not just to excel at something, but not to be intimidated by the bully. Enough of you come and show us, then pretty soon, we don't have no bully no more."

"You're not an inspiration to me," a large man said. "But you're a challenge. I see you and other free blacks who come here, and it is a challenge to me to be like you, free, and if not me, my sons."

"Power, power!"

Downstairs, Don was waiting patiently, just to say goodbye. "Go well, brothers," he said to us, clasping our hands, "go well, go well."

Shame, shame.

# 13

## *These Small Communications*

Ellis Park has been crowded, with record turnouts all week, but I faced Bob Hewitt in the quarter-finals today, and for the first time, the place really tingled. This was the stuff of confrontation, and nobody was missing this.

Hewitt is a native Australian, but he emigrated to South Africa several years ago and is now a citizen, with a beautiful South African wife named Delaille. Harry Hopman, the Aussie captain, never thought much of Hewitt, questioned his gumption and never used him on the Australian Davis Cup team, which is one of the reasons Bob left the country. This was not altogether uncommon with left-over Aussie players who couldn't break into the first string. Ken Fletcher moved to Hong Kong, for example, Nailbags to Paris. But these were just idle pairings of the man and the nation; Hewitt and South Africa were made for each other. Of all the South African players, Hewitt, the Australian, is, well, the most South African.

His politics aside, many people find Hewitt an amiable enough fellow off the court, but he is, by any standard, a terror on it. He argues with officials as a matter of course and, often enough, with opponents and fans as well. Curiously, he has always been on his very best behavior in his matches against me, and I'm sure he has made a conscious effort to bring that off so smoothly. But often he can be unbearable. A few years ago in Berlin, I was in the locker room when he and Roger Taylor came in after an especially aggrieved match. Hewitt was railing at Taylor, and eventually he accused him of cheating. Then he kind of shoved Roger a couple of times. You don't go around pushing the son of a Sheffield steelworker, and you don't call him a cheat. Roger is normally a pretty soft-spoken guy, but this was too much. It took one punch, and Hewitt was down, and the fight, such as it was, was over. Roger's hand was so swollen that he was out of tennis for the next week or so. They had to take Hewitt to the hospital. I remember poor Delaille, outside the dressing room, crying like a baby.

On another occasion, at the Los Angeles Tennis Club, an elderly gentleman became so upset at Hewitt's behavior that he followed him off the court and came up behind him and jumped him.

Hewitt and I are so at odds in our views that we seldom bother with one another. Aside from polite salutations, I really don't believe that we've exchanged four sentences of dialogue since about three years ago when we had a rather spirited discussion of apartheid. The conversation ended rather abruptly when Hewitt informed me that he didn't want to talk about it anymore inasmuch as I was so obviously uninformed since I didn't even know that South African blacks preferred apartheid because "they're happy."

Hewitt's opinions are well known in South Africa, so the fans in attendance appreciated that we stood as opponents in every sense of the word. We even came, by coincidence, dressed quite properly for the occasion: I in rebel red, he in a brown shirt. The crowd was animated and restless, but they were most sportsmanlike, and it seemed that about half of them were for me. It was a good show they came for; back home, it was Thanksgiving, and the tenth anniversary of John Kennedy's death.

The tennis was not so competitive. We held service till I led 4–3, and Bob had me 30–love, but I got him on the defensive with some good returns of his second serve, and broke him for 5–3, then held for the first set. I also broke him straight off to start the second set, but my own serve began to desert me, and Hewitt got his chance to get back in the match when we came to a tie-breaker. But I jumped right out to a big lead and won it easily. I ran out the match 6–3. I've won nine straight sets now, and am really playing quite well.

130

As I came off the court today, I made a point to salute the north-east section of the stands, where only nonwhites sit, and Hewitt, in his own crude way, made something of a facetious gesture toward them when he left the court too. The nonwhites have been cheering brazenly for me, without a great deal of concern for the niceties of evenhanded tennis crowd etiquette. The continued existence of this section has also been the cause of some embarrassment and controversy.

I must admit it: I made a mistake in claiming that I would play before a totally integrated house. Segregated seating is the law of the land, and I was presumptuous to think I could change that. Now, it could be said that Owen lied to me when he agreed that there would be fully integrated seating. Technically, I suppose, I would be within my rights to pick up my rackets and go home, proclaiming that I had been deceived. But none of these things are ever, shall we say, black and white. The South Africans think that I have gone back a little on my word too, because I assured them I would keep my mouth shut about politics while I was here, and they think I fudged on that by writing a piece for the London *Sunday Times* which was reprinted here in the Rand *Daily Mail* this Monday, after I arrived on South African soil. In that article, I stated unequivocally that I had been promised that I would be playing before a fully integrated stadium "with no special sections reserved for Blacks and Whites only."

So, it seems, they read this little tidbit over in Pretoria Monday and as fast as they could started ringing Owen Williams' phone off the hook. Owen is a case study in how to play both ends against the middle. Here is the game he is playing: to keep Jim Crow John Law off his back, the nonwhite section has been retained, as visible as ever. To keep his promise to me (and to his own ideals), he has very quietly distributed tickets to nonwhites for all sections of the stands. Blacks have even sat in the President's box, at courtside, and in every section of the grandstand. I know for sure, because Donald and Carole Dell and the U.S. writers have been taking their own little censuses every day. Also, we have been doing our own personal integrating by bringing along the servants from Brian's house. If the allotted nonwhite tickets are not distributed before the matches begin, Jennifer Williams just goes around handing

131

them out to whatever blacks she comes across.  And if the ushers complain, Owen "takes care of it."

To any logical, rational mind, this probably all sounds very deceitful, but remember that South Africa is neither logical nor rational.  You negotiate the truth along with everything else.  The *Star* is champing at the bit, anxious to write the true story of how the seating arrangements are being finagled.  They feel they got blindsided when my views appeared in the *Mail,* and they want to get even.  We hope they will not risk the progress we have realized just for the sake of a scoop, but it got a little sticky yesterday.

After I finished an interview with CBS out on the grounds, an Asian citizen of South Africa appeared from nowhere, waving his ticket — plainly stamped "Nonwhite" — and screaming that I was being fooled or duplicitous, or both.  This made the matter of seating public, and the press took after Owen, who was not anxious for the attention, especially because he was still coming off a spectacular hangover.  Even without that, he is really getting seesawed, but he can be very proud.  Outside of Wimbledon, the South African Open is run better than any tournament in the world, and the reason is Owen Williams.

*Friday, November 23 — Johannesburg*

I'm enjoying an amazingly eclectic social schedule here too.  Tomorrow night Brian is holding a big bash at the house, complete with entertainment by Sol's dance troupe.  Last night we had dinner with a fascinating man named Mandy Moross, a financier, who is among the richest men in the country.  Tonight, at a party given by John Burns of the United States Information Agency, I met the most famous South African author, Alan Paton.  He is no longer under house arrest and has his passport back, and he flew up from Durban to see me.  Nothing ever makes any sense here.  *Cry, The Beloved Country* is now required reading in many South African high schools.  "The whole world thinks we are odd," Mr. Paton said to me, in something of a spectacular understatement.

There were also several students invited to the party, and many of them — from a couple of banned organizations known as the South African Students' Association and the Black People's Convention — lashed into me, with the usual arguments why I shouldn't be in South Africa. The students I have met here exhibit an exuberance and a vast determination that is not unlike what the students of the U.S. in the sixties possessed. I had to break off the debate at a pretty early hour because I must play Drysdale tomorrow at midday in the semis.

*Saturday, November 24 — Johannesburg*

The spectators spilled onto the apron of the court today, and a few even perched up on the billboards, but if the attendance was slightly larger than for my match against Hewitt, this was an easier, more sporting crowd. It is well known that Drysdale and I like and respect each other, so it is really merely coincidental that I am playing another home boy. As a matter of fact, Cliff has been so outspoken against his government's policies that I suppose to some whites in the audience I am the lesser of two evils. Really, the white crowd has been most generous — although I'm afraid that the nonwhites in their section were not so benevolent toward Cliff. A couple of times during the match, the referee had to ask them to be less restrained on my behalf.

This is the first time in months that Cliff has gotten to the semifinals of a tournament. He was sick early in the year and has devoted much of his attention to the ATP, so he really has not been able to apply himself fully to tennis. At his best, he wins on steadiness. He lacks stamina and has an average serve, but his blocky South African backswing helps his return of service — he can keep the ball in play and wait for you to make the mistake. Cliff's two-handed backhand is his best stroke, so strong that playing Drysdale is really like playing a lefty, because my best shots go to his strength (for example, as they do to Laver).

But today, my ground game was reliable — better, in fact, than my serve, which was spotty. I broke Cliff right off for 2–0 (prompting whistles and hosannas from the northeast corner), but then I fell into what turned out to be my only real slump of the match, and Cliff came back to lead 4–3. But my groundies were working here, and I broke him twice in succession and won 6–4. My serve began to pick up somewhat in the next set, and Cliff moved well back of

133

the base line to receive, but I was just too reliable for him, and I finished out the match, three and two. The crowd cheered us both warmly.

Now I have won twelve straight sets, only two of them tie-breakers, and only Jimmy Connors stands in my path to the title. He appears, alas, a formidable barrier. The tennis gossip is that he and Chrissie Evert will soon announce their engagement, and she is down here also — whether as an inspiration or distraction, I do not know. He blew Okker off the court in the other semi today. Tom said that Connors played better against him today than any man ever had, which is quite a testament. Okker and I are playing as a doubles team for the first time, and we've gotten through to the semis, so I've got a good chance to win two titles. I didn't enter the mixed doubles, although a few mischievous South Africans have suggested that I should have gone into that draw — with a pretty white South African partner (and lots of embracing and even some exuberant kissing to celebrate our victories).

After my match with Cliff, I got an urgent call to hurry to Owen's office. Piet Koornhof was there, waiting with Owen and Donald and Blen Franklin of the Lawn Tennis Association. Since I appreciate that my chances of meeting the Prime Minister are slim, I have been increasingly anxious to see Koornhof, this man who is so responsible for my being here. He greeted me with real enthusiasm, I thought, but holding some reserve. He was an impressive-looking man, although any pretense to good looks would be marred by his hook nose. But he is tall, maybe 6'1", and wore a smartly tailored diplomatic gray suit well. He smokes heavily, and speaks slowly and deliberately, perhaps because he is smart enough to realize that he is not especially articulate. But Koornhof is very bright, a Rhodes Scholar, and it is a fact (though one hardly much promulgated by Pretoria) that his thesis at Oxford was based on the premise that apartheid could not continue to work.

Koornhof laid down the ground rules: we would speak candidly but off the record. This works, obviously, to his advantage; that is, if I keep my word. The man trusted me. It is possible that I could embarrass him. I give him credit for that, and even though this will be published more than a year's time after our meeting, there are statements Koornhof made that I am honor-bound not to repeat. I can say that mainly we were separated not by what must be done in South Africa, but *when* it must. I came away honestly believing that the man who is maybe the next Prime Minister of South Africa is committed to major advances for the black man.

I got the feeling that timing was vital. Then he cited improvements that have already been made since he came to influence and those that are earmarked for the immediate future. Specifically, he promised to take up the matter of integrating the Sugar Circuit the next time we spoke.

He also told me, quite bluntly, that what I said and did would have a great bearing on whatever progress in tennis might be forthcoming. It was a subtle enough reminder that they held the whip-hand. But he indicated on a human level that he knew how I felt for the blacks in his country.

*Sunday, November 25 — Johannesburg*

Besides all the black and white laws in South Africa, they have blue laws too: no sports or executions on Sunday. So today we went to Soweto. We obtained a sort of blanket permission for the whites, so Gordon Forbes asked if he could come too. He has lived all his life in Jo'burg and had never once even ventured near Soweto. "I had no idea what the place was even like," he said. "It took me thirty-nine years to travel seventeen miles."

We gave a clinic, with Bud Collins handling the commentary, and played with some of the best local players on what was advertised as the best court in Soweto. That is damning it with faint praise. There are only about twenty courts in the whole place. We played in one of the better sections of Soweto, known as Pfefeni, by a train station, adjoining a dusty soccer field. The best that can be said of Soweto is that it is spacious; it has not had to double back onto its own filth yet. Perhaps 1500 people showed up, jammed against the courts and under the signs, all around, that read: "LIFE is great." Life in this case is a cigarette. It is one of the sadnesses of Soweto that few people from the outside ever visit there, so my presence

135

was special, no matter who I was or what I did. The main thing: *I came to them.* The large majority of the people who watched had probably never seen tennis played before.

After the clinic, people crowded about me, and handed me their stinkers to autograph. One rather stout lady asked me to autograph her chest instead, which I did, with a blue Flair, right above the cleavage. But then I was also set upon by a bunch of young students who surrounded me and began berating me, as usual, for coming to their country. This was a little frightening too, because a number of other people, who disagreed with the students, swarmed around them, and we bordered on a real physical confrontation. Some of the people were screaming, "Go home, leave us alone," while others were calling "God bless you, Arthur" to me. Gingerly, I kept moving and smiling and managed to reach a car.

We were going to my official welcoming party at one of the swank residences in Soweto, belonging to Dr. and Mrs. Methlane. He is one of the few physicians in the community, and even though this was a major social event in Soweto, and a weekend night, he was never able to get away from his patients to come to his own party. Owen had handled all the catering though, and a loud band had been hired, and perhaps a couple hundred guests jammed onto the property. The house was tiny by the standards of the white community but palatial relative to the rest of Soweto, and it had a comfortable back yard, where most of the party stayed.

Reggie Ngcobo, a neat little man who is one of the top black lawyers in the country and the head of the black lawn tennis organization affiliated with SALTA, stood up on the lawn after a while and spoke. He was, in some respects, embarrassingly pointed. "You can make us or break us, Arthur," he said. But he was also the most gracious of speakers. "You are the pride and idol of us all. You epitomize sportsmanship, for the essence of sportsmanship is to experience happiness in the happiness of others — and to feel their pain and their suffering too. God bless you for coming, Arthur, our Arthur."

And then he called for three cheers — hip, hip, hooray — and they sang "For He's a Jolly Good Fellow" and hung a prized lucky amulet round my neck and gave me, too, an official new nickname to take away from Soweto: *Sipho,* "A Gift."

*Monday, November 26 — Johannesburg*

This is my tenth final of 1973, but only my first since the summer. Connors beat me the only time we have ever met, in the finals of the U.S. Pro at Boston in July, but I played quite poorly that night and still lost a close match.  There are certain inherent advantages I enjoy in our match-up, so I have a fair right to be confident, even if Connors has played brilliantly down here.  My best strokes go to his weaknesses.  My backhand is better than his forehand, so I'll play him down the line a lot, or right down the middle, and refuse to give him the angles he likes.  Also, because he likes to work with speed, I'll try to vary the pace on my shots.  I expect to attack his second serve, and lob him a lot, because his overhead is lacking. I'll hit over the ball too.  Okker's underspin set the ball up in this light air and let Connors control it too well.

The center court was packed again.  All records are being broken, and the total attendance won't fall too far short of 100,000.  The crowds today were completely behind me too.  It was even so embarrassing at one point in the second set that I had to plead with the fans not to applaud when Connors made mistakes.  Much of the response is probably misleading, of course.  Cheer for the black boy and assuage your guilt feelings.  Some of the same people who supported me so warmly on center court today will tomorrow behave despicably toward some poor black man.  And the South Africans have no special lien on that behavior.  Madison Square Garden's best Knick fans will act the same way.  These people live in two different environments, and I can't explain it except to say that the human is a creature of paradox.  I think of the pathologist who cuts up some stiff and then washes his hands and comes home and pops into bed with his wife.

My first reaction to Connors was how strong he is off the ground. This is his recognized forte, of course, but I was even more impressed than I expected to be.  Still, his serve was nothing special, and I had him to break point in each of his first three service games. Unfortunately, I got the break only in the last of those games, and by then I was down 1–4; he broke me twice.  I chased him the rest of the set, but never quite caught him: 4–6.

I also let him get me down in the second set at 2–1 when I reached rock bottom on my serve. But at last I began to work an occasional lob in, and also in here, I found that I could hit with him off the ground. I broke him quite easily for 4–all and went ahead 5–4 and 6–5.

At 30–all on his serve in this game, I threw up a fine lob, caught him going the wrong way and had the set point, but he pulled off a beautiful backhand cross-court that just got past my racket, and then he served his way into the tie-breaker. That was a disaster; I lost the first six points and 7–2. And after that, you could feel that the air had gone out of the match. The third set went to Connors 6–3, with only one break, but I never was really in it. They will have to wait another year for a black man to be champion of South Africa.

*Tuesday, November 27 — Johannesburg / Durban*

At least I got a large measure of consolation today when Okker and I beat Rob Maud and old Lew Hoad for the doubles championship in four sets. In a way, this might have been the most important doubles match I ever won, for now a black's name rests on the list of South African tennis champions. Etched. Forever.

Afterward, we flew to Durban, on the coast, to start a quick two-day tour before I have to return to commitments in the States. We flew on South African Airways. Apartheid seems to break down in the sky. There were no toilets on the plane designated for blacks only. Of course, excepting me, there were no blacks on the plane either.

Bud Collins has left our party now, but we've been joined by a feature writer for the *Star* named Marshall Lee. We were having a magnificent curry dinner at our hotel, on the beachfront, tonight when Marshall told the quintessential South African joke.

It seems that a visitor to a hotel such as this one calls the waiter over and says, "Waiter, tell me, is that the Indian Ocean?"

"Oh, no, Master," the waiter replies. "That is the white ocean. The Indian ocean is down that way a mile, past the Colored ocean and the black ocean."

*Wednesday, November 28 — Durban / Capetown /
Stellenbosch / Capetown*

We had to get up at four o'clock this morning.  We had chartered
a plane to take us into the bush to meet with Gatsha Buthelezi, the
Zulu chieftain, who is probably the most powerful black man in
South Africa — or, anyway, the most powerful black man in South
Africa who is not in jail or banned.  Unfortunately, the landing
strip we had to use is tucked behind a mountain pass, with nothing
as sophisticated as a radio tower, and when the pilot found no way
to get through dark storm clouds, we had to turn back to Durban.  I
did reach Buthelezi later on the phone (dial: Kwazulu 2), but not
meeting him was probably as great a disappointment as losing to
Connors.

We went back to bed, and slept again until we took a midday
flight to Capetown, and there, as soon as we landed, we drove out
into the vineyard country, to Stellenbosch, where a rather fascinating meeting had been set up for me, with an Afrikaner professor of
anthropology named Christopf Hanekom and three students.  Stellenbosch University is the Harvard for Afrikaners.

A word, first, for the Afrikaners.  They take the brunt of the criticism for their nation's racist politics, and, I might say, no one could
be more deserving.  But give the devil its due: the Afrikaners have
the courage of their convictions.  They are the white majority, and
they run the land and support apartheid.  The British just *own* the
land and support apartheid . . . quietly.  Virtually all of the
English-speaking people that I met in Jo'burg were quick to confide
in me their own political thought — and surprisingly, it was always
located somewhere between the ideology of Bella Abzug and Huey
Newton.  It may come as a shock, then, to learn that 99 percent of
the Parliament is elected as proapartheid.  It is one thing to express
righteous indignation, it is another, quite obviously, to vote against
this dandy arrangement that provides you with cheap servants,
cheap labor and complete superiority.  It doesn't take much.  Cliff
Drysdale's younger brother is just out of college, married and
makes about $7000 a year, but he has a full-time black working for
him.  Slavery in the Confederacy only profited the upper white

classes; in South Africa, a majority of the white population benefits from the system. For that matter, it can be argued that slavery in the old south was a more benevolent arrangement than here. The white masters at least felt some obligation to care for their plantations blacks — if only because it was sensible economically. Here, there are no such ties that bind; Soweto is out of sight, out of mind. The practical slavery of South Africa may well be a more efficient and a more immoral system of servitude than was the real slavery of the old south.

But at least the Afrikaners will defend what they vote for, and this afternoon, under massive old oak trees, spreading over a courtyard at a lovely Dutch inn, we ate finger sandwiches and drank tea and talked dispassionately of racial superiority. Professor Hanekom, who was a dark-eyed, olive-skinned man, welcomed me: "I'm glad you're here, Mr. Ashe. You are obviously a sensitive man who has done a lot for the different races and the different cultures — and for that, I thank you."

We talked rather genially that way for a while, feeling each other out. I found quickly, though, that my adversaries delighted in citing U.S. faults and inconsistencies to support their own injustices. One of the students, who was tall and handsome, with the clearest blue eyes, said: "You see, Mr. Ashe, it is so necessary to keep the balance in our country. This way, we don't have the riots that you suffer."

"But perhaps riots are a small price to pay for freedom of expression," I replied. "And besides, every day that goes by with apartheid increases the chances that the riot that does come will be even more violent, a huge conflagration." I turned to Professor Hanekom. "Tell me, professor, are you scared?"

"No," he said, after a pause.

"Boy, I'd be, if I were you," I said, and I laughed to take the edge off that, but none of the Afrikaners even smiled back. Yet they remained loath to even admit the violence, both casual and one-sided, occasioned by the system. I talked of the easy racial murders, of the rapes, of the executions, and Marshall Lee, the *Star* writer, supported my case with statistics, but in defense of these facts, a student wearing glasses responded only by calling my atten-

140

tion to John Kennedy's assassination, and saying, blandly: "No system is perfect."

"You must try to understand, Mr. Ashe," Professor Hanekom added, "that we are still struggling with our colonial past. We are different cultures, different languages, trying to find our way together, and that is not an easy task."

"I agree with you there," I said. "That sort of thing is true everywhere — as much of the tribes in Burundi, as the Protestants and Catholics in Ireland, the Flemish and Walloons in Belgium, the French in Quebec — "

"So you agree with me, that cultures should stay together?"

"Sure," I said, "but only if they choose to — not by arbitrary fiat."

"We think we are on the road to diverse equality," the professor said somewhat later. "A voluntary multiracialism." .

"We are not so static a society as it may seem," said the tall student. "But at the moment, we just do not believe that racial equality would benefit the whole society."

"Oh? Can I ask you who you sampled in the whole society for that conclusion? Did you go up to Soweto for any soundings? How do you justify the whites' making all the decisions?"

"You can't justify it except on the basis of evolution," the student with glasses said, and there he went, around and around. The third student, a theology major, told me — whether meant as a compliment or condescension, I'm not really sure: "But of course, Mr. Ashe, you're culturally white yourself."

"But one more thing," I said, as time ran out. "All the sophisticated evolutionary arguments aside, all the intellectual and political position papers forgotten — in your heart, do you think it's right?" The students looked toward the professor, and he replied, but only with more general mumbo jumbo. "No, wait," I said, and I pointed a few seats away to Conrad Johnson, a Colored tennis official, a salesman who wore a suit as fine as the professor's, and spoke as well as he. "Forget all that. Just what about this man? Why can you vote and this man can't? Why are you free and this man isn't?"

Professor Hanekom looked briefly at Conrad, and then at me, and

141

then quickly, in distress, his eyes dropped to the ground. "Mr. Ashe," he said, "that is an ace up your sleeve. I cannot defend that."

I remembered Nikki Giovanni: "These small communications are necessary . . ."

We met Christiaan Barnard later that afternoon, at his hospital back in Capetown, and he escorted me about, showing me the biracial facilities (at least at this one hospital) and carefully instructing me in the South African medical policy, which will welcome any patient in the world to one of its hospitals for $8 a day. We had dinner that night too with Dr. Barnard (and also with the head of the Progressive Party), and we talked of heart transplants, and what he envisioned soon, a body transplant. You see, as he explained it, you can't transplant a brain, because a brain is legally what constitutes life. So you keep the brain and give it a whole new body to work with.

"You mean, doctor," someone at the table said, "that I'm six-foot-four now, but you might give me a five-foot-eight body."

"Yes, and your vife will lof you all the more."

Chris was one of the rare South Africans honest enough to admit to me that he is not in favor of one-man, one-vote. He still characterizes blacks as "children" and believes that the government must "take a child's hand to help him cross the road." But then, in contrast, as we passed by the magnificent new opera house in downtown Capetown, he assured me that he had never been inside it and never would so long as apartheid were practiced with its seating.

And this time I remembered Alan Paton: "The whole world thinks we are odd . . ."

*Thursday, November 29 — Capetown / Pretoria / Johannesburg*

We flew back to Jo'burg and came into the airport just as Cardinal Mindszenty was coming through on a visit. Then Donald and I took a car to Pretoria for a final visit with Dr. Koornhof. He spoke bluntly with regard to the black players getting onto the Sugar Cir-

142

cuit but so did I, and I did change a few phrases in my departing statement.

When I got on the plane, Carole Dell brought over to me a message, on a photograph, that she had smuggled onto the plane in a newspaper. It came to her from the relative of a political prisoner, and it bade me tidings and thanks and urged me to go well. And then, just before the plane took off down the runway for the trip back to New York, an official courier came on board and handed me a huge bouquet of flowers. It was from Dr. Koornhof.

We learned today that nonwhites will be permitted to compete on the Sugar Circuit. The situation isn't perfect. The players must be affiliated with SALTA, the approved white tennis organization, to have their entry considered, and also, the Sugar Circuit is a relatively high class of play. If the South African Open is pro ball, then the Sugar Circuit is the equivalent of major college, and you can't succeed in big-time college athletics any more than you can in the pros unless you can compete freely at all lower levels of play. But there may be some advantages to starting out at the top. You get more publicity. And maybe you learn faster out of embarrassment. When Dr. Johnson finally got his black players admitted to the interscholastics, it took three years before one of his boys so much as won a game. But they got the chance — and hardly a decade later I won the title.

I've decided to set up a foundation for the nonwhite South African players. Those who show promise will get money for equipment and coaching. Also, all the used rackets and clothes and any other tennis paraphernalia that I have left over will go to black South African players. I've already been criticized by a black American newspaperwoman for making this decision and for not providing for the tennis players of Harlem first. Funny how people like to make up your mind for you.

I still have the resolve that contact with an adversary is better than isolation of him. Boycotts, particularly, are an antiquated and limited form of pressure. Simply because a boycott will crack open a door does not mean that more boycotts will open it wide.

Dennis Brutus, a Colored South African who was first jailed and then expelled from the country and now teaches at Northwestern and works for SANROC, is one of the more persuasive advocates of a boycott policy. The last time we argued, I finally said: "Look, Dennis, you want change in South Africa, and you believe that your way will effect change — "

"Absolutely."

"Okay, do you honestly believe that change will arrive in a split second, a whole big complete national turnover, like when Sweden switched from driving on the left to driving on the right at the stroke of a clock?"

"No, of course not."

"Then damnit, Dennis, if change will be gradual, then logically, the pressure must fit the situation. At different stages in the progress, you apply different procedures. Besides, a total one hundred percent boycott is the only kind that ever works, and you'll just never obtain that. It's realistic to expect only marginal progress at first when you're on the short end of the stick."

Personally, I saw hopeful signs in South Africa that the whites must accept a faster rate of change than presently seems likely. In favor of that are these realities:

(1) every day Black Africa gets stronger
(2) the numerical African superiority in South Africa itself is simply too great to be suppressed forever, particularly since the master-servant relationship is pulling taut. As Nikki Giovanni says: "They really don't make the best of friends."
(3) the world has been diverted by the horrors of Vietnam, of the Mideast, and other crises for a long time, but the odds are that attention will soon swing back to examine and deplore the injustices that emanate from Pretoria.
(4) how you gonna keep 'em down on the farm after they've seen TV?

I believe that the criticism applied against my trip is more emotional than logical, and more frustrated than anything, and I'm convinced that my way can produce results. Arthur Ashe is not going to topple a government, but the very nature of sports is such that I believe that progress can be made in this frivolous area first. Perhaps if I were a politician or a businessman or a clergyman, or whatever, there would be compelling reasons for me not to go, but I am a tennis player, and it seems proper for me. For one thing, I do not have that much more time when I can provide leverage. I've only got a few more years before I'm a has-been. I'm a valuable commodity now. You have to be missed if you are *not* there to do any good when you *get* there.

And cliché or not, sports can bring change. Look at it in the United States. The white guy who will sit next to a black spectator at the ball park and root for a bunch of black athletes wearing *his* city's name across their chests may have a conniption fit if you asked him to sit next to a black at work, or in school, or in church. But maybe next time, after the ball game, it won't seem so bad, or unusual.

I know this, that South Africa cannot be a lost cause. Not from what I saw at Ellis Park. It's not normal, I'm told, for a white kid to ask a black man for an autograph in South Africa, and I'm sure this is so, because asking for an autograph anywhere is a sign of humility. I always make every effort to sign every autograph because I understand that the person asking has humbled himself, if only in a very small way, to ask me. Not anywhere do I want some white kid growing up hostile to blacks because he humbled himself to me and I turned his humility into humiliation. Well, there were a lot of young South African whites who asked me for my autograph, there are a lot of humble South Africans growing to maturity and there must be a better future in the hands of those people.

Tennis, or boxing, or any sporting event can, if only for a moment, in that cursed, bizarre place, bring a diversion. Maybe that is what South Africa needs above all — a little escape. The place is so intense, so scared. Fear is the real currency of the land. Everybody is afraid, although I suppose the Afrikaners most because they are afraid of *being extinguished.* On the other hand, I found, in South Africa, that the black man — for all his agony — has a better sense of humor than the white man — for all his guilt — and humor is great sustenance. It is obviously, above all, just a matter of time. Sooner or later the black man is going to rule South Africa, and the white man knows it. But more important, the black man knows it.

Read this: "Freedom is the most ineradical craving of human nature; the denial of human rights must, in the long run, lead to a cataclysm." That was written by Jan Christiaan Smuts, the South African Prime Minister, in 1934, when he was minister of justice.

And read this:

> Banning will not stop the revolution.
> It will come,
> When it comes, unheralded,
> To fashion a new Utopia,
> Where our offspring, black and white,
> Come together in common brotherhood,
> Undefiled by your guns,
> Untouched by enmity,
> When the seas and mountains are still,
> And a free people inherit the earth.

That was written by Don Mattera, in the small hours of the morning on the day they banned him.

146

Arthur Ashe, Jr., with some early trophies, 1953.    *(Scott L. Henderson)*

Clark Graebner, Arthur Ashe and Bob Lutz with Davis Cup trainer Gene
O'Connor, 1968.   *(Russ Adams)*

OPPOSITE PAGE

*Top:* Ashes, son and father, share a joyful moment at Forest Hills, 1968,
the year Ashe won the U.S. Open. Robert Kelleher and Alastair Martin
preside.   *(Russ Adams)*

*Bottom:* Longwood Cricket Club, Boston. Ashe beat Bob Lutz to win
the amateur singles, 1968. Walter Elcock, President of Longwood, is on
the right.   *(Russ Adams)*

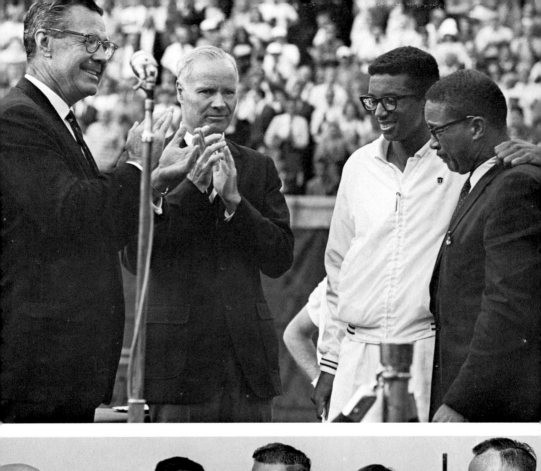

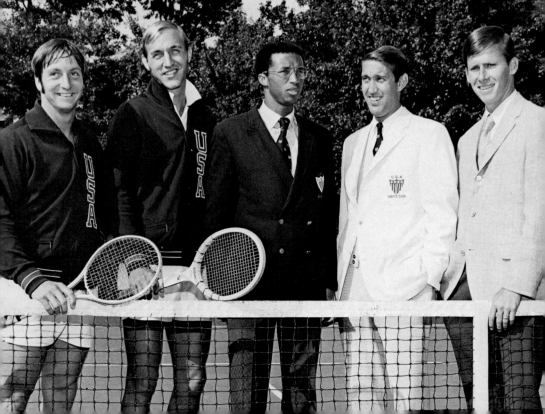

Tom Okker, runner-up, with Ashe who won the singles at Forest Hills, the first U.S. Open, in 1968.   *(Russ Adams)*

OPPOSITE PAGE

*Top:* Ashe is interviewed by Bud Collins, tennis commentator and sportswriter for the Boston *Globe*.   *(Russ Adams)*

*Bottom:* The Davis Cup team in Cleveland in 1969 against Rumania. Bob Lutz, Stan Smith, Arthur Ashe, coach Donald Dell and captain Dennis Ralston.   *(Russ Adams)*

Rod "Rocket" Laver and Arthur Ashe, Forest Hills, 1969, the year of Rocket's Grand Slam. Ashe lost the match.   *(Russ Adams)*

OPPOSITE PAGE

*Top:* Davis Cup Challenge Round against Germany, 1970. Arthur accepts cup while teammates Stan Smith and Cliff Richey look on. *(Russ Adams)*

*Bottom:* Dennis Ralston, Charlie Pasarell and his wife enjoy dinner with Ashe on tour.   *(Russ Adams)*

Donald Dell, former Davis Cup captain, advises his client and friend.
*(Russ Adams)*

OPPOSITE PAGE

*Top:* Ashe in South Africa: A Time to Serve Black and White.
*(Gerry Cranham)*

*Bottom:* Ashe meets fans in Soweto, South Africa, 1973.
*(Gerry Cranham)*

Ashe and Bjorn Borg, Forest Hills, 1973. Ashe lost the match.
*(Russ Adams)*

Ashe presents American Express award to Rodney Harmon at Forest
Hills, 1973.    *(Russ Adams)*

Stan Smith, his fiancée (now wife), Marjory Gengler, and Ashe relax at a WCT film.  (*Russ Adams*)

The serve.  (*Bruce Curtis*)

The forehand.   *(Christopher W. Morrow)*

The backhand.   *(Christopher W. Morrow)*

Ashe, poised for the next serve.  *(Bruce Curtis)*

# 14

## Different Strokes for Different Folks

*Friday, November 30, 1973 — New York / Durham*

Awful flight. Sometime after we left Dakar, we hit some turbulence, and we must have dropped two or three thousand feet.

Anyway, after that, things were fairly quiet and we landed at Kennedy at six this morning. Donald caught a plane to Cleveland, where he is going to be one of the commentators for the U.S.–Australia Davis Cup finals. I came on down here to North Carolina. It's a Junior League kind of thing. We had a clinic this afternoon and I played Roscoe tonight. Nice crowd too — but I'm too screwed up from the time change to make much sense of things.

*Saturday, December 1 — Durham / Newark / Princeton / New York*

Kathy met me at the Newark Airport, and we drove down to Princeton University with Roscoe for another exhibition. We also played some celebrity doubles, with Dustin Hoffman and Burt Bacharach. I heard we lost the Davis Cup, but what can I say? When you lose to Newcombe and Laver you never have anything to be ashamed of.

*Wednesday, December 5 — New York*

I've just been catching up on business for the last few days, so today I went out and ran in Central Park. After so many years of

147

staying in shape, my body is tuned so that if I just miss a couple of days of exercise, I start to feel the cobwebs. A lot of it is mental too.

I do think it's good for my game to get away from tennis occasionally, as I am now. It doesn't really matter anymore whether this is true or not — I believe it is, so the absence provides a placebo effect. When Stan wants to get away from it all, he can go off and play golf for a week or more and come back to tennis the next day and play near his best. I don't have that resiliency, and besides, it only takes me a couple of days away from the game to become eager to come back to it. The guy who never quits is Onny Parun of New Zealand. He must play a tournament every day of the year. If they had the South Pole Open on New Year's Eve, he'd be there — and he never seems to get stale. Different strokes for different folks.

The only time I can remember when I tried to even temporarily give up tennis for a while was once in high school. By that time, I could beat everybody black in the Richmond area, so there was no incentive; more important, there was peer pressure. Boys didn't play tennis; tennis was a sissy sport. So, I went out for the baseball team and made it as a pitcher. I was doing okay too, but after one game I got a message to see the school principal. His name was J. Harry Williams. It was a very brief discussion we had. J. Harry Williams said: "Arthur, I'm kicking you off the baseball team."

He knew that I might be a pretty fair high school baseball pitcher, but that any substantial future I had in athletics would be in tennis. If a hundred little things like that hadn't have happened, I never would have made it. My development was fluke piled upon coincidence. But people never want to hear that when they keep asking me why there aren't more black tennis players. The more valid question would be: how in the world did even one black male player emerge?

*Friday, December 7 — New York / Richmond*

Tonight I went home to Richmond. My parents and I live such completely contrasting life-styles that it is necessary for us to see each other every now and then to get to know each other again. I

don't mean that I have to come down here to learn to love my parents again, but we all have to get together every so often so that we can remember how much we do share and how much we love each other.

*Saturday, December 8 — Richmond*

I helped build this house. This was around my junior year in high school, somewhere in there. When I was very young I was quite uptight about laboring, about working for a living with your hands. I was a very bright little kid, and I worked this out in my mind early on: the blacks did all the menial work and suffered all the abuse and degradation; therefore, being black and degraded were connected. I accepted, as an article of faith, that any man in a coat and tie was better off than any man in a work shirt. Thus, on my scale, an insurance salesman was, by definition, a finer person than a plumber, a shoe clerk a better human being than a brick-layer. You can imagine what kind of havoc this thinking can play with you, especially when your own father is black and a working man. It took me several years to sort it out.

My father built this house, with just Johnny and me and a few friends helping, after his father-in-law (my stepmother's father, Edgar Kimbrough) gave him five acres out here. Technically, the place is called Gum Spring, but it's really just a post office address. When we built the house, we just used materials that we picked up in Richmond, where they were undergoing a lot of urban re-newal — urban *removal*, we blacks call it — in order to build a new expressway. Everything was just lying there — bricks, cinder blocks, good lumber. We built the whole house out here in the country with what was destroyed back in the city.

My father's always been a country person, with a country sched-ule, even when he lived in the city all those years. If my father stays up past ten or sleeps past six, it's a real event. And his hob-bies have always been hunting and fishing and fiddling around in his tool shed. As a boy, living in downtown Richmond, I would be up before dawn and then we'd drive up to the Rappahannock or down to the James, and we'd fish for catfish or perch or spot; or in the spring, in the spawning season, we'd go for shad and herring

149

with nets.  We'd hunt a lot too — squirrels and rabbits and some-times deer.  We'd clean what we caught or killed ourselves and then pack it away in salt.  We keep a deer four/five years in the freezer.  It's tastier after a long time, more tender.  Somehow the freezing breaks down the tendons — something like that.  I'm not at all squeamish.  Even as a kid, I gutted deer.

Now, when I think back on it, I lived a sort of dual life as a boy. I was city, but I was raised country by an old-fashioned country fa-ther.  Maybe that's why I can manage so well as the black in a white world.  It's the same sort of experience.  I've never been the kind of sonuvabitch you ever could put in any particular niche.

Anyway, this morning my father woke me up for a deer hunt. We were going out on a no-nonsense hunt, where the purpose is not strictly a sporting one, but the very real matter of trying to put meat on the table.  It used to be this way all the time.

There were possibly twenty of us altogether, and the ironic thing to me was that only about five of us were black.  Just four or five years ago, you never would have gotten blacks and whites hunting together in Virginia, especially out in the sticks like this.  Anyway, whatever the colors of the hunters, you set up in a semicircle and use the dogs to flush out the deer.  It is a very well organized, ef-ficient operation.

My father and I were located pretty far over to the right end of the semicircle, with maybe only one or two more hunters to my right. The first deer came very quickly after we got set.  He was off to my right and behind me, and he came that way, out past me, and then he veered off and cut in front of me, going right to left, toward a creek.  That was when the hunter from the next stand over to my right fired.

Right away, I felt the shot in my leg.  I had never been shot before, but I knew what it was.

It hurt like hell, but I already had the deer in my own sights, so I squeezed off and got him.  There was no question but that I was the one who shot him.  He only ran about another thirty yards before he keeled over and died.

Naturally, I was more worried about myself, but down here they don't use rifles and slugs, only shotguns and pellets, so I knew I would live.  And for God's sake, I remembered that my brother had been hit twice with real bullets in Vietnam. I had only been grazed in my inside left thigh, and although it didn't even break the pants, it was bleeding some, and it really hurt for a while.

Finally we set about splitting up the prize. Everybody gets a little something, but the guy who did the actual killing wins the best part, the hindquarter. We took it back to our freezer.

*Monday, December 10 — New York*

Too often, I'm afraid, some of us blacks in this country are more interested in methods than in objectives. There is much rhetoric, without any follow-up, or as David Halberstam said, "Lose gallantly rather than win pragmatically." It may be emotionally satisfying to stand up on a soapbox and have a television camera pointed in your face for five minutes, but how often does that help anyone who follows you?

Some blacks — and some whites too — get mad at me because they feel that I don't make enough waves. You'd be amazed how often I hear that I'm not arrogant enough. But how in hell is that going to help — particularly in my situation where I am a single black surrounded by whites. There are many ways of accomplishing things in the white world without compromising integrity.

I mention all this because today I had lunch with Joe Cullman at 21. Joe is the chairman of the board of Philip Morris, and I've known him for years. I told him that I wanted to meet with the proper executives at Ford and IBM to discuss their South African policies. Joe is on the board of both of those companies. He said fine, he would arrange it, and later he called to say that I would soon be hearing from the company vice presidents of Ford and IBM who have the responsibility for that area of the world. He said that both of them would be delighted to meet with me. Perhaps something substantive will come of it; at the least, IBM and Ford will hear a black view, and they will have to confront a black man with a defense of their own policy.

I think this is an accomplishment. However small, I am sure that this profits the black cause more than if I called a press conference and then proceeded to scream for thirty seconds on the six o'clock news that Ford and IBM were racists. And equally important: while accomplishing something, I sacrificed nothing. I retained my dignity, my credibility and what punch I have. And I did not shut any doors behind me for those who may follow.

*Tuesday, December 11 — New York / Miami*

Christmas shopping. Kathy flew in. We have to fly over to Jamaica tomorrow to finish up shooting the South African film.

*Friday, December 14 — Kingston*

We selected Jamaica to finish up the film because we wanted to have me talking in a place where there are a lot of blacks around in a natural setting. It's kind of like the time I was with Okker in Bologna and he looked out the window and said: "Have you ever seen so many Italians in your life?"

Anyway, today we went out to film in a little town named Lucea, where we shot a lot with the high school kids. I was rather impressed with their awareness of the South African situation. Several of them even had a sophisticated enough understanding of the problem to protest that I should not have gone, but most merely responded emotionally. One kid told me he'd like to go over there and smuggle in a machine gun. Another said he wanted to get out of Jamaica and go join the guerrilla liberation movement that seeks to free South Africa.

No matter where I go, in and out of the U.S., it always seems the same way with so many young blacks — they see only one way to skin a cat. There are other ways to complement and supplement the liberation movements. In the final analysis, it cannot be guns alone, but diplomacy, that provides the real answers — and these young people must be made to see that. Where the hell is Kissinger today? I wish more people — blacks especially — would study his philosophy.

*Saturday, December 15 — Kingston / San Juan*

I'm hurting. At the conclusion of the shooting this morning, all the guys working on the film decided to celebrate by throwing me into the pool, which they did.  Almost.  One guy dropped me, and I scraped my knee on the edge of the pool as I bounced in.  This has been a rough week for my poor skinny little legs.  Shot on one Saturday, scarred on the next.

*Wednesday, December 19 — Miami*

The people are already starting to crowd into the Doral for our special holiday tennis program, but I don't have to start working full-time on it till the weekend.  I give free group lessons to anybody who has signed up and generally oversee the whole program. We have a social hostess working with us, and there are three teaching pros working full-time on twenty courts.  We have to charge $8 an hour for our members just to use a court.  I don't like it, but the way this tennis boom is going you have to sort of embargo the courts to give everybody a chance.

*Thursday, December 20 — Miami / New York / Deer Lake,*
*Pennsylvania / New York*

Practically speaking this was about a thirty-hour day.  The sun is just coming up now in Miami the morning of the 21st.

It began at 1:30 this morning (Thursday morning) when John Marshall, our film director, called me to say that he had just managed to set up a meeting with Muhammed Ali at his training camp in the Poconos, where he's working on his fight next month against Joe Frazier.  For our film, Marshall wants to get a sequence with Ali and me talking about South Africa.

So, I got up at 6:30 for the first flight up to New York.  I met John at my apartment, where I picked up some warm clothes, and then we went down to the street and hailed a cab.  John got in and said, "Deer Lake, Pennsylvania," as if he were asking the driver to take him over to Lexington Avenue.

John is British, but he is so brash and forward that he is more American, really, than most Americans.  As far as I can tell, the only reason we are getting to film with Ali is that Marshall outtalked him.  Or so he says.  Anyway, they're a good match.  Before he went into films, John was a press agent, capping his career when

153

he handled Nina Van Pallandt. Remember her? The woman Clifford Irving went to Mexico with when he traveled there to meet with "Howard Hughes"? Of course, as John tells it, it almost seems as if he created Clifford Irving and the whole hoax in order that Nina's career eventually would be advanced. I love to kid him about this.

It was a three-hour cab ride to Deer Lake, and by the time we got there, a light snow was falling in a midday dusk. I had never met Ali before, but apparently he had always wanted to talk with me too, and we had a good chat for a couple of hours, most of which John's crew filmed.

Ali spoke in his usual folksy way, with the bad grammar and the colorful idioms, but there certainly is no doubt in my mind that a very natively clever man lurks behind this façade. If anything, I think he may even overdo the ignorant put-on. What impressed me most was that there were no pretensions. Despite occasional bursts from his routine act — a sudden flurry of pantomime slugging, that sort of thing — we had a most forthright and intelligent discussion.

For one thing, unlike a lot of blacks, Ali was honest enough to admit some unfamiliarity with the South African situation. He was willing to shut up and listen to me on the subject — which is more than I can say for a helluva lot of educated people. Ali told me that he had himself very nearly gone to South Africa a couple of years ago to box exhibitions, but that when the word leaked out, several UN ambassadors from various Islamic countries visited him and urged him not to go. And he acceded to their pressure and called off the trip.

"Me representing the whole Islamic world," he told me, "I had to listen to these people. But you going as an individual, Arthur — I support everything you did as an individual."

I got back to New York to catch an 11:15 flight, which took off at 4:30, which is why I am going to bed at sunrise. So, I went round the clock just to get a few feet of film with Muhammed Ali. But I think it was worth it.

*Friday, December 21 — Miami*

Dennis Ralston called. The first round of the 1974 Davis Cup takes place next month in Colombia. That's hardly a month after we played the finals for '73. The Davis Cup has become impossible — a revolving door. A lot of the countries had to play '74 matches as early as the summer of '73. The Davis Cup nations have got to change the format and make it something like the World Cup soccer, with all, or most of the matches played like a huge tournament at one venue.

Stan has begged off the Colombian match, which he has every right to do. He's been crammed with tennis, carrying our Davis Cup all this year. I couldn't play this year because I was ineligible, due to an obscure contract technicality, and I can't play in Bogotá either due to commitments I made months before the match was scheduled. Connors, as I understand it, won't play for his country so long as Dennis is the captain. Dennis is represented by Dell, and Riordan won't let Connors be contaminated that way. Dickie Stockton can't make it either — out with a bad back — but Dennis thinks we're in pretty good shape.

The big match, looming sometime in the spring, I guess, probably will be South Africa vs. the U.S. They're entered in the American Zone.

*Saturday, December 22 — Miami*

Juan Farrow arrived with Mr. Hudlin to play the Orange Bowl junior tournament. Juan has problems with his serve but otherwise is hitting the ball well. He has also settled down personally, and I can hardly wait till he gets on the circuit. Juan wears big apple caps, the flashy clothes, the two-toned high heels, the works. I can just see the day when he shows up at some country club like Longwood. All those tennis officials are going to be walking around saying, "Whatever happened to that nice little colored boy Arthur Ashe?"

155

*Tuesday, December 25 — Miami*

Well, it certainly doesn't look like Christmas today; the Doral Country Club is not exactly your Currier and Ives print: no sleigh-bells, and for that matter, no Christians. Kathy and I did see a cute bunch of Jewish kids opening a bunch of presents up in the lounge.

It's a strange thing, which I really can't explain, and which did not even occur to me until I started getting serious with Kathy, but all my life I have been inclined toward Jews. For whatever reason, I feel quite comfortable — or am made to feel comfortable — among Jews. Curiously, my father had the same experience, and perhaps that somehow influenced me. His closest white associates were almost all Jewish.

Anyway, the curious thing about how prominent Jews have been in my life is that I never sought them out. The Jewish people have always made the most fuss over me. Well-meaning whites at the country clubs are forever trying to *put me at ease*, but Jews have usually been better at it or more sincere than the Gentiles. It is the Jewish women's organizations that are invariably the ones that ask me to speak and to help out with charity.

And finally, thank you, Mrs. Goldlust.

She is a dear lady who lives in the apartment next to the one I use in New York. Now I am seldom there, and, of course, it is an article of faith in the big city that it is gauche to be neighborly. I used the apartment for months without meeting Mrs. Goldlust, and then one day we happened to come off the elevator together and to walk down the hall together. At last, as we were putting our keys into our locks, we introduced ourselves and went into our respective quarters.

It so happened that day that I had a bad case of laryngitis. Fifteen minutes later there was a knock on the door. Mrs. Goldlust was standing there, holding a huge bowl of hot chicken soup, homemade, guaranteed to cure my throat. Of course, I don't look Jewish.

*Friday, December 28 — Miami*

This is the last day of the holiday tennis program. I have been on the courts eight hours a day since last Saturday and am sick of tennis, which is just great, because I have to start training for the '74 season on Monday. I had hoped to use December to change my forehand grip, but, as with so many other things, I never had the time. But the program really did go well here at the Doral. No ulcer this time, no knots in my stomach. Today we had a staff meeting about the off-season Arthur Ashe weekends that we're planning for next summer.

*Saturday, December 29 — Miami*

Very important entry in the diary: I shot an 88 today. Wow, I was really hitting it. That's the second-best I ever made; I shot an 86 once. I wish Stan had been here.

*Sunday, December 30 — Miami*

When Daddy came down the other day, he brought the hindquarter of the deer I shot up in Virginia a few weeks ago. We gave it to the chef here at the Doral to fix, and then I invited the owners and some of the guests I know well to join us for dinner. The deer was just delicious, too, but there were several people in our party who simply couldn't bring themselves to eat it. It wasn't venison to them but a cute little deer. The same people don't think of a nice, juicy sirloin steak as Elsie the Cow, but they think of venison as Bambi. Oh well, I can understand that.

*Monday, December 31 — Miami*

This may be New Year's Eve, but it also fell on the Monday I promised myself that I would begin working out for the '74 season, so Brian Gottfried came over around 10:30 this morning, and we just about killed each other. Brian never stops practicing, so he is a very good influence on me. The first day you try to get back into

157

shape is always miserable, and I was ready for bed by eight o'clock tonight. I've never cared much for all the horn-blowing and the funny hats anyway, so Kathy and I decided to go to a movie. Afterward, we went back to the Doral, though, and joined my father for the midnight celebration. He probably had a token glass of champagne, but he really has never drunk or smoked. We never kept any liquor in the house, except perhaps for a little homemade wine. I have no idea where my father got his strict Calvinist ways. His own father, Pink Ashe, the guy with the thick mustache — he would drink and raise hell with the best of them. But that strange mixture of the stoic and the emotional was, apparently, also evident in my grandfather — although he and Daddy are otherwise totally different types.

In comparison to his father, my father is slow to anger, and he practically never gets mad anyway. Yet otherwise, he can wear his heart on his sleeve; he will laugh or cry easily. Still, most times he appears nearly impassive, and he is, above all, a preeminently practical man. For a time, Daddy was a chauffeur in Richmond to a Jewish man named Schwartzchild. My father and Mr. Schwartzchild got along together quite well, and one day Daddy mentioned to him how surprised he was that Mr. Schwartzchild took so much crap from so many people (that is: Gentiles) that he didn't appear to have to. Mr. Schwartzchild just replied gently that he didn't mind having to suffer a certain amount of crap since he generally got what he wanted in the end. That made an impression on my father. He has great pride, but he leaves something for posterity. His favorite expression is: "You'll never know the difference a hundred years from now." No matter what he has on his mind, he goes to sleep like a baby as soon as his head hits the pillow. He is at great peace with himself — which must be a wonderful way for a man to be.

After Mother died, Daddy probably was overprotective of Johnny and me — but that is natural enough. What the hell: you've just lost your wife, you don't want to lose the kids too. He did some things that embarrassed me to death. In the summer, he always made me come home and take a nap in the middle of the day, which the other kids teased me about unmercifully, and he made Johnny and me eat whole-wheat bread and brush our teeth in baking soda because that's what he had done as a kid, and he had never gotten any cavities. And I'll tell you: I've never had a single cavity my whole life.

Daddy did loosen up with us after a while, though, and he never tried to create us in his own image. There was not a lot of *don't*. We were expected to know what was wrong. The first day I could go by myself to the elementary school, Baker School, my father walked it off with me. It took twelve minutes, so he told me that he expected me back at the house twelve minutes after school let out. That meant: twelve minutes, not thirteen. And I obeyed. Johnny was more mischievous. He was nothing bad at all, but by comparison with me he seemed a real hell-raiser to Daddy, and it worried him. Or baffled him. Finally, though, he caught on that I was the abnormal child, that Johnny was more typical — so he stopped worrying himself about him.

I really was unusual. I mean, from the first, I adored school. Loved it. I was crazy about all my teachers, even Mrs. Poindexter in the sixth grade, who made it her point of honor never to award any A's. I can still even remember all my teachers: Mrs. Mary Branch in junior primary; Mrs. Thomas, who would rap you across the knuckles with a big green pencil; Mrs. Jordan (now Mrs. Jones); Miss Clark — hell, I can even remember all my home-room teachers in high school. I was bananas about school and teachers.

Different as Johnny and I were, we always got along. We were five years apart, so there was little direct competition, and if he suffered from some of the teachers because little Arthur had been such an angel and good student, Johnny knew that he was a much better athlete than I. My distinction was that I was excellent in one sport, but Johnny was very good in them all. He was all-service football in the marines. We don't see much of each other, but we love each other as brothers and friends; I would say that the Ashes are a very loving family.

When people ask if my father is bothered by my going out with girls of different nationalities it just shows that they know nothing of my father. I say this unequivocally: of all the people I have met in my life, I have never met one who can apply himself so evenly across the board as my father does. He treats everybody absolutely equally, and seeing this principle applied so thoroughly has, ob-

159

viously, had a tremendous effect upon me. "Respect everyone," Daddy has always told me, "respect everyone, whether they respect you or not."

So when I see where some people like the British call me a militant, and then I hear that some blacks call me an Uncle Tom (if never to my face), I figure that these obvious contradictions can exist only because I am being the same person with everyone.

The values that my father instilled in me will never go away. And I recognize that the possession of them made it possible for me to succeed. Without them, you see, I never could have accepted Dr. Johnson's procedures. Without Dr. Johnson, I never could have made it in tennis. It's as simple as that — so Happy New Year, Daddy.

# 15

## "You must be a loner in tennis"

*Thursday, January 3, 1974 — Miami*

I practiced again with Gottfried this morning. Now get this: he's such a fanatic on conditioning that since he's getting married Saturday, he asked me if it would be okay if we just worked out in the morning because he had to reserve the afternoon for getting married.

*Saturday, January 5 — Miami*

You'll be relieved to learn, I'm sure, that Gottfried was able to get Harold Solomon to come around and practice with him today, his wedding morning.

I don't know who I'm going to marry or when I'm going to marry, but I know that I'm sure not going to play any tennis that day. Golf maybe, but tennis, no —

*Sunday, January 6 — Miami*

This is the first day of a tennis convention here, and the place is packed with manufacturers — gut, shoes, rackets, everything. Donald came in, and we sat up till 2:30 talking, largely about this point in my career. I've set two special goals for this year: I want to

161

win the World Championship of Tennis finals at Dallas in May and
Wimbledon in July.  I've never won either.

### Tuesday, January 8 — Miami / Washington

Today was the first time I've been on an airplane in eighteen
days.  That's got to be some kind of modern record.

### Wednesday, January 9 — Washington / Buffalo

They're having a little four-man one-night tournament up here —
eight-game pro sets, $10,000 pot.  Smith, Okker, Riessen and
me — and 4700 people turned out.  Incredible.  I won too.  Beat
Marty and then Stan.

### Friday, January 11 — New York / Greensboro

Stan and I played an exhibition match down here as preliminary
to the Carolina Cougars' ABA basketball game.  Beforehand, we
were paying for our dinner at Howard Johnson's, and a white girl
who was the cashier recognized me and said that this was an
incredible coincidence and that — guess what? — her name was
Ashe too.

I said no, it probably wasn't any coincidence at all.  In fact, we
were almost certainly related to each other.  Oh, did she blush at
that.  But I wasn't putting her on.  Sam Ashe, the governor of
North Carolina from 1796–98, owned my people and presumably
made some very personal contributions to the line too.  Asheville,
which gave us Thomas Wolfe, was named for old Sam.  I've never
been there myself.  You see, you can't go home again.

A funny thing is, though, that most blacks still think of their old
home down south.  Some guy may have lived in Harlem for forty
years, but if you asked him where he was from or what was home,
he'd reply North Carolina or Mississippi or whatever.  We are
called so many things by whites, and we call each other so many
things: *brother, my man, blood, ace boon coon,* even *nigger* in an endearing way (especially *bad-ass nigger*).  But the fondest term is
saved for those we actually grew up with back south: *home* or *home*

162

*boy.* If you see two black guys meet and say, "Hi, home" and "Hey there, home boy" to each other then you will know automatically that they are really close.

*Saturday, January 12 — Winston-Salem / Greensboro / Atlanta / Dallas / Austin*

We came down here near Austin to Lakeway, the WCT resort, where CBS is video-taping another tennis "classic" that will be shown next summer. Well, I'm making up for lost time with the airplanes: seven in the last five days.

This is the first time that Kathy and I have ever traveled together in the south. There have been a few stares, but they have only been curious, not hard — and certainly there have been no incidents. It's really amazing. It's just like anywhere else in the world.

I don't presume to be an authority on morals, but I am an authority on hotels, and let me tell you: either morals or hotels are changing. Few hotels in the world cock eyebrows now when an unmarried couple registers together. Kathy always uses her own name too; I think most of the girls traveling with players have also stopped playing that charade. There's always a few girls on the tour. Ove Bengtson, Andy Pattison, Dick Crealy, Colin Dibley, Geoff Masters are the guys I can think of with girl friends along now, but at one time or other it's the custom for all types, except the Latins. That kind of stuff is still taboo for their girls.

The hotels still practice one flaming double standard though. Whereas they will let you check in with a girl, they frown on your bringing one in later in the evening. They'll get the house dicks after you in that case, or at least have the desk man or the hall porter call you. If you pay for her then, though, the hotel will immediately drop its moral interest in the matter.

Marjory Gengler, who was the top woman's player at Princeton a couple of years ago, has been going with Stan now for some time and is with him on this trip, but the betting is that Masters will be the next bachelor to go. This will kill Snake Case since he and Geoff are practically inseparable. Snake holds the tour record, though, for easiest score.

163

He arrived for a WCT event last spring with the understanding that housing would be provided. This young girl of about twenty — and not bad looking — comes up to him in the airport and says: "Mr. Case?"

"Yes," says Snake.

So then she introduced herself and said that the housing committee had assigned him to stay with her. Snake said fine, threw his bags and rackets in her car and got in to drive off to her parents' house. Only she stopped at an apartment building and when they got upstairs and opened the door, Snake noticed that it was a very small apartment.

"I'm sorry," the girl said. "I have only one bed, so you'll have to sleep with me. Is that all right?"

Snake allowed as how it was.

"And don't worry," she said. "If you meet another girl and don't want to come back here with me some night, that's perfectly all right."

"Oh thank you," Snake said. Up until that tournament, Snake hadn't won a single WCT match. He ran through a series of upsets that week, though, and got all the way to the semis before I beat him — and he's been a respectable force on the tour ever since.

*Sunday, January 13 — Austin*

Lakeway is a magnificent place, but it's still somewhat unfinished, and the grass on the hill behind the court isn't green enough for CBS, so the network was out painting the hill today. I never saw anybody paint a hill before.

*Tuesday, January 15 — Austin*

I drew Cliff Drysdale, who is the host pro here, in the opening round, and beat him 6–4, 2–6, 6–4. I was very eager, and I'm pleased because Cliff played well.

*Thursday, January 17 — Austin*

Riessen beat me three and three. I had a 3–1 lead in the first set, but then I just collapsed. I can usually beat Marty by overpowering

164

him. He's a top athlete, always in great shape, and he'll run every-thing down, but he's never had the big game. That's very curious for a guy who's fairly tall and strong, and whose father is a pro, but Marty never developed a great serve. I've never understood that.

Anyway, it was very windy today, and I seldom handle that well. Alan King says that all you have to do is blow in Ashe's ear and you're up three-love. But seriously, folks, the wind does tend to hurt my game somewhat more than the average guy's because I slap at the ball and really must hit it in the middle of the strings in order to control it. When the wind is whipping the ball around, I have a smaller margin of error.

*Sunday, January 20 — Philadelphia*

I've gotten some good practice in the last couple of days, which is especially important here because I'm going to be very busy this week with ATP meetings. Nowadays, it seems as if each major tournament is as much a political convention as it is a competition. The tennis world is so fragmented now that only on a few occasions in the course of a year will most of the players all be together. The point is, everybody is spreading themselves too thin. We're forgetting the things in tennis that really count.

Just about everybody will be here in Philadelphia though. The Indoor has an eighty-four-man field, all the WCT players. Today, for example, I saw Torben Ulrich for the first time in months and made the mistake of saying, "Hey, Torben, how are you?"

He said, "Well, I don't know, Arthur. But I'll think about it and let you know in a few minutes." And in five minutes he came back and said, "Not bad."

Torben, of course, is our preeminent tour character. Even Tiriac or Nastase pale in comparison. I've never met anyone so different as Torben. Even his wife thinks he's different. He's completely true to himself.

He is Danish, with a heavy beard that he was wearing years before beards were considered acceptable. He is forty-five years old and has been playing at Wimbledon since 1948, but he remains in top shape. Torben plays some parts of the year with us, and then he'll go off and play on the Grand Masters tour with Gonzales

165

and Segura and the other old-timers.  He'll play a fifty-five-year-old one week, a teen-ager the next; Torben is ageless, I suppose.  Certainly, he doesn't play tennis for the same reasons that the rest of us do.  Winning seems insignificant to him.  A few years ago he was defending his national title but decided he would rather watch the World Cup of soccer on television, so he just left the court and finally they had to default him.  Torben gets his high from having a ball hit perfectly in the middle of his strings.

Everybody adores him, and he pays the world back in kind.  I have never heard this man say an unkind word about another human being.  He just goes his way and lives his life honestly.  Even when he is with someone, Torben is really alone, but one of his closest friends, and sort of a pupil, is Jeff Borowiak, a Zen from California who has shoulder-length hair.  Both love music.  Torben is a special authority on Eastern music, he has his own radio show in Denmark and is a jazz critic; he writes quite a lot.  Jeff draws intricate parallels between tennis and music; he gives, for example, a very detailed analysis of Rosewall vis à vis Bach.

What frightens me is that as tennis becomes more businesslike, more stylized, it will increasingly tend to attract only the businesslike, stylized sort.  Perhaps our greatest strength (or is it a beauty?) is our eclecticism.  We are a mob of individuals.  Probably you must be a distinct kind of individual to succeed at a game by yourself.  There must be more of the loner in tennis players than in team-sport players.

I remember one time when somebody idly asked Torben what he did when he was not playing tennis.  As he always does, he considered the question at length before he finally answered: "I think a lot, and I listen a lot."

We'll all be the poorer in tennis if the game becomes so professional that a man like that cannot find a place in it.

*Monday, January 21 — Philadelphia*

My wake-up call to Room 1212 of the Bellevue-Stratford came at seven o'clock this morning.  I struggled up and dressed and when I went downstairs for breakfast I noticed that it was still pitch black dark outside.  I was scheduled to meet Jean Chanfreu at 10:00 A.M.,

166

and this was the first time in my life that I had to get up to play a tennis match when it was still dark.

But here was the real kicker. By the time I got down to the coffee shop it was all of about 7:15, but there, sitting at the counter, already halfway through his breakfast, was Laver. Rocket and I have both been assigned to the same WCT unit — the Green Group — and if I had any doubts about my competition, they were dissipated this morning. Rocket is obviously anxious for WCT; it is the only major title that he has never won. We just smiled at each other; besides "good morning" there was really nothing to say.

I beat Proisy, serving very well. It's not easy to play that time of the morning before an empty house. It's the same as being shunted away to a back court somewhere for a match. When you get used to crowds, you depend on them for feedback. It's easier to call up reserves when you're playing before people, when they respond to your game. It doesn't really matter, in that sense, whether they're for or against you.

*Wednesday, January 23 — Philadelphia*

I beat Patrick Proisy, another Frenchman, today. I served beautifully again. We're having ATP meetings every night, and we're going to have to come to some accommodation with Team Tennis; their money is too good. At a break in our session tonight, Drysdale took me aside and he got a very sheepish expression on his face and he said: "Look, what do you think — I want to sign with Team Tennis."

"Well, since you're the president of an organization that's on record as being opposed to it, I'd say it would look pretty funny," I replied, but I smiled. WTT has the tide now, and it's just a matter of how we decide to adjust. Any way, I lose. Kathy is hardly speaking to me because of all the time I'm devoting to ATP. Second prize is spending one week in Philadelphia with Arthur Ashe.

But the tournament here is terrific. After Wimbledon, it's as well run as any in the world.

Playing in large public places like the Spectrum is the best thing for tennis too. Everybody makes a big fuss over the tennis boom, but it is somewhat deceiving. While it is true that more people are

167

watching the sport and playing it, tennis remains very much a country club game. Basically, it is just more *of the same people* playing it. Only now is the boom finally beginning to reach down into the public parks and the public schools.

*Thursday, January 24 — Philadelphia*

I'm through to the semis; beat Panatta today.

At our ATP meeting we decided officially to reverse our stand on Team Tennis and to take a position of neutrality. Eighteen months ago, when we drew up our constitution, we thought that it was crucial to come out against guarantees, to stand for the principle that every player must earn prize money on the court. But WTT is a new concept that confuses that issue; also, money talks. If our members want to play Team Tennis, then our first obligation is to them. Essentially, we're changing our goal from protecting tournament tennis to protecting the ATP. We've dispatched Jack Kramer abroad to talk to the European tournament directors and explain our position.

*Saturday, January 26 — Philadelphia*

I beat Tony Roche pretty easily this afternoon to get to the finals against Rocket. This is the best tournament Rochie has had in years, maybe since he was in the finals at Forest Hills in '70. He's another one with the twist serve — and then a bad back and a bad elbow. It's a shame too, because he would have been one of the best.

He says some faith healer in the Philippines fixed up his elbow — opened it right up by magic and had it all cured by the time the skin zipped itself back up. Well, however, it is good to have him back. I didn't give him much chance, though. My serve is just silk smooth now, and when it is working like this, my whole game falls into place.

I feel as if I have a good chance tomorrow afternoon in the final against Rocket. But then, I always feel as if I have a good chance against him, and most times I play a good match. The only thing is, *every* time he wins. Laver has won seventeen straight from me

168

without ever losing. That goes back to our first meeting at Forest Hills when I was seventeen years old. It's an incredible thing for any world athlete to be 17–0 against another in any sport — especially when we have been playing each other over a spread of so many years.

*Sunday, January 27 — Philadelphia / Tampa / Rotunda, Florida*

18–0.

It took him four sets, and we both played well, but the result was the same as ever. People ask me why I don't change my game when I play Laver. Sure, and what am I going to do? Ice the puck? Run out the clock? Put in a designated volleyer? The trouble is, the strengths of his game just dovetail perfectly into my weaknesses.

For instance, his best return of first service is a slice back and cross-court, which goes to my forehand volley, my weakest shot. Then, my second serve is a twist which just hops right up onto his racket, a setup for his left-handed forehand. So he returns very well against me, and I don't happen to return well at all against most left-handers.

A great lob can neutralize Laver — and I don't have an outstanding lob. This will sound silly, too, but I get into a match and forget completely about the lob. I'll talk to myself about using a lob for hours before a match, and then I'll get out there and draw a blank on the shot.

And it's all very relative. I beat Riessen regularly — even if I did lose to him last week — but Marty returns well against left-handers and he can throw up a good lob, and so he does quite well against Rocket.

To try to make me feel better, some people have consoled me with the rationalization that my game might have been affected by all the ATP work I did this week. But that is a specious argument. I would go out of my mind if I only played tennis, the way Rocket does. There is simply a limit to how much straight tennis I could endure. I could never even consider becoming a teaching pro when I'm through playing.

When I think of tennis, when I think of the pleasure I get out of it, I think of a whole existence — playing and traveling and meeting people and being with the guys and all that. When Rocket thinks of tennis, he thinks of one thing: playing tennis. He even relishes practice. He is like a pig in mud out on that court, even if it just means chasing balls until he is literally out of breath. We both love tennis very much, but we love it very differently.

*Monday, January 28 — Rotunda*

Rocket and I flew down here together after our match last night. It's a new development near Sarasota, which is holding this so-called Superstars competition, where a lot of top athletes compete against each other in events other than their own. Bob Seagren, the pole-vaulter, was the winner last year. You have a list of ten events, and from those you must select seven to compete in. But, of the ten, my profession disqualified me from picking the tennis, my body disqualified me from the weight lifting and I've just never been very adept at swimming, so I really didn't have much option. I entered golf (nine holes), the half-mile bicycle race, the half-mile run, baseball hitting, bowling, the hundred-yard dash and the obstacle course.

I met a lot of the guys last night, and then, of course, we competed against each other all during the day, and I really liked this bunch. Bill Toomey, the Olympic decathlon champion, took it all pretty seriously, but everybody else — even Kyle Rote, Jr., the soccer player, who came best prepared for the competition and is obviously going to win the damn thing — made a lark out of it. We had a helluva bunch of athletes in our group too: Rote, Rocket and Stan; Jerry Quarry, the heavyweight; Jean-Claude Killy, the skier; Larry Mahan, the rodeo performer; Dick Anderson of the Miami Dolphins; Bobby Allison, the stock-car driver; and five baseball players — Reggie Jackson, Brooks Robinson, Jim Palmer, Pete Rose and Tug McGraw, who also served as the class comedian. All of us had a ball, with all these hotshot athletes acting like kids, everybody whispering, "What'd you get?" and "Did you hear what so-and-so did?" and "Who's faster, Jim or Pete?" — stuff like that. It was like YMCA field day.

The funniest thing happened this morning when I went out to

play golf, my first event, in a threesome with Rocket and Jim Palmer, the Oriole pitcher. They have those billboards being carried along with the players' scores on them, just as they do on the pro tour, and as I was strolling down the first fairway, I saw Stan's threesome some distance away, coming down the third fairway. Out front was the billboard, and I squinted through my contacts and read: "Smith +1" — which isn't bad; just one over after two holes. But then I got a little closer and saw that it was two one's, as in: "Smith +11."

He bombed. So, I beat him today. You needed to finish one, two or three in the whole group to collect points, and I picked up a few in golf by shooting a 47, which tied me for third with Brooks Robinson. But damnit, I would have been an undisputed third if I hadn't blown a four-inch gimme on the last hole. I'm not exaggerating: four inches and I roll it up short. I'm always short.

In the half-mile run, I finished a respectable fourth, but I was way back in the bicycle race. I don't have the thighs for that.

Tonight we went to a bowling alley in town and really put on a show. It's funny, but except for Quarry, none of us turned out to be regular bowlers. It's never had any appeal to me; I don't think I've bowled once in the last decade. But we came on like pinbusters. The local people couldn't believe it. I bowled a 168 myself and couldn't break into the top three. Quarry had a 191 and Mahan and Rose also snuck in ahead of me. The spectators were flabbergasted.

*Tuesday, January 29 — Rotunda / Tampa / New York*

Not only were we all still goofing around today, but we've also begun to take a great pride in our division. Men in groups. Somebody found out that 140 or something *won* the bowling in another division, and here we had men with 150s and 160s who couldn't make a point. We're quite pleased with ourselves and have developed a real camaraderie.

In the hundred-yard dash, I finished way up the track, and I ended up sort of in the middle of the obstacle-course event. The funniest performer here was Bobby Allison, this big old country boy who drives the stock cars. The obstacle race began with a wall you had to scale, then a football blocking dummy, tires for you to

171

high-step through, hurdles, water hazards. Allison could never manage to get up the wall. He finally loped around it.

Killy was one of the few guys here whom I knew in advance because he worked for Head Ski, but he dropped out after a couple of events. He said his stomach was hurting. I saw him later and asked him what was wrong, and he said an ulcer had been troubling him off and on. "What's the cause?" I asked. "My main problem is, I don't have any problems," he said.

Actually, the competition is strongly culturally biased against the athletes, like Killy, who come from countries other than America. There's not a single event where you have to kick a ball. Laver entered the baseball hitting, and he didn't have a clue what was going on. I did pretty well in that; I have quick wrists. I hit three home runs to finish just back of Rote and Smith in third place.

Reggie Jackson came over and stood behind the cage as we were taking our turns swinging, and he was ragging us pretty good until somebody made the mistake of saying, "Well, why don't you come out here and show us?" And, oh he did. We thought we were hitting the ball. Reggie yanked some of those pitches completely out of sight.

The whole thing was really a lot of fun. Nobody's ego got in the way, and everybody took it in just the right humor. I'd love to do it again any time.

*Wednesday, January 30 — New York*

Bill Cosby and Stan Smith came by the apartment this afternoon, and we took a cab out to Brooklyn to play an exhibition at a buffet cocktail party to benefit the African Student Aid Fund. Obviously, this is a quote black unquote charity, and I help because it has a special appeal to me. It really burns me up when blacks *expect* me to have certain preordained interests, to structure my life only as a well-defined black-tennis-player-person.

That means that it is understood — accepted — that my main social concern should be with junior tennis — specifically with young ghetto blacks playing tennis. As people outline my life for me, I should spend most of every day sticking rackets into young black kids' hands, as if I were some kind of recreational Johnny

172

Appleseed. That really annoys me. Nobody ever asks Stan Smith why he's not out helping poor little Presbyterian white kids to play tennis. I'd like to choose my interests like any white player, any white man. I spent the first twenty-five years of my life, through my time in the army, having whites tell me what to do. I've spent the years since having blacks tell me what to do. When do we get to the point when Arthur can tell Arthur what to do?

Cosby expanded on another aspect of this. He pointed out that if any picture ever appeared in a newspaper of him and Camille just vacationing on the Riviera, blacks would have a fit. He would be accused of being insensitive, uncaring, greedy, of deserting the black cause. It is like now, when all the blacks are down on Sammy Davis Jr.'s case because he supported Nixon. Politically, I don't like his choice, but is it inscribed in stone somewhere that every black must vote Democratic? And how quickly have they all forgotten the many things that Sammy has done for blacks?

It's a curious thing. The white man who is a success is considered foolish if he does not take some of his money and enjoy himself. Then later, when he has grown old, he is expected to show some gratitude to society by giving something back to society. It is the reverse with blacks. Those of us who have made it are not permitted to enjoy ourselves until *after* we have paid our arbitrary dues. Even then, blacks expect us to adhere to certain limitations. It would be considered proper, for example, for the Cosbys to vacation in Nigeria.

My own case is complicated by the fact that I'm the only one. I am *the* black tennis player, a bloc by myself. Some black basketball player or black minister or black educator can announce a decision much easier than I because he does not carry the weight of his whole community. I've sometimes thought that a black American who runs the gauntlet similar to mine is Senator Brooke. He's the only black senator in a white senate — and he's married to a white woman too. Of course, it's still probably not so tedious for him; presumably everyone isn't always asking him why there aren't more black senators.

But I understand why blacks place an additional pressure upon me, because I feel myself doing the same thing to Senator Brooke or to Thurgood Marshall. To paraphrase Lyndon Johnson, Brooke is

173

the only senator we got; and Marshall the only justice; and Ashe the only tennis player.  I realize that other blacks will identify with me — even if they've never even seen a tennis match.

Not long ago, shortly after I lost a TV match, I received a postcard.  It was from a black guy, and in essence, all it said was: look, Ashe, if you can't win, get out of the game; we can't afford to have any losers so visible.  Imagine writing somebody a thing like that.

# 16

## Playing Europe and the Zone

*Sunday, February 3, 1974 — Paris / Nice / Monte Carlo / Nice*

Kathy and I are here for a few days of fun before the Green Group starts its WCT schedule. First, Roscoe and I are going to warm up in a little doubles tournament in Turin. Then, for WCT: Bologna, London, Barcelona, Hartford, São Paulo, Tucson (for an ATP tournament), Palm Desert, Tokyo, Houston and Denver. If I should make the singles finals in Dallas or the doubles finals in Montreal in May, I'll be a yo-yo by then.

*Monday, February 4 — Nice / Monte Carlo / Nice*

You should see the bathroom we have here. It's almost as big as the bedroom. Kathy is in ecstasy. She's a bathtub freak, and she's turned me into one too.

If you think about it, there's much in common between the philosophy of American bathrooms and restaurants vis-à-vis European bathrooms and restaurants. Bathrooms in our hotels are just like McDonalds. They're constructed only with traffic in mind: just to get you in and out. Bathrooms in U.S. hotels are cramped, unimaginative and inhospitable. God knows they *are* antiseptic enough with all the crinkly paper on the glasses and the little paper strips across the toilet which are supposed to certify its cleanliness, but

175

our hotel bathrooms have no charm, no ambience. I don't want my appendix out; I just want to take a bath.

But most U.S. hotels tacitly encourage you *not* to take a bath by putting down those gritty little nonslip strips on the floor of the bathtub. These do keep you from slipping in the shower; of course, they also keep you from sitting in the tub unless you are anxious for spinal lacerations.

By contrast, European hotel bathrooms look clean enough even without crinkly paper — and more important, they are spacious, gracious, comfortable places that encourage you to relax and dawdle. For the first time ever, I am even faucet-conscious; after all, the location of faucets dictates seating arrangements in bathtubs. Just as Europeans take so much more time and care with eating (and with playing a point in tennis), so do they attend to themselves more in the bathroom.

European hotel bathrooms are exactly that: rooms with a bath. American hotel bathrooms would be more correctly named "shower closets." I would think that if somebody would come along and construct a new chain of American motels — but with European-style bathrooms — they could appeal to a substantial minority of the population that, like myself, enjoys the pleasures of the tub.

*Tuesday, February 5 — Nice / Turin*

I covered the hotel bill with some money I won last night playing blackjack, and then Kathy and I set out for Turin in our rented car. We got to the hotel at four, and Roscoe and I had to play the first match against Paulo Bertolucci and Antoni Zugarelli at 6:30. I think the promoters were setting us up for the kill from the local boys, but we beat 'em. Bertolucci comes from near here. The Pasta Kid, we call him.

*Wednesday, February 6 — Turin*

I've only been in Europe a week, but already I have the feeling that the whole world is quieting down. Somehow, when I'm at a place where nobody is calling me on the phone and I can't even

176

carry on a conversation with most people, I become convinced that nothing much could be happening anywhere else either.

### *Thursday, February 7 — Turin*

We lost in five sets after being up two sets and 4–2. That's shameful of us. But the crowds were great, and the home boy won, so they were happy. The place could only seat 4500 and it was packed.

### *Friday, February 8 — Turin / Bologna*

You know, you really don't need a watch anywhere on the Continent (except possibly Scandinavia) because every building of any size has a clock on it. It seems as if every hotel I stay in in Europe has a clock right out my window.

We took the afternoon train to Bologna, and it left and arrived on time.

### *Sunday, February 10 — Bologna*

It's a shame Bologna has to be associated with a lunch meat, because in fact it is a very pretty little city that has fantastic restaurants. We're eating ourselves Bolognese to death, but I'm very lucky in that regard. I never gain weight. I have my mother's build; she was very slim. My father is stocky, and my brother too. Pasarell claims that I have a tapeworm in me — named Oscar. I do eat like a horse.

### *Tuesday, February 12 — Bologna*

I hadn't played a singles match in better than two weeks, so tonight, when I walked out on the court with Tom Leonard, it was more of an event, and it occurred to me that tennis must surely be the only sport in the world when you walk to the competition with the man you're going to play. Also, it must be the only major sport left where serious disagreement is settled by playing the point over.

177

Can you imagine the Miami Dolphins and the Minnesota Vikings playing a let?

It was very late when Leonard and I started, but hell, in Italy or Spain it might be one o'clock before the final match goes on. Everybody eats such a late dinner here that nothing can begin until later still. I've figured out that lunch is the key to it all. People in Europe eat such a big lunch that they can't possibly be hungry for dinner until nine o'clock or so.


*Wednesday, February 13 — Bologna*

I beat Onny Parun in the last match of the afternoon session. Poor Onny. He got married last Saturday to a Czech, but she has visa difficulties and is stranded in England with her six-year-old son. So now Onny has a son who doesn't speak his language and a bride a thousand miles away. He's a nice guy too — so conscientious, very frugal and probably the single worst dresser on the whole tour. I don't know, but he plays so many matches he probably never has time to shop. Actually, Onny's a lot like the Aussies and he sure looks like he's been chiseled from that same piece of granite, but the worst thing you can tell a Kiwi is that he reminds you of an Aussie.


*Thursday, February 14 — Bologna*

I'm playing so well I can't believe it. I beat Stilwell four and four, so here it is Thursday afternoon and I'm already in the semis. I'm serving beautifully, I'm not afraid to take chances, and every time I gamble it pays off. I'm unconscious out there — I don't feel a thing. This is the way life should be, just coasting.


*Saturday, February 16 — Bologna*

This was my first tough match, and I even lost a set, but I won the third 6–4. I was playing Roger Taylor, and he beat Laver yesterday and is playing well, so it was a very good win for me. For a long time after Wimbledon the guys pretty much ostracized Roger for being a scab, but he paid his fine, and that's all nearly forgotten now.

The crowds here are really going bananas — wilder than Turin. Laver really lost his cool the other night. He was playing Zugarelli and was down 5–4, 30–15 in the third on Zugarelli's serve, and the fans were berserk. Rocket pulled out the match, but he came into the locker room screaming that the people were "animals." I never saw him so worked up before.

Myself, I think this is one of the great crowds in tennis. They're excited, but they're not mean or vicious.

*Sunday, February 17 — Bologna*

Hey, I finally won a tournament — my first since last July in Washington. I beat Mark Cox 6–4, 7–5. He had me 5–3, 40-love in the second set and I still won it. I tell you, just about everything is breaking right for me now.

Cox has always been sort of my bête noire too. The last time we played, it was also in a finals, at Denver last year, and he ate me for lunch — one and one. But Marcus is something like me in that he thinks too much. A brain certainly doesn't have to be a liability in tennis. On the contrary, Newcombe is one of the smartest guys in the game; Drysdale's another; and Kodes is a pretty bright boy too.

But Mark uses his brain against himself. He's too bright, too rational. If Newcombe, say, or Drysdale, get beat, they shrug it off. Their brain tells them — what the hell, it's only a game. But if Cox gets beat, he starts analyzing why. He knows that he is more naturally gifted than many of the people who beat him, so he worries about it and tries to figure out why. Well, the reason he gets beat by these people is that he worries about it and tries to figure out why.

I have the same kind of problem. My mind has gotten in my way all along. I know that I should have won more than I have in my career, and it bothers me, especially as I get older and realize that my chances are running out. It's nice to win a Bologna; hell, it's nice to win anything. But I want a Wimbledon, I want another Forest Hills. Those are the victories people measure you by.

179

*Monday, February 18 — Bologna / Milan / London*

It's nice to be back where they speak English. So, as soon as I got to my room in the Westbury, I ordered the eggs Benedict.

*Tuesday, February 19 — London*

The best news is that the tournament at Queen's, the one we all hated which is played the week before Wimbledon, has been replaced on the schedule by a $100,000 event at Nottingham.

Donald arrived last night from Paris with the word that the French, Italians, Germans, Spaniards and possibly the Swedes are all going to ban World Team Tennis players from their tournaments. Jack Kramer had just explained to them the change toward WTT in the ATP position, but these countries feel that they should attack Team Tennis now while it is still relatively weak.

*Friday, February 22 — London*

I thought I was playing unconscious, but Borg beat me 6–4, 7–6 tonight, and he is in what we call *the zone*. (That comes originally from "twilight zone" and translates, more or less, into "another world.") The kid has no concept of what he is doing out there — he is just swinging away and the balls are dropping in. He has no respect for anybody. Hell, he should win the whole tournament.

*Saturday, February 23 — London*

John Marshall, the producer of my South African film, lives on an estate in Hampshire, west of London. We went out there today to see some rough footage of the movie, and I ended up being totally immersed in a British experience.

The house first of all: simple, elegant and loaded with tradition. The Duke of Wellington had it built and two prime ministers died in it: William Pitt and Neville Chamberlain. And then: a fox hunt. Mrs. Marshall is a very accomplished rider, and there were about forty other hunters there, a dozen or more dogs, a field master and a master of the hounds. It is, when you think about it, as much a tribal rite as anything you would find in the most primitive land. What struck me most were the women — riding sidesaddle, but game as hell, stiff upper lip, bouncing along like so many sacks of potatoes, all dressed in various outfits that designated their level of experience (like colored karate belts).

The British do these sort of things just right, which is probably why they have so many traditions. The hunt made me think that Wimbledon should not change a thing. Particularly, when I saw all the hunters dressed in their magnificent riding outfits, I became convinced that Wimbledon should be the one place that should toe the line and retain the all-white clothing rule.

I was one of the first pros to wear colored clothes, and it is obviously the fashion of the day, but that is all the more reason why Wimbledon should stand alone and maintain the all-white tradition. Nobody else could get away with it but the British, and then, nobody else should get away with it but the British.

I read a magnificent comment from Lord Snow the other day. He wrote: "The English are still really good at three things: ceremonies, where we are unparalleled; there's no one in the world who could put on a show like the English, such as, for instance, the royal wedding. The sheer production is marvelous. That's one thing. Two, we are very good at acting, and three, we are, *pro rata*, still very good at pure science. Pure science, not applied."

And that is the British, all right — pure, not applied.


*Sunday, February 24 — London / Madrid / Barcelona*

Room 411 of the Diplomatic Hotel. The bed here is typical of those in Continental Europe: it sinks in the middle and makes it seem that you are inside a banana.

The ideal hotel room would have a Continental bathroom and shutters; an American bed, telephone and Coke machine; and be attended to by British personnel.


*Monday, February 25 — Barcelona*

I beat Dibley 6–3, 7–6. Just barely; it was tight. We played a sudden-death tie-breaker in the second set. I won the point, and

181

the set and the match, and he just rushed to the net to congratulate me — so genuinely.  Colin may be the typical Aussie: nice and fun, loves to practice, to punish himself, and the same way, win or lose. He loses as well as anyone I've ever played; and I mean that as a large compliment.

*Tuesday, February 26 — Barcelona*

We tried the zoo and the Museum of Modern Art — nothing, either one.  I'm not exactly crazy about seeing animals all penned up, but with a lot of time on my hands, I see a lot of zoos.  Budapest has the best zoo I've seen in Europe.

*Wednesday, February 27 — Barcelona*

I creamed Solomon two and love.  My serve is just out of this world.

*Thursday, February 28 — Barcelona*

I just keep rolling on.  Beat Taylor four and two.  I'll be home in three or four days at the most now, and it may sound corny, but my pace always quickens when it's getting time for me to go back to the States.  I get itchy.  I do.

*Friday, March 1 — Barcelona*

I found a little packet of detergent for five pesetas, so I went back to my room and washed all my laundry.  I'm going stir crazy.  Most hotels, the things you can wash out and hang up one day will be dry the next.  Lamps will often throw off enough heat to dry small things in a hurry — socks and jocks.  The main thing to do is wash as you go.  Once you get behind four or five pairs of dirty socks, you better get on the phone and call for the laundry.

*Saturday, March 2 — Barcelona*

I beat Dibbs in the semis, and now I've got to play Borg in the finals. I forgot to tell you what Borg did to Laver the other day. He beat the Rocket one and one. Incredible.

*Sunday, March 3 — Barcelona*

What a way to go home. I beat Borg in three sets, 6–4, 3–6, 6–3, and then Roscoe and I made it a double for me by beating Tom Edlefson and Tom Leonard in straights.

Roscoe and I celebrated by taking Kathy and Nancy out to dinner at a place called Oliver's. Stuffed ourselves. The bad news is we have to fly back Iberia.

*Monday, March 4 — Barcelona / Madrid / New York*

As soon as I cleared customs I hurried over to my apartment, just long enough to take a shower and change and get to the New York Hilton to attend a fund-raising dinner for Senator Javits. I received a wire a few days ago in Bologna asking me to speak, and I accepted without realizing what a big deal it was. Every Republican to the left of, oh say, Howard Baker, was there, as well as a number of prominent Democrats. I was seated at the table with the Javits family and spoke between Percy and Brooke.

I've always been fascinated by politics, by the science of power, but I suspect that I'm too private a person ever to put up with the hail-fellow-well-met stuff that you must endure to succeed in politics. But then, for that matter, I think I've been spoiled so long by the good life I've lead in tennis ever to even settle for a nine-to-five corporate life. What I would really love to become is an ambassador, especially to some African country.

I know you can say, well what the hell qualifications does playing tennis have for becoming a diplomat, but in fact, I've had the chance to use my tennis travel. I've met people, little and great, all over the world and tried to learn firsthand about the cultures and idiosyncrasies of different peoples. In a way, I've had the chance to

183

learn more as a world-class tennis player than some lower-echelon Foreign Service Officer would have had over the same period of time.  And I'm an American black with an international aspect, which is not exactly ordinary.

Besides, I'm sure I could learn to play a pretty good game of social hit-and-giggle tennis with the other diplomats.

*Tuesday, March 5 — New York*

I've always loved films.  I'm especially crazy about documentaries.  Right now I'm thinking seriously about producing a documentary film series myself about Africa that would be pointed for American schoolchildren.  It looks like a real possibility too.  The New York State Board of Education has shown some interest in the idea.

What we want to do is a really serious, educational, thematic work about Africa — not another damn travelogue with the water buffaloes and pygmies.  For instance, my partner, an Englishman named Graham Lowe, and I were talking today about how our pilot film might be on the subject of how nationalism in Africa is so often thwarted by tribalism.  Our idea would be to have the various segments narrated by popular blacks like Cosby or Poitier or Bill Russell, so that the kids would be more willing to listen.

Very few Americans, whites or blacks, have any real concept of Africa.  The place has hundreds of languages and is almost four times larger than the U.S. — Kenya and Nigeria have about as much in common as Sweden and Albania — but most people tend to think of it as one big country with people all much the same.  When I've been in Africa and told the schoolchildren there that most Americans up till now had no image at all of Africa much past Tarzan and elephants, the kids invariably laugh at first because they think I'm putting them on.  It's the same every time: very quickly the laughter turns to nervous giggles as they realize that I'm on the level.

Another truth is, ironically, that white American kids have a greater comprehension of Africa than do the blacks.  If I speak in some white suburb, a Scarsdale or Chevy Chase, I will get more questions about Africa — and more sophisticated questions — than

184

if I talk to a bunch of inner-city black kids.  Of course, the general black ignorance of Africa gets back to the business of the luxury of being the majority, of being more able to *select* your interest. Largely because of economics, most American blacks are obliged to concentrate on things next door.

But I'm convinced that most black American kids want to know more about Africa.  You see so many of them, for instance, wearing the green-red-and-black armbands of African liberation, but without any real understanding.  And the "authentic" Afro haircuts, which are nowhere to be found in Africa; African names, African clothes.  The thinking, the desire is there, if it can only be focused. I think it will help if we can make films about the real Africa and get kids interested for the real reasons.

I get depressed at the strangest times.  I've had a helluva start this year.  I was in the finals at Philadelphia and I've had two wins already.  I'm the leading money winner, and everything else is going fabulously.  And yet I get so down, especially if I can't do things I want to, or whenever I lose.  It seems like I take my losses harder all the time.  I know I'm still in peak shape and I don't have any weight problem so I have another six or seven years left, I suppose — there's no sense of urgency — but still, I feel more vulnerable all the time.

It's harder in an individual sport.  It's just you out there.  But it's not just me.  Before he won Forest Hills last year, Newcombe was down for a long time.  Nastase is so incredibly talented, and a year ago he was nearly invincible.  Now he is in a real slump, and — check this later — I have this feeling that he's not going to get any better this year, that he's going to fall off more.  We've never had this situation in tennis before where players at the top have been challenged year after year.  It used to be that you played a few years in the spotlight as an amateur, but where no real money was involved and while you were still very young, and then you either packed it in or started barnstorming as a pro, with no pressure to speak of.  But now, suddenly, it's a whole new ball game: you're on the line, week after week, year after year.

And the money cuts two ways.  If you make the top you get the side money, the endorsements, and that is bound to make you a

185

little complacent.  But the kids coming up are scratching for the prize money and you have to fight them off to keep the ranking, the name, which gives you the extra dollars.  People are saying: look at what this kid Borg can do at seventeen.  He might be the greatest ever.  But the way things are, he might be over the hill at twenty-one or twenty-two.  Nastase was so great just being himself, out there scrambling all around, laughing.  And suddenly he was on top and everybody started looking at him and picking him apart, and then, it seems, it wasn't fun anymore.  It was a tough job.  I think that may be what has happened to him.

Jack Nicklaus, or any top golfer, can go to a tournament and shoot a bummer one day, a 74 or a 75.  And he is still there.  He has three more rounds to make it up.  If a high-ranking tennis player shoots, figuratively, a 75 on the court, he's through.  Somebody named John Bartlett or Edison Mandarino or fifty other guys can shoot a 74 against him, and he's out in the first round.  There's no catchup in tennis.  They're at your heels, barking, every day.  There's never been anything like this before.

I was so anxious to get back here, but it hasn't been at all like I expected.  I remember the last time I saw Bill Cosby's wife, Camille, and she was talking about how I must have just about the ideal life — single, some money, living in New York, all that.  I said, "No, Camille, I'm just not that type.  I'm not a typical New York single."  And this time when I came back, when I walked into the apartment, for the first time I wasn't really glad to be in it.  It looked so damn boxy, so much like just another hotel.  Right now I wish to hell I was out of here and could see some grass and trees.

# 17

# *The Aussies*

*Wednesday, March 6, 1973 — New York / Hartford*

We're playing the World Cup, which is not a World Cup at all but a match between Australian and American professionals. It was inaugurated five years ago at a time when the pros were locked out of the Davis Cup, but now that that prohibition has ended this competition is pretty superfluous.

There's also talk of starting something called the Continental Cup, which would pit God's land masses against each other instead of just nations or cities, the way it is now. The tennis calendar already runs about seventy-four weeks a year, so we might as well add a few more cups.

*Thursday, March 7 — Hartford*

The World Cup, as opposed to the Davis Cup, has a format of seven matches, five singles and two doubles. Stan and I will each play two singles for the U.S. against Newcombe and Laver, while Gorman and Rosewall will play the fifth match.

Tonight Stan lost to Rocket, 7–5, 6–3. Stan was just a little bit slower than he should have been all over the court. Now I play Newcombe tomorrow.

*Friday, March 8 — Hartford*

Tennis, of course, is not really a team sport. When it is played as a team sport, it is a forcing of the issue; it is just a number of separate matches totaled up. Still, the Davis Cup has been contested for almost three quarters of a century and college team tennis in this country has a long tradition, so that all of us who play the game have a certain experience with the concept and spirit of team.

I talked earlier about the U.S. team in '68 that won the Cup back. That was a unit in the highest athletic sense. But as an ongoing team, an entity, a tradition, nothing in tennis has ever approached the Aussies. They have an esprit no other country's players have. They are a breed apart.

For one thing, which is more important than it sounds, the Australians travel better than the rest of us. In fact, because their country is so far away, they must travel. Some kind of a selection of the species sorts them out back home. We never see the homesick Aussies; if an Australian makes the tour it is understood that he cannot be homesick.

This sets the tone for their whole philosophy, for just as they can accept traveling as part of the game, so they accept every other variable. Rarely, if ever, will an Aussie bitch about calls. They play the game, not the lines. Interestingly enough, the only one I've ever known who does complain with any degree of frequency is Nailbags Carmichael, who has lived for several years in France. In private, the Aussies will complain about the money — aside from buying beers, they are a nation of tightwads — but never will they complain about conditions or use them to alibi. If the lights were bad or the crowd was noisy or the surface was slick or whatever — they keep their mouths shut. If you have an injury, you can default; if you play, you don't have an injury. You're playing aren't you? "You walk on the court, you have no excuses," Roy Emerson told me once, and that is the credo.

The whole world has tried to adopt their training methods, and while they are no secret, they have never worked as well for any other nation. The rigorous exercises have been just right for the Aussies for a couple of reasons. First of all, and simply, the Austra-

188

lians are good athletes; they are athletes who happen to be tennis players. They didn't learn in country clubs. Secondly, though probably more important, it is part of their culture to endure. By their own definition, they are a nation of "mutton-punchers" and "sod-busters" and so it was relatively easy for them to accept the Marquis de Sade exercises that, in the main, Harry Hopman devised.

Hop is the father figure of Australian tennis — or the godfather figure. He was captain for most of thirty years, beginning in 1938, and while he had been a world-class player himself, he made his mark as a team leader. He wasn't just captain, he was everything: coach, administrator, trainer, warden, chaperon. He even wrote his own newspaper scoops. He is the one constant in the Aussie story, and while many of the guys who played for him still hate his bloody guts, they all give him credit. Actually, since I never played for Hopman, he was always very kind to me. It was only his own players he treated like dogs. He was the first person to suggest that I try Butazolidin for my tennis elbow.

Of all Hopman's training devices, the most maniacal is the two-on-one drill: just two guys on one side of the net hitting to the target player on the other. It's as simple as it sounds and it's a universal procedure now, but it is absolutely the most grueling exercise.

Yet probably as important as the training methods that he created was the sense of team, of continuity, that Hopman developed. Among the stars, a tradition of responsibility grew early, and each of the big players passed something on: Sedgman and McGregor to Anderson and Cooper to Laver and Emerson to Newcombe and Roche — when the string ran out. The younger Aussies, the ones who never had the benefit of Hopman, are different. They don't have the same spirit and outlook. The money has changed a lot of things. Hopman probably couldn't run things his way anymore. He treated newcomers to the squad with contempt. Here was some hotshot kid, junior champion, the comer, and Hopman made him into an errand boy, an orange squeezer. The reserves on the team didn't hit a ball unless Hopman deigned to let them. On the other hand, if he thought one of his stars needed work, he'd bring out a reserve and use him as a ball machine for as long as it suited his

189

purposes. One time I saw Bill Bowrey serve to Roy Emerson for better than a half an hour straight.

The players came to him pretty much as stoics, but Hopman conditioned them to go further, to play when they hurt. I can see any one of them now, say down 30–40 after a hard-lost point. One deep breath and right back at you — and all the time exuding confidence, sure that they'll win this point, make it deuce, sweep the next two and the game. Hell, ace you the next two. You felt that across the net; still do when you play one of Hop's boys. Tired as an Aussie might be, he will always make it a point to cross over standing straight up, breathing easy. It is a matter of pride never to let you know they can be tired. And with Hopman sitting there watching them during Davis Cup matches, they were like the little Spartan boy with the fox eating his stomach out. Probably they were more afraid of Hopman than anybody on the other side of the net.

He would never get out of his chair. Just sit and watch. But after all the harassment and hectoring in practice, when it was a match, he was a model of reassurance. No matter how badly a guy would be playing, he'd say, "Keep going for the lines" — hit out, don't ease up and play safe. Stolle told me that in the key '64 Challenge Round match against Ralston, when he crossed over down two sets to one and a break in the fourth set, Hop just said: "Go for the lines." Stolle broke Dennis next game with a lob just in. *Go for the lines.*

Hopman was a long time coming around to playing Stolle. He didn't think Fred had guts enough. One year Stolle made the Wimbledon finals, but Hopman still wouldn't use him. When he finally did select him for an important match, against Mexico in '65, he never gave Fred a clue to his intentions. Stolle didn't know he was playing until his name came out of the bowl at the draw.

Fred's case was unusual. Most times, if you got behind Hopman's eight ball you never got out. A lot of good Aussies finally gave up and left: Marty Mulligan moved to Rome, Bob Mark and Bob Hewitt to South Africa, Nailbags Carmichael to France, Ken Fletcher to Hong Kong. Hewitt has won the Wimbledon doubles four times, but Hopman wouldn't tolerate his temperament, no matter how good he was. Fletcher was like Kilroy. Even Onny

190

Parun is no match for Fletcher. He must have played every court in the world. If you got to Katmandu you'd find out Ken Fletcher won the tournament three years ago. He was like a one-man Harlem Globetrotters of tennis.

What sets the Aussies furthest apart from the rest of us is that they never stop being a team. They are traveling alone in the world, and so they look out for one another. It does not matter which one of them is playing, at least one other Aussie will be watching, and if you lose, there will also be at least one mate to console you over a few beers. "We always know there will be one of us there," Stolle told me once. "It's never that way with you bloody Yanks."

The Aussies even evidence something of an adolescent element, like schoolboys off at camp. They almost all have nicknames or, at the least, are known to each other by affectionate diminutives. Lew Hoad, a bull of a man, is Hoadie. *Hoadie!* And there's Newc and Emmo, Creals, Dibbles, Dave-O and Philby.

On the tour, outside of the Aussies, there's only a handful of nicknames that have taken hold. We call Eric van Dillen "VD" (of course) or "Drifty" because his mind wanders and Tom Leonard "Spacey" for fairly similar reasons; Torben is "The Guru" and Roy Barth is "Tub" (which comes from Barth to Bath to Tub). Lutz was "Lust" in his single days, and Richard Evans, the ATP PR man, is "The Creeper" because he has a well-deserved reputation for snaking anybody's date. But most of these nicknames are seldom really used. Not so with the Aussies. They use their nicknames. Everybody actually calls Rod Laver "Rocket." I'm Arthur, he's Stan, he's Cliff, and there's Rocket. It would be like calling Babe Ruth, the Sultan of Swat, "Sultan" or saying "How's things, Slammin'?" to Slammin' Sammy Snead.

And the Aussies accept their own nicknames and use them. I'll get a call from Carmichael and he'll say: "Nailbags here." Or Case will ring me up and say, "Arthur, it's Snake." And there's "Muscles" for Rosewall, "Hesh" is Ray Ruffels, "Fiery" is Stolle, "Country" is Mal Anderson (who married Emmo's sister), "Boy" is Tony Roche. Bill Bowrey fell off a horse once, somebody laughed and called him "Tex," and that's been his name ever since.

I first went to Australia in 1965, and I've spent better than a year

191

of my life down under — plus no telling how many years made up of days and nights with Aussies all over the world.  The Australians are among the nicest people I've met, and if they call us "the bloody Yanks," they have a great affinity for Americans — certainly much more affection than for the British, whom they sneer at as "pommie bastards."  (Although *bastard* is pronounced "bostad" in their dialect.  Since there are so many Aussies and since they use the expression rather often, the foreign players who learn English on tour invariably pronounce the word Australian style.  Nothing is more disconcerting than to hear Santana say "you bostad" with a Spanish accent.)

The first place I ever stayed in Australia was Brisbane, in Queensland, where Roy Emerson comes from.  Lennon's Hotel; I still remember.  Brisbane is the furthest north of the large Australian cities so, in the Southern Hemisphere, that puts it closest to the equator.  Australia is about four-fifths the size of the United States (with hardly twelve million residents), and it is shaped pretty much the same way as the U.S., so that if you think of a map of our country with Australia overlaid on it, then Brisbane lies about where Washington is.  But hot — like an oven, a sophisticated cow town.  A few years later I played an exhibition nearby at a place called Toowoomba, where Snake comes from.  Never been hotter. And I never saw so many flies in my life.  I thought they would eat the tennis balls.

Sydney is the largest city and the geographical equivalent to Atlanta.  Melbourne, around the bend, about where Mobile is, is nearly as large as Sydney and more of a cultural center, but for some reason many more of the best players come from Sydney.  Rosewall, Newcombe, Hewitt, Dent, Alexander, Crealy all come from Sydney, and Margaret Court, Roche and Goolagong from nearby, but Nailbags, Stone and Dave-O are my only contemporaries from Melbourne.  Laver comes from the town of Rockhampton, which would be our Portland, Maine, way northeast, right on the Tropic of Capricorn.  After growing up in that climate, anything else must seem mild to him.

The fourth city of the country is Adelaide, where we won back the Cup in '68.  It is located about where New Orleans would be. West of that is nothing but kangaroos and aborigines until you get

192

way out to Perth, all by itself, on the southwestern coast, like Los Angeles. The aborigines stay out in the sticks, and there are almost no blacks in the cities because, until recently, Australia followed a discriminatory immigration policy that allowed in only a few non-European people.

I must say, though, that I have never had any problem whatsoever there with regard to race and, according to Newcombe, the government and the people don't give a hang about blacks like me, one way or the other. The immigration policies were, he says, aimed strictly at keeping the Asian hordes out. Of course, it all amounted to the same thing.

The Aussie players tend to have very little interest in politics. Newcombe, who is among the brightest of them all, is the exception, and Stolle also has some strong political opinions. The players are usually conservative, as nouveaux riches tend to be everywhere — the British have an expression for it: "Bang the bell, Jack, I'm on the bus." The rest of us are laughing at the Aussies now because a Labour government was voted in recently for the first time in many years, and it is raising taxes. I mentioned this to Rosewall in the locker room today, and with a perfectly straight face, he replied: "It doesn't concern me too much, of course, but they are taxing the rich a bit much." As if he were not among the Australian rich.

Muscles still has every dollar he ever made, and he still dresses like a farmer come to town. On those rare occasions when he cracks a joke in the locker room, the whole place falls silent in shock. But he owns the complete respect of the players, as a man and as a player. Unlike Laver and Newcombe and Emerson and several of the others who have tennis interests and homes in the U.S., Muscles does not have as many ties to America. He is strictly an old-fashioned family man and an Australian and a man unto himself. He plays much as he lives, never changing his game for anybody.

It is interesting to note, for instance, that while both Muscles and I have backhands as our best shots, I have three different backhands, and he has only one. I can hit a flat backhand, on top of the ball or under it. Muscles just hits every backhand the same — perfectly. He also never has to hurry a shot. I have no idea how he manages it, but 99 percent of the time he is in perfect position to hit whatever you send back. This gives him an edge few people are aware of too. It gives him the time to disguise his shots; you seldom can tell what is coming. His lob, particularly from the forehand side, is bouncing back by the base line at approximately the time when you figure out that he has lobbed you.

Rosewall came up with Lew Hoad two decades ago, the teen-age whiz kids, but they were, and are, temperamentally opposite. Also, as great as Rosewall is, it is important to remember that Hoad was considered the better, and even, for a brief spell, possibly the best player ever. Gonzales always told me that if there was a Universe Davis Cup, if Earth had to pick one man for all time to play one match for the planet, he would pick Lew Hoad in his prime. But Hoad is another who was done in by back trouble.

A lot of people think that if Lew had stayed healthy, he could have been tennis' equivalent to Arnold Palmer and hastened the tennis boom by a decade. Hoad was surely the strongest player who ever lived; he completely contradicted the lingering effete tennis image. And he was colorful and charismatic. He would stay out drinking beer till five in the morning and then beat your brains out on the court by noon. Whitney Reed was an American who could do that, but of course he was not even near Hoad's class. Emerson is another one who could carry on all night, then play at top speed the next day.

There are two absolutes I think you can lay on Emmo. One, he was the fittest player who ever lived. Two, he is the most popular. Every tennis player loves Roy Emerson — in the richest sense of the verb. He is a "great bloke" as they say, completely selfless and genuine. In the locker room, after you have played a match, he is sure to come by, whether you won or lost. If you won, he says, "Well done." If you lost: "Bad luck." A smile in either case.

Emmo has bad teeth. So does Muscles. So do a lot of the Aussies. The men are purposely plain, with no artificiality at all. There are a lot of long faces and jut jaws — a very determined-looking, down-to-earth type. The Aussies wouldn't care about the cosmetics of teeth as long as they work when it comes to eating. They even rather pride themselves on their ordinariness; showing off is

194

the gravest Australian sin.  The worst they can call someone is a "high noter," meaning a person who flaunts money.

I don't believe that any of the players have ever invested in anything more exotic than an apartment house back home.  The whole continent must be sinking under apartment houses owned by tennis players.  Given a choice, they'll stay in the cheapest hotels.  For Wimbledon, they all go way out to Cromwell Road and find cut-rate deals at small hotels out there.  Their dress is neo–Goodwill.  I swear Nailbags wore the same sweater almost every day for five years.  The Aussies will always play Rome at least once every other year so they can stock up on shoes to last them till the next time they're there.  And it's probably just as well they never buy any clothes, because they don't care about fashion to begin with.  The only good Australian dresser I've ever seen is Newcombe's wife, Angie, but then, she's from Germany, so she really doesn't count.

Native Australian women know their place.  "Sheilahs" they're called.  "Come on, you bloody Sheilah," Emmo will scream, pulling some other player's wife up by her arm.  That is an invitation to dance.  Stolle, who likes "to get through you" (pull a fast one on you), has raised hell with me because he says the American soldiers who go to Australia for R&R are spoiling all the Sheilahs by talking to them and listening to them and spending money on them.  Making them think they're bloody queens.  The Australian idea of a great date is to take a Sheilah to a pub, park her in the corner and then go over and drink all evening with the boys.

Of course, in self-defense, the Aussie girls learn pretty quickly to be beer drinkers too.  Davidson, Newc's buddy, also married an Angie, this one from Houston, and she's already more Aussie than American.  I expect Angie Davidson to be saying "piss off" — but endearingly — very soon now.  Dave-O is the most direct of the Aussies.  We call him "Mr. Warmth," after Don Rickles.  But he always makes himself understood — he is fair and forthright, so everybody likes him.  But he is an anomaly: a bad Aussie drinker.  Two beers and Dave-O is, as they say, "pissed as a parrot."

Hoad has the reputation as the most indomitable drinker, but Newcombe and Roche are leading contenders.  Newc is not invincible though.  In 1967, the first time he won Wimbledon, he celebrated by filling a bathtub full of ice and beer bottles — Foster's, the favorite, direct from Australia — but the evening concluded when he threw up all over Angie. The year before, New Year's Night, January 1, 1966, I was playing down in Australia, and a bunch of us went over to a place in Sydney named Herman's Haystack. Pretty soon, after an awful lot of Foster's, we were all pissed as parrots, and Newc tilted back in his chair and fell right out of it and injured his back. I think he'd like to forget that.

I've never seen an Australian order anything like a martini. Hell, they call you a "lardy" (snob) if you ask for wine. If you do join a group of them drinking beer, there is only one rule — the newcomer must be prepared to "shout." That means to order a round. "It's your shout, mate. What's the matter — your arms too short or your pockets too long?" Economic status has no bearing when it comes to shouting. The poorest man at the table is expected to match shouts with the richest. And as tight as the Aussies can be, they are not necessarily clannish at the bar. If you want to join them on their terms and give a shout or two, fine. They love having Cliff Richey sit in. He's such an intense, humorless creature on the court, but after a few beers with the Aussies, he gets all bugeyed and turns into a regular comic.

As egalitarian as the Aussies are, however, they take a monarchist pride in their champion. They show no jealousy toward him and are more anxious to build him up than to watch him fall from his perch. At the very peak of his career, when he was winning his second Grand Slam, Laver would get coaching tips from lesser players like Stolle. When Newcombe assumed the leader's mantle but then fell into a slump and took some bad losses, Stolle came right up to him and, well, reprimanded him. "You got to shape up, Newc," he told him. Another time last year, when Newcombe wanted to give up the tour because he was going so badly, Allan Stone and Ray Ruffels kept him up drinking beer till three in the morning, calling him "a quitter" to his face. At last, they beat him down and he stayed on tour. The next day, Dave-O volunteered himself to practice with him.

Newcombe has the best court presence. He emits vibrations that he is on top, and particularly for big events and under pressure, he is capable of raising his game. John is not a pretty player, but he is much smarter than he is given credit for. One of his greatest assets is his ability to win five-set matches. Yet, he cannot go top speed for five sets. He looks stronger than Laver or Emerson, but he doesn't possess their stamina. So Newc must pick his spots and save something for the fifth set — which means that his accomplishment is all the more impressive. He doesn't just outlast opponents; he outthinks them.

Tonight in the World Cup he beat me 6–4 in the third. In the Davis Cup at Cleveland he beat Stan 6–4 in the fifth. He got the break off me in a way he often does. Newc has a great forehand, you know. Many people who are strong on that side will often run around their backhand, but Newc will play it straight. He'll hit backhands he could work to run around. Then suddenly, you are serving and he gets the edge — 30–40 on your second serve, as he did tonight. So now, for the first time in the set he slides over into the alley and glares back at you. He is announcing to you: I am going to hit my forehand. And you must serve to it or risk a double fault by trying to hit his far backhand corner on a dime. In the Davis Cup, at match point, in a similar sort of situation, Stanley double-faulted. Tonight, I get my serve in, but Newc hit the forehand and won the point. Break.

In ways like this, Newcombe distracts you and makes you think ahead, wondering what he is going to come up with next. It's a great psychological trick, for you may do more damage to yourself worrying about when he going to run around his backhand than when in fact he does it. Matches with Newcombe may never look subtle, but there is much more there than is apparent.

And now I've got to play Rocket tomorrow.


*Saturday, March 9 — Hartford*

Hallelujah!

1–18!

I beat him 6–3, 6–3. It was the first time since 1959 that Laver lost a match playing for his country. Since Gorman had beaten Rosewall last night, this gave us a 2–2 tie in the Cup, and we should have gone ahead in the next match. Stan and I had Newcombe and

Roche 3–0 in the third, but we let them pull it out at 6–4. So my participation is ended and the Aussies are up 3–2.

As far as the Laver match was concerned, it was just my turn. He wasn't playing very well at the start, and I sensed this and concentrated just on getting the ball in and letting him make the errors. I remembered to lob too and used it to good advantage. I was hitting a sharp backhand slice from the base line, and I was putting more volleys away than I usually do against him. He often makes me hit my first volley up, without much velocity, and then he comes in a step or so and passes me, but tonight he was just off and I could hit down on my volleys.

Still, no one can ever feel secure against Rocket. People talk about me being a streaky player, but there is no one who can blow any hotter than Rocket. In 1968 in the finals of the Pacific Southwest, Rosewall beat him 7–5 in the first set and then didn't win another game — love and love, a double bagel. When Laver goes on one of those tears, it's just ridiculous. He starts hitting the lines, and then he starts hitting the lines harder — and harder and harder. No one can stop him.

So, in the second set, I went up 5–1, and damn if he doesn't break back and all of a sudden it is 5–3 and I'm down love–40 on my serve. Well, I am not a defeatist, but after eighteen straight losses to the guy, you can imagine what was going through my head out there. And I am aware that everybody in the building, Laver included, is probably thinking the same thing.

But this time I steadied and held. Laver has one fantastic little shot that serves as sort of a weathervane for him. If this shot is working, you can be sure his whole game is on. It is a soft backhand underspin lob down the line. He doesn't hit it high but just sort of scoops it up — and he never uses it except to your backhand side. When that shot is on, it goes, diabolically, exactly one inch past your backhand reach and lands just inside the base line. Rocket missed one of those tonight near the end, when he was coming back at me, though, and that was when I finally believed that I really might beat him at last. As the Aussies say, the game was up. But let me tell you, mate, if he had beaten me again, I would have gone round the bend. As it is, I'm buggered, and Laver's probably so surprised you could stuff him up a gum tree.

198

# 18

# *The Jaybird Stopped Singing*

*Sunday, March 10, 1974 — New York / São Paulo*

Welcome to Brazil. We just got into our room in this fleabag and I've already been cheated twice. Problems. No bathtubs — just showers. Kathy is mad already.

*Monday, March 11 — São Paulo*

They've got new money since the last time I was here, and a new president was installed just last Wednesday. Pat Nixon came down as the President's representative, and the city went bananas over that. But then, things are going so well here, I get the feeling that nobody much cares who's president.

Roscoe and I lost to Munoz and Zugarelli in the first round today, which is not smart. We're still comfortably in second place in the Green Group standings behind Borg and Bengtson, and the top two teams in each group qualify automatically for Montreal (as well as two other teams with the highest total), but there's some good teams close behind us, and it's just not a very bright thing to go getting beaten in first rounds.

*Tuesday, March 12 — São Paulo*

I bought a Portuguese phrase book and discovered that, correctly, it's pronounced Sown Pal-o. It's also the beginning of the rainy season — showers every afternoon around three-thirty or four — which only serves to remind Kathy again that there are no bathtubs.

Jun Kamiwazumi and I had lunch together at the Hilton. We had to play each other afterward, so it made sense to eat and go out to the courts together. I beat him three and one. The WCT surface is too fast for his best game, but, like a lot of foreigners, Jun could beat almost anybody on clay. The public in America doesn't have a clue yet to how many really top players there are floating around now — especially foreign clay-court players. If the grass courts at Forest Hills are dug up and replaced by the composition clay-type courts for the '75 U.S. Open, the quarter-finals could easily be made up of eight foreigners, none of whom the average U.S. sports fan has ever heard of.

Well, maybe Mutt and Mutt would win a couple of spots for the home country to go along with, oh, say, such household names as Jaime Fillol, Juan Gisbert, Zeljko Franulovic, Guillermo Vilas, Antoni Zugarelli and Alex Metreveli. The sports fans of America would be tearing the gates down to get in to see that action, wouldn't they? That's an extreme example, I know, but it could happen.

Metreveli, the Georgian — Tbilisi, Georgia, not Waycross — is an interesting guy. He was good enough to make the Wimbledon finals last July against Kodes when the ATP pulled out, but he is better on clay than grass. It is typical of the Soviet system, though, that he would be instructed carefully to play any surface. There is very little individuality to his game; he stands out because he is Russian . . . and because he is one helluva good tennis player.

He gets along quite well with everyone. Of course, he can never keep any of his prize money — it goes to his federation — and he's always accompanied by a coach, either Serge or Simon. Old Serge is particularly fascinated by me, as there are few black men back in Minsk or Moscow or wherever. I remember the last time Alex and I were together at a tournament at Albert Hall, Serge's eyes just popped as he watched me comb my hair after a shower. I could see him staring, but I couldn't figure out what the hell it was he was so fascinated about.

Finally, he couldn't stand it anymore. "Vat is dat? Dust?" he asked. What it was was simply flicks of water flying off my hair as I combed it. He was downright disappointed when I explained it to him.

### Wednesday, March 13 — São Paulo

There's just not a helluva lot to do here and everybody is finding that out. It's very sterile and lethargic. But the crowds for the tournament have been fantastic — and it's on TV every day too. Tomas Koch, the Brazilian player, is in charge of the tournament (as well as playing in it), while a sugar company is sponsoring it.

I beat Roscoe tonight in the second round. Three sets, all 6–3, but he won the first. He gets tougher all the time, but he's yet to beat me, and I want to keep it that way. Once a guy beats you, the psychology of the competition is changed significantly. The first kiss is the toughest one, but after that it's often easy.

### Thursday, March 14 — São Paulo

There was a pro-am scheduled this morning at a club some distance from the hotel, so I dutifully dragged myself up, and so did Roscoe and Ove Bengtson, Borg and Laver, and we all went out there, and not a single amateur bothered to show up. There was no mistake in the schedule; just nobody could be bothered.

It's funny about this town. The people couldn't be nicer, the tournament has looked after us all well, the crowds have been enthusiastic, but, to a man, the players can't stand the place and want to get the hell out of here.

São Paulo has a couple of shopping streets, but there's nothing really very special — jewelry is the only good buy — and otherwise it just seems to be a lot of tall buildings and concrete and cars. It's nearly reminiscent of some average U.S midwestern city, where you have to buy a newspaper to remind yourself of where you are. I'll get back to the States and I'll meet somebody and they'll make a big fuss over the fact that I've just been to São Paulo, Brazil, and if I try to tell them that it was a really dull experience, like going to Cincinnati or something, they'll think I'm trying to be blasé and putting it on. But the truth is that travel shouldn't be measured just in sheer distances anymore.  Sometimes, like this, I don't feel I'm traveling, I feel like I've just been *shipped* somewhere.

*Friday, March 15 — São Paulo*

I beat Solly 6–1 in the third tonight, and now I get Zugarelli tomorrow in the semis.

*Saturday, March 16 — São Paulo*

I have to tell you what Zugarelli did to me one time tonight.  I hit a beautiful lob past him right into the backhand corner and followed to the net, and he ran back, and I swear to God, he passed me cross-court by hitting the ball backward on its bounce.  Understand what I'm saying: he's running one way, and he hits a bouncing ball underhanded the other way, and sends it cross-court, like an arrow, for a winner.  I just stood there and looked at that ball, and said to myself: Zugi, baby, if you can do that, I'm not even going to wave at the ball.

Zugi can really handle a racket.  You know, he's one of those guys who can hit half-volleys from the base line — like Hewitt, or Nicola Pietrangeli, Santana.  Herbie Flam and Ron Holmberg were the best two Americans I ever saw who could *use* a racket that way.

Zugi's a really handsome guy — the women players have voted him, after Newcombe, the player they would most like to see streak — and he's playing awfully well now.  He beat Rocket yesterday, and tonight he won the first set from me with a 7–2 tiebreaker, and we came to a tie-break in the second as well.  But I won that one 7–2, and he fell apart, and I ran him out 6–1 in the third.  The place was packed, too, almost ten thousand people, because Koch was playing Borg in the other semi.  Tomas carried him to three sets too.

*Sunday, March 17 — São Paulo / Rio de Janeiro*

Bjorn beat me in three sets — he just was a little better than me — and I'm getting out of here at 8:40 tonight.  The people have been nice, and there was another good crowd today, but I'm just

202

ready to go. It's a different spirit playing tennis in a Latin setting like this. There are only three ball boys so everything moves at a slower pace to start with. The linesmen sit there casually with their legs crossed and they may pay attention if the spirit moves them, and the officials generally make no effort to show they are in control. Nobody wants to get too involved. Sometimes I felt like I was playing in slow motion out there.

*Monday, March 18 — Belém, Brazil / Miami / Tampa / Dallas / Tucson*

Finally, this afternoon, we got in. This is the ATP tournament with American Airlines sponsoring. We're staying in a motel called the El Dorado — Room 34 — looks a little like a bordello with red velvet walls. Not the greatest place for what they're charging.

It rained today. The locals swear it hasn't rained in three years.

*Wednesday, March 20 — Tucson*

I beat Ruffels 6–4, 7–6, but I was really annoyed at myself because I was serving for the second set at 5–3 and let him break me back. Then I had appearances to make for both Catalina and Head, the second one in a shopping mall right down the hall from where Newcombe and Riessen were making an apperance for Samsonite. I grabbed a hero sandwich and a chocolate malt at a 7–11 Store and hustled back for an ATP board meeting, but I left before it was over, I was so pissed off.

Thirty-one members, including seven guys on the board, have now signed with World Team Tennis. Guys don't seem to care. They'll take anything untested as long as the money's there. Ahh, but then I'm being unfair. It's easy for me to sound off so righteously, but I'd probably do the same thing myself if I had a wife and a couple of kids and I didn't have all these endorsements and business deals.

*Thursday, March 21 — Tucson*

This was the first time in about fifteen years, since I was playing in the juniors in Ojai, California, that I had to play two singles matches in the same day. I was playing so well, though, it didn't make any difference. First, I beat Vilas two and four on the center court. But let me tell you, although this is the first time I've played the kid, a lot of guys have warned me about him, and I can see: he could be really tough on clay. Afterward I beat Gerald Battrick one and two. I just couldn't miss a ball.

There is a shop here in town selling some magnificent Indian turquoise jewelry, and I bought some for myself and for Kathy. She wore the ring and bracelet tonight and looked just beautiful in them.

*Friday, March 22 — Tucson*

Can you believe this? I beat Rocket for the second time in a row — 6–3 in the third. Basically, it just seemed that he doesn't have my number anymore. Funny match too. No pattern. I won a tie-breaker, then he beat me 6–1, and then I won the match with just one break in the third.

He's been practicing with me a lot too. The last three mornings, he's dragged me or Roscoe out and has really been working. Laver's been off since he won Philadelphia, and now he's slid all the way down to fourth place in the Green Group, behind me and Borg and Kodes. And he wants to win the WCT championship, so he's really hustling his ass. Theoretically, four guys could get in from one group, but it's a long shot.

More meetings tonight. ATP and business. A lot of it's beginning to bore me now. I've got to cut down on my affiliations. Essentially, I'm just not happy. I'm spreading myself too thin. It's that simple. I've got to establish better priorities. What *will* make me happy in the long run?

*Saturday, March 23 – Tucson*

I beat Okker one and four in the semis. I served thirteen aces and just blew him off the court. He's always saying that it's a bore to play me because I'm always the same slam-bang stuff, point after point, and since we both play at a fast tempo, it didn't take long in the sun today.

*Sunday, March 24 — Tucson*

Well, here we go again. I lost another final — and on national television. Newcombe beat me, and now I think anyone would have to agree that he is definitely the best player in the world. But damnit, I could have beaten him here.

He won the first set 6–3, with one break at 3–2, when my serve all of a sudden deserted me and I played two bad volleys as well. But still, three times in the set I carried his serve into a deuce game — but he always pulled out.

You've always got to be thinking against John. I like to push him, make him quicken his pace, because he prefers to play very deliberately. Connors is the same way; he even has the most meticulous pattern at the crossover — he'll use a towel and then fold it neatly into five or six sections. In contrast, I don't want to dilly-dally at the crossover. Often I won't bother to stop and rest. My main purpose during these breaks is to think. I very carefully plan the next two points, with an alternative if/come strategy for the second point depending on whether I win or lose the first.

You can get a helluva lot more rest in bits and pieces than people generally realize. If I am a bit tired, when my opponent is taking time getting ready to serve, I'll bend over and let my arms drop loose for a few seconds. That posture helps your lungs and diaphragm to hang loose too and get a break. Whenever I do sit down at the crossover, I'll always make it a point to sit up straight — that opens your chest up. If you slouch, it constricts your breathing.

Anyway, after the first set loss to John today, I came right back at him and went up 4–0. This was one of those streaks of mine that people love to talk about. I broke him twice at love in the process and won sixteen straight points overall. But it never occurs to me how many points I've won (or lost) in a row. You don't have the luxury of thinking cumulatively on the court.

John is especially dogged. A lot of guys who won the first set and then were down 0–4 would forget the second and plan to throw everything into the third. But, in fact, that's dangerous thinking. For one thing, in a three-set match, you're almost always better off coming to the third set if you've won the second (or won the fourth in a five-setter). It's a tie, but you're coming into the last set with the tide. And besides that, it's always tough to regain control from a guy who's hot and running amuck, as I was.

So Newcombe wasn't really out to beat me in the second set after I got up 4–0. All he wanted to do was to slow me down, bring me back to earth, remind me that he was still in the match, so that when we did start the third set we were back on even terms.

What happened, though, was that as he stiffened, at the same time, my serve cracked on me. All of a sudden, it wasn't just 4–1 or 4–2 as John had hoped; he got the two breaks back, and had tied the set. And then he beat me in the tie-break to win in straights. The difference between Newc and a lot of other players is that many of them would not have been in position to take advantage of my lapse when it came.

*Monday, March 25 — Tucson / Tombstone / Tucson /*
*Palm Springs / Indian Wells, California*

We drove over to Tombstone this morning to see Boot Hill and the O.K. Corral, and then came back and flew to Palm Springs and drove over here to Indian Wells for this week's tournament. Where we are staying, the Erawan Hotel, has a jacuzzi, one of those portable whirlpools, right outside our room. The water is hot, 117 degrees, and it has seven nozzles, and just sitting in it was heaven.

This afternoon, we drove to the Desert Inn Motel, about a mile away, and Kathy and I played some tennis. The Desert Inn has reciprocal privileges with the Erawan. But when we got over there I discovered I had forgotten to bring any balls, so I had to buy a can. As best as I can remember, *this is the first can of tennis balls that I ever bought in my life.*

It was twenty-four years ago in a very different place, when I learned that my mother had died. And let me tell you, when you are six years old and find out that your mother is dead, you don't ever forget that.

It was early in the morning, and my father came into the room where Johnny and I slept, and he woke us up, and then he grabbed us and hugged us until it hurt. What scared me the most was his crying. I had seen grown people cry before, in church, when they had baptisms — immersions: *head to toe, in you go* — and I didn't understand that either, except to appreciate that adults were not acting normally. But it is much more frightening when it is your own father who is crying so. And then he told me that Mother was dead.

I said, "Well, Daddy, as long as we're together, everything will be all right."

Johnny was only about a year old, too young to take anything in, but later my father asked me if I wanted to go to the funeral. As I think back, I think that was an extraordinary thing for him to do, to let me decide myself whether I wanted to see my mother buried. I said, no, I didn't. I'm not sure why I decided against going, but it was probably because of another funeral. That one was when I had been four, and it is the earliest recollection in my life. It was when they buried my grandfather Pink Ashe. To this day, I can still remember going up and seeing him lying there in the casket — and his great gray mustache. And so very vividly, I can remember my mother holding me all during the service, and my Aunt Lola, from Mississippi, just carrying on, near hysteria.

I only recall a little of my mother, of the person in the picture in the living room, the tall, delicate lady in pink whom the family all called "Baby." Her real name was Mattie Cunningham, and she was twenty-seven when she died. I do remember that she taught me how to read by the time I was four, and that she taught me manners and about angels. My mother told me quite a lot about angels.

The last time I saw her was on the first day of spring that year, 1950, at the house in Brook Field. She was standing at the side door of our house in a light blue corduroy robe. I can still see her there, framed in the door, with a big tree at her back, where a jaybird was singing. My father had to carry her to the hospital later that day.

I always understood that Mother died of high blood pressure, but the last time my father saw Kathy, she asked him about my mother, and he told her that the trouble went back to complications from Johnny's birth. Maybe Daddy didn't want Johnny to feel as if he had anything to do with his mother's death. I don't know, and I don't suppose it matters much now anyway.

The jaybird had been making a lot of noise for several days, and Daddy always told me that it suddenly stopped singing the one morning, and that was the time when Mother died at the hospital. And we never heard that jaybird sing in that tree again either.

*Tuesday, March 26 — Indian Wells*

Hey, what do you know, I won a match in the wind. Beat Onny one and four.

Kathy and I went to the Foreman–Norton TV fight tonight with Ray and Rose Moore. That Foreman will kill Ali, won't he? Bob Wagner was at the theater and Kathy went bananas. He's her real hearthrob; she met him once in London too. So much for Michael Landon.

*Thursday, March 28 — Indian Wells*

I beat Kodes 3–6, 6–3, 6–4 in the quarters, and if you can believe it, I broke him to win by hitting two of my worst shots: two forehands down the line that dropped right in. I thought Kodes was going to throw a fit. He has enough trouble playing on cement even under the best of circumstances.

I didn't know any of this either, but his father had died in Czechoslovakia a few hours before the match. The Czech embassy had reached Mike Davies, the WCT executive director, and he called Cecil Eager, the Green Group road manager. Cecil decided to hold the news from Jan until after our match, and then he got Vladimir Zednik, Kodes's doubles partner, to break it to him.

Kodes must be made of iron. He said he'd stay and play his doubles match because he felt that he owed that to Zednik. And they won too.

I'm at a loss ever to explain Kodes. He generally seems motivated entirely by selfishness. The British players despise him so that you can feel the tension when they're in the locker room with him; it becomes uncomfortable. Kodes is convinced the Americans are cheating him. For that matter, he's convinced that he's the only

208

guy on tour ever to get a bad call. He can be such an incredible fighter out there, but he's also capable of being a complete crybaby, of just quitting. One year I played him in the finals at Stockholm, and he got a bad call very early in the first set. He complained, then pouted, sulked and finally just gave up. I won the set 6–1. Only then, when the whole set was over, did Kodes seem to revive himself, and for the rest of the match, he was a tiger; he carried me five long sets before I finally won. He'll bitch about one bad call for a whole damn match.

The funny side of that is Kodes's compatriot, or ex-compatriot, Milan Holecek, the fellow who left Czechoslovakia and now wanders stateless. Holecek not only remembers every bad call, but every point, every stroke of a whole match. If you ever make the mistake of saying, "Hey, Milan, how'd ya do?" he'll say, "Well, he serve the first out, then his second serve go wide to my backhand, and I swing under the ball and hit too long. Bad shot. But I make next a good return on deep serve to forehand, hit it right at his feet, and make him hit shot into net. So, at fifteen–all, he serve to . . ." and on and on like that through the whole match or for as long as you stand there, whichever ends first.

The other Czech here is Zednik. Big blond — 6'3", two hundred. I always shake my fist in his face when I pass him. It's a standing joke; I wouldn't threaten anybody that big under any circumstances. In return, Zednik curses in English. He has picked up the curses better than the rest of the language. Zednik can really do a job cursing in English. The best of that sort of thing, however, is Patricio Cornejo, the Chilean. I have got to get him on the stage. No matter what someone says or how they behave, Cornejo just shakes his head, and in this great Spanish accent, says: "Well, nobodees perfect." Whatever: "Nobodees perfect."

It's just beautiful. It's always great just being around Cornejo anyway, because he is positively the happiest person I have ever met in my life.


*Saturday, March 30 — Indian Wells*

In the semis against Rocket today, it got so windy they had to suspend the match. That's the first time that ever happened to me.

Literally, neither Laver or I could throw the ball up to serve. But I was ahead 7–6, 3–3, and so we'll pick it up there tomorrow, if the winds die down.

The celebrities have been trickling in all week: first Bob Wagner, of course, Cosby, Dino, Dan Rowan, Rod Steiger, Burt Bacharach, Ed Ames, Simon of Simon and Garfunkel, Ron Ely, who once played Tarzan. For two weeks running now we've had celebrity pro-ams, and these famous guys are starting to crawl all over our tournaments. A few of them really take it seriously too. I'm not going to say who, but one of them actually criticized his professional partner for not practicing enough for their match. Can you imagine that?

*Sunday, March 31 — Indian Wells / Los Angeles*

Rocket and I started to play again at 10:30 this morning. And with no wind. Remember, I had won the first set 7–6, and we had played to three-all in the second before the winds just got too strong. Then this morning, he won that set in a tie-break and beat me easily in the third set 6–2.

In both the first two sets, we played the tie-breakers to double sudden death, six-all. I won the first one, and I'm still kicking myself that he took the second. I had him five points to four with two serves coming. Hold my serve, I win the tie-break 7–4 and the match.

Twice I went for the big first serve, and both times I missed. At 5–4, I sent my second serve to his backhand down the middle, and he passed me down the line. Then damn if he doesn't also pass me at 5–5 on the second serve with another backhand.

Now there, I suppose, was a mistake *twice.* I should have gotten the first one in. The tie-breaker is an entirely different circumstance from anything we've ever had in tennis. For instance, the understanding that the server has the edge may not be true in the tie-break. Particularly late in a close tie-break, it seems that the player receiving serve has the advantage.

The key is to get the first serve in, preferably safely down the middle, even if it means taking something off it. If you miss that first one and have to come in with a second serve, you better have a

210

lot of confidence. I've seen some real cream-puff second serves in a close tie-break; I've seen some terrible double faults too.

Now in this match, I was suddenly down five points to six to Rocket, but he had to serve. And he muffed his first one, just as I had before him. Now, the percentages favored me to go for a winner if he got his second serve in. And I made it. I passed him. Now: 6–6. It's set point for him, but it's match point for me.

Would you rather be serving? I have to figure that he wouldn't, that the pressure is on him, on the server, and when Laver missed his first serve once again, my instinct is to think that he must play it safe to get the ball in, and that I should play to win. We were playing the right court (my choice — another edge for the receiver) and Rocket served medium deep down the middle to my backhand. Not that much on the ball. Damnit, this is the kind of shot you work to obtain. Everything in my system, in my training, in my subconscious, tells me I have got to try to hit a winner off this shot. And so I try.

And I hit it just out.

Maybe you should always play it safe in the tie-break. Hell, so many times I've seen a tie-break settled in the first three or four points, when one guy gets ahead and the other starts gambling to try to catch up — and only falls further behind. In this case, today, for the *last* four points, both servers missed all four first serves and then dumped in second serves, all of which were slugged back as attempted winners. Rocket made both of his, and I only made one of my two, which told the difference in this match, but specifics aside, it all only offers more proof that the advantage lies with the receiver. He, not the server, was the man on the attack.

So the tie-break is not only a very different kind of tennis, but it may well be a totally unique sports overtime. Traditionally, possession and attack have been the cornerstones of overtime victory, but in tennis the edge in overtime seems to lie with a patient defense.

*Monday, April 1 — Los Angeles / Atlanta / Richmond*

I got into Atlanta at five this morning and checked into the Hyatt House for a couple hours' cat nap. I had a full day of appearances for Catalina, but I did run into this old friend, a black girl I've known for years. She mentioned to me that she was going with a white law student, and I made some passing comment like "that's nice" or "what's he like?" and she replied instead that she was going to have to end the romance because her black friends were getting down on her case. "Why?" I asked.

"Just because it's not right," she said.

I beg your pardon. *Right.* There's that damn word again. Who's right to say it's right?

I believe that what we blacks need now more than anything else is a black Kissinger. He takes almost a Zen approach to problem-solving, always seeing concepts instead of issues. Kissinger never seems to get hung up on rights or wrongs or to let his personal feelings cloud things. We blacks seldom seem able to think globally. We're still very provincial. I wish more blacks would pay attention to the way Kissinger does things, or the way Ralph Bunche did things before him.

### *Tuesday, April 2 — Richmond / Tampa*

It was a gorgeous Virginia spring day this morning, so I dropped over to see the neighbors, Mr. and Mrs. Edgar Kimbrough; they're my stepmother's parents, the people who gave Daddy his land. Mr. Kimbrough has lived in this same place all his life, and he's in his seventies now. His family bought their house from some white people for $800 back in the 1890s, and he's been in it all this time.

He and Mrs. Kimbrough just had their fiftieth anniversary. Imagine that: seventy years in the same house and fifty years with the same woman. And when I went over to say hello and congratulate them, I found them out by the barn, picking salad together. Fifty years, fifty thousand times they've done this, and there they still are, so happy doing something simple together.

In my life, my father represents the only real continuity I can perceive. The unique circumstances of my experience have bred a certain distance into my relationships. Some people think I'm aloof, even cold and uncaring. I know that. The newsletter from Lakeway, the WCT resort, where I played in January, came out recently. I had written Lakeway a little thank you note, which they printed in the newsletter. Obviously, they were delighted and were trying to say nice things about me, yet the best they could manage was to describe me as "remote, yet sincere."

I doubt that I would be this way naturally, remote yet sincere, if tennis hadn't come along. If, say, I had ended up as a high school teacher in Richmond or an insurance salesman, I think I would have been quite a different breed of cat. But because I have been caught up in this strange social limbo for so long, what I once put on defensively is now me naturally. I'm just afraid I guess.

I am not surprised at the way I am. It is not surprising that I seem remote, *am* remote. I've called three women in my life "Mother." There was my real mother first, of course, and then an elderly lady named Mrs. Otis Berry who died not so long ago. She looked after Johnny and me after my mother died. When my mother realized that she was quite sick, the one thing she impressed on Daddy was that he must never let the family split up. She didn't want Johnny and me with different grandparents, or even the same grandparents; she wanted us both with Daddy. So Mrs. Berry served as his housekeeper and our surrogate mother until he married again. And I've always called the second Mrs. Ashe "Mother" too. Very few children have, effectively, sequential mothers.

It is so easy — and simplistic — when it comes to minority persons to explain that their every move is due to their minority. The fact that I was black, however, counted relatively less in my early development than the fact that I had no mother and that my father was a special park policeman (who sometimes had to impound the unlicensed bicycles of my schoolmates). The most magnificent thing that Bill Cosby has shown white people is that childhood is universal, that growing up is the same wonderfully frightening experience, regardless, as they say, of race, color and creed.

Especially in Richmond in the early 1950s, where my whole world was black, I probably spent no more time dwelling on race than some white kid who lived in a one-color suburb. What I did worry about was my size, what there was of it. I was called Bones or Skinny, or Ears, because mine stuck out (although later they got rather small and stuck to my sides so I was then called Tighthead; you can't win). I was scared to play football and could not fight worth a damn; the only fight I ever won was when my opponent slipped and bumped his head against a locker door. Worst of all, I panicked when I had to go to gym class and wear shorts, thereby revealing my spider legs and knobby knees. No matter how well I did at my studies, it never compensated for my size. Perhaps the single greatest influence upon me as a child was that I was ashamed of the body I resided in.

When I was twenty-four years old, a lieutenant in the army, stationed at West Point, I spent several months working with weights. I never had before, and I've never had the time since. I got incredibly strong that winter and in March — March 10, 1968 — I gave a very pointed speech about racial inequality. I was called in by the chief of staff at West Point and told that, as an officer in the United States Army, I could not speak that way about the country, and so I was required to hold my tongue for the few weeks remaining of my tour. Perhaps a psychiatrist would say that skinny little Arthur Ashe could not make himself speak up until he no longer felt physically inadequate. And maybe he would be right, maybe there was a connection.

214

# 19

## *Valencia Is for Love*

*Thursday, April 4, 1974 — New York / Anchorage*

At midday today I have to go out to the airport for Tokyo, and after that, although I come back to the States, my schedule is such that I cannot expect to return to the apartment for a month or more.

Aside from a tennis bag, holding four rackets and ten sets of string, I only carry one large bag. Sometimes, especially in the warmer seasons when there are fewer heavy clothes to lug around, I can fit the rackets in my large suitcase. I've got pretty temperate spring climates ahead, so I can do that today. Here is what else I'm packing for the month: one sport coat and one tie, four pairs of pants, four street shirts, four pairs of shorts, three pairs of socks, one pair of boots, six tennis shirts, eight jocks, a sweat suit, two pairs of tennis shoes, five sets of sweatbands, seven pairs of tennis socks, and a pair of rubber heel inserts.

I am wearing a pair of shorts, a pair of pants, a sport shirt, a belt, a pair of clogs and a necklace of beads that everybody assumes has some African tribal origin, but which actually I bought on King's Road in London for $3.00.

I don't like wearing a tie, or, really, dressing up at all. Kathy likes to see me dress up, but I think it's a pain, so I seldom do. I don't own many clothes at all. I don't own any shoes. I wear only boots and clogs, and since you don't need socks with clogs, I seldom wear socks.

215

I never take a bathing suit, since tennis shorts will suffice, but in the winter I will wear an overcoat and also take along an extra-warm coat and a sweater. I always think I've forgotten something after I pack in the summer.

Anyway, it is not my clothes that take up most of the weight in my suitcase. The bulk is in books. Also on this trip I am taking sixty-five tapes, each worth ninety minutes of music — plus the cassette player itself. I'll also bring some jewelry, vitamins, toilet articles, plus my paperwork and magazines. You have more time on your hands out of the U.S., especially out of an English-speaking country, when you're limited by language and custom. At most, we play tennis four hours a day, so that even if you sleep too much, which many players tend to do abroad, we are left with excessive time on our hands. So I'm carrying a lot to read; I'm just about to finish *The Stranger* by Camus, and I'm also bringing along *The Idiot* and *The Liberated Marriage* (that's two titles, not one long one). I also picked up a bunch of magazines that have been piling up while I was away and bought the latest *Newsweek*. I much prefer *Newsweek* to *Time*. And, as much as I travel, I'm bananas about travel magazines. I've also got some crossword puzzles packed.

All of the players are trapped together when they're traveling abroad, so we spend more time just talking to one another. You become an in-group. I learn most of my tennis gossip abroad; I sort out the cliques again; and I start using the inside nicknames and tour argot more. To beat somebody six–love is, for instance, a *bagel*; 6–0, 6–0, naturally, a *double bagel*. A *no-brainer* is a shot so spectacular that it could only have been done unconsciously; I think Ralston gave us that expression. To *grease in* a shot is to make it delicately; or, in the adjective form, like this: *Jesus, what grease*. An ugly girl is an *Alpo* — which I think also has something to do with the fact that Solomon screams out "dog meat" whenever he misses an easy shot. Well, "nobodees perfect."

I carry my passport and tickets and cards and other incidentals in my pocketbook, which Kathy bought me in Italy. At first I was reluctant to carry a pocketbook, but it is unbelievably practical, and now, just about everybody on tour does except the Australians. I think they're afraid their countrymen wouldn't let them back in if they were carrying one.

Very few of the tennis players are especially clothes conscious. For one thing, you're always on the move, so the main thing is getting clothes cleaned, not color-coordinating them. We think in terms of wash-and-dry, not alpaca. Pretty soon, we stop dressing for each other, and since you only see other people for a week at the most at any one time, you need little variety. Of course, some guys overdo it. Nailbags and that same damn sweater. And Marty Riessen has been wearing the same pink shirt almost every day since he turned pro in 1968. I've pleaded with Sally to do something about it, but what does she care? She doesn't travel with him all the time and have to face it every day.

Of all the players on tour, Ray Moore may be the most clothes conscious. Solomon tries hard to keep up, and Graebner dresses meticulously, by the book. The Italians, Zugarelli and Panatta, dress the most seductively. Of course, Stan Smith believes he is a regular Beau Brummel ever since *Esquire* magazine cited him as the token tennis player on its list of best-dressed athletes. That is such a ridiculous, impossible choice that it has made us wonder, ever after, if you can believe anything you read in *Esquire*.

*Friday / Saturday, April 5 / 6 — Tokyo*

We lost a day, passing the International Date Line. It's different being a blasé, sophisticated globetrotting tennis player. A sportswriter told me once that when the St. Louis Cardinals took a charter to Japan to play an exhibition series a few years ago, the pilots had a couple of the players come up into the cockpit with their cameras, so that they could get a good picture of the line itself as the plane passed over the International Date Line.

My advice for travelers. Move around a lot on long flights. At least, get up out of your seat. I'll stand up and read for an hour or more at a time and maybe also do some basic isometric exercises. Moving around keeps you in better shape. Stewardesses have told me that they're less tired at the end of crowded flights when they had to be up and around a lot. If you don't believe me, just sit on a long flight for a sustained period, and you'll notice that your legs will be sort of numb below the point where your thigh touches the edge of your chair. Your blood just kind of drops to the bottom, or something.  I'm not kidding.  If you take your shoes off on a long flight, you will have trouble squeezing them back on when you land because your feet are all puffed up with blood.

On any flight, there are two things I will never do.  One, I will never wait until I get to the airport before buying my ticket.  Ideally, get it from a travel agent — but always, in advance.  Two, I will never carry a bag.  I'll bet I pay several hundred dollars a year in airport tips — and I'm a good tipper — but it is money well spent.  I've hurt my back and arms twice trying to lug big suitcases, and just the other night in Tampa, I think the reason my bag broke was that there was nobody to carry it for me at the airport hotel and I had to half drag, half carry it to my room (and I was hurrying not to miss any of the Academy Awards).  I look upon baggage tips not as an extra charge, but as a final, regular airplane fee.

One thing I will *not* do, however, is arrive at an airport as far in advance as the airlines want you to.  That is one of the great time rip-offs in the world.  I make most planes about five minutes before they take off, and I have yet to miss a single one since I turned pro.

There are vast differences between airlines, particularly the international carriers.  Right now, I'm traveling Japan Airlines, which is easily one of the two best service airlines in the world.  The other is Air India.

The worst airport is Hong Kong, where you have to come between two mountains and then right over the city.  Rio's a little like that too, and Bombay and Saint Maarten, Netherland Antilles, are the other two scariest landings.

Now for the good news.  Amsterdam and Frankfurt have the best duty-free shops.

Copenhagen has excellent airport benches; I've spent two nights sleeping on them.

Hong Kong really is a shoppers' paradise, but if you're going to get a suit there, don't do it unless you have nearly a week or so for them to fit it and make it.  Otherwise, it'll pull apart like cellophane as soon as you get back home.

Here's the best places to get other goodies:

    diamonds — Antwerp (below wholesale)
    all other jewelry — Beirut (best by far), Florence

218

leather — Italy or Spain
alligator — Buenos Aires
suede — Spain or Sweden
crystal — Czechoslovakia, Hungary, Sweden
pearls — Tokyo
custom-made suits — London
off-the-rack suits — Italy, France

If I ever buy a car, I'll buy one in Germany.

If I ever want someone rubbed out, I'll get a trigger man in Manila. That has got to be the toughest city in the world. The last time I was there, you could buy a certified hit for $200, although I suppose that inflation has driven that price up too. Nothing's really cheap anymore.

If you are ever going to visit someone in Sweden, or just going to meet a Swede on business, pick up as much booze and cigarettes as you can coming into the country. There are so many high taxes in Sweden on liquor and tobacco that any Swede will gladly buy whatever you have purchased; in fact, they'll love you for it.

The best train I've ever seen is the one in Japan that goes from Tokyo to Kyoto at 130 miles per hour in two and a half hours. I think trains are coming back.

The best caviar I ever had was in Teheran, from the Caspian Sea. Four dollars a serving.

The best Hilton is the one in Hong Kong.

The most striking hotel in the world is the Ivoire in Abidjan, Ivory Coast. It is one of the great hotel structures anywhere, but it is the setting that really makes it distinctive: a huge pool and lake on two sides, and just beyond, the most incredible human squalor you have ever seen.

Paris is supposed to have the best restaurants in the world, but for my money, both Brussels and Bologna match it.

My favorite restaurants are:

The Colorado Mining Company, in Denver; The Underground Railway in Toronto; The Trident in Sausalito; Le Chateau in Melbourne; The Boondocks (for soul food) in New York; Joe's Stone Crabs in Miami; Alexander's in London. It's an Italian restaurant in a basement out on King's Road in Chelsea, and all the players eat there a lot during Wimbledon.

I'm sure I've forgotten some, but the list of the places I've played includes all the continents of the world except Antarctica, forty countries in all, plus thirty-seven states of the Union, Washington, D.C., and Puerto Rico.

Of the eighty-two cities where I've played outside the U.S., I remember these experiences best:

> Dakar — water-skiing on the Atlantic Ocean.
>
> Fiji — almost getting killed falling off a horse.
>
> Libreville — Riessen was bitten by a dog on the beach, and he had to have two weeks of rabies shots.
>
> Vientiane — this magnificent grass court in the middle of the Far East.
>
> Bermuda — the last time I ever doubled-bageled anybody; I beat Charlie love and love; I also refused to do a clinic at an all-white club.
>
> Valencia — the greatest weekend I ever spent in my life with a girl. It was at a Coca-Cola appearance. We had a two-month affair and this was the peak of it. We went dancing, walked on the beach, stared dreamily at the moon reflecting off the Mediterranean. People ask me, of all the places I've ever been to, what was the most romantic, and I always answer right away: Valencia, Spain. But I'll tell you something, to be honest, if that girl had spent that particular weekend with me in New Jersey, I'd probably be walking around answering that question: Bayonne.

*Sunday, April 7 — Tokyo*

This is my fourth trip to Tokyo, and I always find it very clean and a little aloof. You still find the very traditional juxtaposed to the very modern: the kimono walking down the street next to the hot pants, that sort of thing.

The Japanese, with all their money to spend, are now going bananas over our upper-class sports: golf, skiing and tennis. I had two store appearances today for Head; Sunday is a big store day in Japan.

*Monday, April 8 — Tokyo*

Roscoe and I are rooming together — Hotel New Japan, Room 994 — but he'll be delighted to trade me back for Nancy. I was sick all last night with an upset stomach, some diarrhea and an awful urge to throw up — which I couldn't.

*Tuesday, April 9 — Tokyo*

More rain, no tennis. I'm taking vitamin C tablets, resting and swallowing soup. I could use some of Mrs. Goldlust's best.

*Wednesday, April 10 — Tokyo*

I lost to Paul Gerken. I felt wobbly, and this is some kind of a weird court, made of rubber or some damn thing, that really gives you a lot of funny bounces. But I had plenty of chances; I won one set and had some break points.

*Thursday, April 11 — Tokyo*

Roscoe and I won our doubles today from a team that tanked. Both of them had already lost in the singles, and so it was obvious they didn't care. In fact, the system encourages them to lose, because there's not that much prize money in the doubles, and the next tournament is on a different surface a long distance away (the clay in Houston), so it's to any player's advantage to get in early and practice.

"Tanking" in the doubles is becoming more and more prevalent on the tour. The creation of the doubles tournament at Montreal helps provide a stimulus to win and so does the fact that the Grand Prix has started awarding some points in its tournaments for doubles, but throwing matches is still a sad fact of modern tennis life. For most, it is not considered wrong or immoral or whatever; guys talk about it openly and loudly in the locker room.

Our opponents didn't hurt themselves by not trying today, but everything is now so interrelated in tennis that you cannot consider only your own best needs. For example, Roscoe and I are second in the Green Group in doubles, which guarantees us a spot at Montreal and at least a minimum bonus. When somebody tanks to us, that affects the chances of the teams who are also still in contention and trying to displace us in the fight for the spot at Montreal.

The trouble is that tanking is a lot like rape. It's very hard to prove. Hell, one time in Barcelona, a player had a dental appointment that he wanted to meet, but he and his partner played the match out to 7–6 in the third before losing in a tie-break. There wasn't a person in the building who could tell what was going on.

What we've got to do in the ATP is create a guilty-till-proven-innocent situation, where if there is enough circumstantial evidence to suggest that a team had a reason to tank, then they have to prove that they did otherwise, if they lost.

Incidentally, just for the record, there are a lot of guys who would never think of tanking. Roscoe, for one. Brian Fairlie, who is one of the great natural athletes on the tour, and highly competitive — he could never lose intentionally. Nor could Cliff Richey or Raul Ramirez or Jaime Fillol, who is highly principled and perhaps the fairest-minded of all the players.

*Friday, April 12 — Tokyo*

Roscoe and I played Roger Taylor and Juan Gisbert today. Taylor seemed sort of half in the tank; he couldn't make up his mind whether to hang around or not, so he and Gisbert were having conferences regularly to determine whether they should try or not. We certainly should be able to win under those circumstances, but we just could never figure the damn court out. We were stumbling around so that Stolle and Laver, sitting on the sidelines, were laughing out loud at us.

And worse, Ray Moore came up to me in the locker room afterward, gave me a big wink and said: "You and Roscoe have your fins on out there?"

It's pretty awful when you play so badly that the other players think you must be fixing.

*Friday, April 12 — Tokyo / Los Angeles
again, over the Date Line*

Flew with Ove Bengtson. Nice guy — tall and handsome. Looks like the map of Sweden on his face. If the little girls think Borg is an idol — my God, if Borg looked like Bengtson, he could never even get near the court.

222

*Sunday, April 14 — Houston*

After I practiced I went out to the airport to pick up Kathy. She almost didn't get in, because the immigration people have become very suspicious of her. She is a beautiful blonde making too frequent trips into the States. Usually, that indicates hanky-panky — the Toronto connection, for sure — and she was detained and grilled for so long in Canada that she was lucky to make the plane.

We're staying with Gladys and Julius Heldman. She's the founder and publisher of *World Tennis* and the guiding spirit behind the Virginia Slims' women's tour — and just a super lady, one of my favorite people. It's always great to see her and Julius, and also to see Mrs. Laura Haywood, their maid.

This is not the case with Mrs. Haywood, but sometimes I'm the first black who has ever stayed in a house as a guest, and the maid gets very jealous of me.

*Tuesday, April 16 — Houston*

Gisbert's wife had their first baby today. Juan is a lawyer, but he has prematurely gray hair, looks very old and distinguished, and so we call him "The Doctor."

I don't know what we're going to do with more babies on tour; it's starting to resemble a movable day-care center. You see, in years past, most players left the tour at an early age to go take an honest job. In fact, if your wife had a baby, that was usually the reason you had to quit tennis. Now, the kids are just included on tour up to school age — and often beyond during the summer. Torben has a teen-aged son he sometimes brings along. The tour is a home. People like Nancy and Roscoe Tanner are making all this nice money and they don't even have a house.

*Wednesday, April 17 — Houston*

In our first-round doubles match today, one of our opponents was a guy named Jimmy Parker. Amazing — I haven't seen him in

223

about ten years, at least, but we played as a doubles team together in the juniors. He lives down here in Houston now; he's married now and has a kid and a southern accent.

Jimmy was like most of the good juniors, then and now; he was born to tennis, it was in the family. He and his father even won a couple of national father-son championships. So did a lot of my contemporaries: Dennis Ralston and his father, Frank Froehling and his, Bill Bond and his, Clark Graebner and his. I met Donald Dell's parents several years before I met Donald because they gave me a lift back from Wheeling, West Virginia, to Washington. The Dells had gone to Wheeling for a tournament with their son, Dickie.

It is still a fact of tennis that most of the good players started in it because it was the sport in their parents' social set. So far, even with the tennis boom, it has not been the case for the best young athletes to drift into tennis, to discover it and choose it, as they do with other sports. When tennis really does become a universal sport that naturally attracts the best athletes throughout the population, I think we're going to get some fantastic players.

People like to argue now about who the best player of all time is, could Laver be the greatest. I don't think it matters because I think that ten or fifteen years from now, when the tennis boom has really attracted natural athletes to the courts, we're going to have any number of players better than Rod Laver at his peak. I think we'll have guys with the size and strength and reach of a John Havlicek or Walt Frazier but with the strokes and moves and quickness of a Rosewall. I'm glad I'll never have to play a 6'5" Rosewall. But there's somebody like that on the horizon. He may be five or six years old already, and he'll play tennis instead of basketball or football because it's now becoming a respectable, popular mass game.

If the court near my house in Brook Field was the coincidence that brought me into tennis when I was very young, the divine intervention was that a young black player named Ronald Charity spotted me, recognized my potential and touted me to Dr. Johnson in Lynchburg. "Dr. J" we called him, long before Julius Erving appropriated that name in basketball.

Dr. Johnson died a few years ago, but to the end, he not only taught his pupils tennis, he taught them a whole way of life on the

224

court. His assumption was that if you wanted to get into a poker game, and there was only one game in town, you had better learn to play by the prevailing rules at that table. Dr. J not only wanted his black kids to sit in for one deal, he wanted them to be able to come back again and again.

We were schooled in the strictest manners and taught an unshakable oriental calm. We were not instructed to be sportsmen, but to be downright benefactors, to give any reasonably close decision to an opponent. Dr. J even gave us complete lessons in the proper way to pass an opponent while switching sides: with a warm smile and then only after retrieving all the balls and handing them to him. If any of this failed to help us win at tennis, Dr. J believed that it would, anyway, assist us in winning friends to the black cause.

He was a physician himself and had been an athlete of some note — Whirlwind Johnson they called him when he ran halfback in college at Lincoln. He was a firm, contemplative man, and when those black kids he collected in the summers came to play tennis, they did precisely as they were told or they were sent packing. Responsibilities about the house and the yard were meticulously assigned and were given as much attention as the tennis regimen. New players were not, for example, even permitted on to the court until they had demonstrated sufficient proficiency in hitting a tennis ball that was suspended on a string in the garage — and they were given only a broom handle as a racket.

This military-style discipline was easy for me to accept, because I was accustomed to a similar arrangement in my own house. In fact, in the several summers I spent with Dr. J, our only conflict came in the very first week, and then it was basically with his son, Bobby, who did a lot of the actual coaching for his father. Bobby Johnson probably had as much technical influence upon my game as anyone, but at that time, since Ronald Charity was the first good tennis player I had ever met, I held his ideas about tennis with a special awe and with a natural loyalty.

So, one day that first week in Lynchburg, when Bobby told me to do something that conflicted with what Ron had told me, I automatically responded with: "But Ronald Charity says — "

Furious, Bobby cut me off, and the lesson proceeded grimly.

Then, near the end of the first week, I came off the court and saw my father's Ford in the driveway, with him standing ominously beside it. He spared no pleasantries on me. "Arthur, Jr.," he said, "do you or don't you want to stay in this program?"

"Yes sir, I do."

"Fine," he said, and he got back in the car without any more to-do and drove the one hundred and twenty-five miles back to Richmond. I stayed with the program.

*Friday, April 19 — Houston*

Parun upset me today after I just rolled through the first set 6–2. Then he started passing me. He was up a break in the third and I broke back to four-all and even had an ad on his next serve, but he held on and then broke me for the match. The crowds have been fantastic here, and I'm still in the doubles.

*Saturday, April 20 — Houston*

Roscoe and I beat Kodes and Zednik 7–6, 7–6, and it was really crucial. We're still in second place in the doubles behind Borg and Bengtson, but if we had lost this match, we could have dropped to third, with just one more tournament left.

Rocket is really coming on in the singles. He destroyed Onny three and one, and now, if he beats Borg tomorrow in the finals, he takes the lead away from me in the Green Group. I'll still qualify for Dallas, but damn, I wanted to win this thing. We had the best players and the toughest schedule, and it meant something to me to come out on top.

And then, Kathy and I had a helluva fight today too. I mean, it was really a beauty. In fact, she would have left for good, but the firemen have gone on strike in Canada, so all the flights to the Dominion have been canceled.

I'm recording this in the bathroom.

# 20

## Coming Apart at the Seams

*Sunday, April 21, 1974 — Houston*

The Rocket gave Borg a lesson in how to play clay-court tennis in the singles finals, and then he and Dibley beat Roscoe and me 6–4 in the third. It rained the whole time, but there was a network commitment; we finished the doubles on a side court under lights at seven-thirty.

Poor Bjorn. The pressure on him must be terrific. The Swedes have shipped in the Davis Cup captain, Lennart Bergelin, to baby-sit with him and improve their chances of keeping him from WTT. Apparently, the Swedish Lawn Tennis Association is pressuring industry to chip in so they can come up with a counteroffer to Team Tennis. Also this week, he had his parents with him, and they don't speak a word of English.

*Tuesday, April 23 — Denver*

I beat Tito Vazquez five and four. Lights are just awful, and everybody is bitching about them.

*Wednesday, April 24 — Denver / Boulder / Denver*

I spent all morning at the main national Head offices here in Boulder. We're bringing out a new model of my racket in the

227

fall — the Arthur Ashe Competition II.  It's really a beautiful thing, if I say so myself.

Our first-round doubles was also scheduled in Boulder, where some matches in the early rounds are being played, and we drew two qualifiers, Roy Barth and Bill Brown.  It should have been easy for us.

Well, we struggled through the first set and finally won on the tie-breaker, and then we lost the second 6–4 — mostly on my errors — and we were lucky to get them to a tie-breaker in the third. They went ahead six points to five, with Brown serving twice. First, to Roscoe.  This was set point and match point for them, and season point against us as well.  And even if we won this point, we had another chance to lose on his next serve.

Anyway, at 6–5, I told Roscoe that if Bill got his first serve in, just get the ball back and we'd go from there . . . somehow.  If he missed the first serve, return the second one hard down the middle. Brown did miss his first serve, and on the second, Roscoe swung and damn near missed the ball altogether.  It's all over.  But by the grace of God, the ball caught the wood, and looped over Brown's head as he came to the net for a "lob" winner.

But now it was six-all, sudden death.  We had the choice of court, and I said I would take the serve.  Again, Bill missed his first one and hit the second one down the middle.  I don't know why I did this — I have no idea yet — but suddenly, for the first time in literally years, I was struck with this urge to run around my backhand, my best shot, and hit a forehand.  And I did — cross-court winner. Roscow was as dumfounded as I was.

So, by the skin of our teeth, we are in Montreal.

*Thursday, April 25 — Denver*

I beat Solomon, and Laver just did get by Zugarelli, so he's still ahead of me, but it's official now that we'll both make the Dallas finals, and so will Borg and Kodes.  That shows you how strong the Green Group is; we'll contribute both wild-card finalists and have half of the eight players at Dallas.

I heard an interesting thing from a couple of the Aussies today. They say that there is talk that if Gough Whitlam's government stays in power — which I suppose is dubious to begin with since there doesn't seem to be a government in the free world capable of maintaining itself in office these days — then Australia would refuse to compete against South Africa if the two countries qualified to meet in the Davis Cup finals. South Africa still has to beat Colombia in Bogotá and then play the European qualifier to reach the finals, but the possibility is certainly a real one. Still, it's difficult to imagine any country actually defaulting in the finals of the Davis Cup. If you won't play South Africa — or any country for political reasons — you shouldn't enter a competition with them.

### Friday, April 26 — Denver

I've been very edgy all week. I was upset with Laver's passing me in the singles and I've been concerned with us making the doubles, and I just haven't been playing well. The altitude here is about the same as Johannesburg, but the court and the balls are much faster, and so I've been very conscious about not hitting the ball out. As a result, I've played very tentatively, especially with my volley.

But tonight I got my touch back against Ray Moore and I served just beautifully, so I'm in the semis. Not only that, but Kodes all of a sudden rose from the ashes and beat Rocket two and four, so that clinched the number one spot for me in the Green Group. I'm very satisfied; that is a point of great pride with me.

And not only that, but I won my dinner from Joe Zingale. Borg officially announced that he would not sign with WTT; the Swedes were able to get up a lucrative enough package to keep him at home. So, it was a good day.

### Saturday, April 27 — Denver

Everything was coming apart at the seams today. We're tired and edgy. We've been playing all over the bloody world together since February. I've been acting like a child myself, and tonight, when I beat Cox in the semis, I got upset at one point over some little thing and blasted a ball up into the balcony. I don't lose my temper very often, and then, when I do, it's only around people I'm close to — Kathy or Donald or Charlie, someone like that. To begin

229

with, there's few things in life worth losing your temper over, and a tennis match, a game, is surely not one of them. But I blew up tonight — and I can't remember the last time I did a thing like that on the court.

But also, let me tell you the truth: when I smashed that ball up into the balcony, it was terrific. It felt like a million dollars. Nobodees perfect.

Roscoe beat Kodes in the other semi, so we play tomorrow in the finals. Kodes has never beaten Tanner. We're also in the doubles finals against Cox and Kamiwazumi. They haven't been past the second round all year, but Cox blew up in the locker room at Kodes, and it seemed to inspire him. Marcus just erupted, and started screaming at Kodes about what a narrow, selfish sonuvabitch he is. I thought he was going to fight. But just like that, Cox came back to his usual serene self, and then he and Kamiwazumi went out and beat Kodes and Zednik on the court. Temper tantrums seem to be paying off around here.

*Sunday, April 28 — Denver / Chicago*

It had to happen. If I can beat Laver, Tanner can beat Ashe — which he did, three and three on national TV. I couldn't buy a serve. Well, we did win the doubles.

And then Kathy and I almost broke up again. I took her to the airport — and I was sure this was it. After she left I went to see a movie by myself. She'll meet me in Montreal.

*Monday, April 29 — Chicago / Detroit / Chicago*

I'm so tired I can hardly think straight. But I'm so depressed. And everything went well too. I got up at 6:15, made a plane for Detroit for some Catalina appearances, saw some friends and then I came back here to Chicago and we really had a great crowd for an exhibition at Northwestern. I can't imagine why anybody would pay to see an exhibition, but they did, and we played some mixed doubles and then Pasarell and I went a couple of sets. Afterward, I had a good interview with Ron Kisner, an editor of *Jet* magazine.

So it was a long day and a good one — except for this one thing.

230

There are these great people, the Warrens from Highland Park, a suburb out here, who come to Doral every Christmas. I had heard that Mr. Warren had cancer, but I just wasn't prepared for how badly he looked. He must have lost sixty pounds since I saw him in December. And I knew he could see the distress in my eyes, but I just stood there and talked about the weather and my forehand volley. And all the time I'm thinking: you've got terminal cancer, Gerry, and I'm never going to see you alive again, damnit. It just destroyed me.

*Thursday, May 2 — Montreal*

One of the things I've always regretted is not being a good doubles player. I've reached the finals at Wimbledon with Ralston and at Forest Hills with Andres Gimeno — a real pickup team, but that was 1968 when I couldn't go wrong. Of all things, I won the French with Marty Riessen in 1971, and I've also won two U.S. Indoors with Charlie and a national clay courts with Graebner. That's certainly not a bad record, but still, I was never really taught to play doubles at a young age, brought up on it, the way they are in California, so that to this day I'm always concerned in a doubles match that I am *looking* like an ass.

I know that's silly, but it's the damned truth.

I don't have good doubles sense. A really top doubles player has a greater insight into interpreting spatial relationships, while I play doubles the same as singles. Also, I need a partner who plays a game much different from mine. Dennis was the best I ever teamed with. I'd love to be able to play the backhand court for a long time with somebody like Emerson, or Newcombe or Smith. I've never had the advantage of teaming with one player for an extended period, and few guys can succeed when they're always changing partners.

And then, another reason why I'm not a really good doubles player is simply because I'm not a confident volleyer, and there is more volleying in doubles.

Roscoe and I can never be an outstanding team because our games are too similar. We're like a volleyball team that has nothing but spikers. It is quite a tribute to us that the two years we've

231

played together, we made the tournament here both times.

The first time we ever played together was February 1973 against Rosewall and Stolle at Albert Hall, and Roscoe was so nervous he was damn near shaking. Nervousness will affect your game more in doubles, because it is more a quick exercise in reflexes, and nerves will show up more. I would say that hand-to-eye coordination counts a third again as much in doubles as in singles.

And I think it's important to be friends or, at the least, to be friendly with your doubles partner — and Roscoe and I do get along extremely well. I feel that it's even more crucial nowadays to be close to your partner, because on tour, playing every week, often traveling together, you're thrown together all the time. Also, with so many wives and girl friends traveling now, there is always the chance that the women can drive a wedge between the partners.

But you certainly don't have to be blood brothers to be successful. Lutz and Smith are one of the favorites here, and they've played together since they were kids — and they have very little in common. Hewitt and McMillan is the team to beat here, and they seldom even see each other off the court. They're both South African, but temperamentally they are complete opposites.

A tricky thing for a doubles team to handle comes when the relative ability or celebrity of the players changes. Players enter into a doubles relationship with an acceptance of each other's ability, particularly as that relates to his own. For example, in the first round tonight we meet Snake Case and Geoff Masters, who are fairly equal in ability. But a team like Newcombe and Davidson is clearly one-sided. No problem in either case; everybody knew what they were getting into. But suppose over the next year or so that Snake became a far superior player to Geoff. That could place real strains on the team chemistry. A decade ago, Riessen and Graebner made a top team at Northwestern, with Marty the superior player. He was number five in the country before Clark ever broke into the top ten. In time, though, Clark caught up, and his personal improvement may have shattered the original fine balance and the effectiveness of the team — although both men have gone on to have good doubles careers with other partners.

Obviously, in the case of Ashe–Tanner, I am the dominant figure: more experienced, better known, higher ranking. I was the one who called up Roscoe and invited him to play with me. There's an obvious protocol in these matters. But I'm not suggesting that I run things, that Roscoe is subservient to me. In a way we might get along better because we are not on an equal plane of age and experience; we're not so directly competitive.

Roscoe's not nearly as naive as he looks, but then, he still is a kid in many ways. In fact, we were coming back from a crepes restaurant tonight, where we had taken Kathy and Nancy after the match, and Roscoe started singing along with the car radio. I said, "Hey, where'd you learn that?" and Nancy popped up — much to Roscoe's chagrin, I'm sure — and said: "Oh, Roscoe used to sing in the Chattanooga Boys Choir." Well, damn if he doesn't look like a choir boy. And even now, going through a door, Roscoe will rush up and open it for me — although I think a lot of that is generic to the south and its manners, with black and white people.

But don't be deceived. The face is one part of Roscoe and that big left-handed serve that comes out of nowhere — hardly any toss — is another. He's as strong-willed as his serve, and, in the Aussies' vernacular, "You can't get through him." One time Roscoe was asking me about playing Nastase; by chance, he's never met him. And it occurred to me that Roscoe would do very well against Nasty, because he would not be conned by any of his crap.

Tonight, in the first round, we should have lost. We giggled our way past Snake and Geoff 7–6, 3–6, 7–6, 7–5. Those tie-breakers keep saving us.

Doubles is a game of percentages, as well as it is one of reflexes and angles. It is more important to get a lot of first serves in than a few screamers. For one thing, there are no singles stakes to hold up the net in doubles, so it sags a little and it is easier to get the ball in simply because the net is not so high. When things were going bad tonight, I told Roscoe: "Use a high kick serve, and then just get the volley back. We'll go from there." You can't gamble too much in doubles, and you've got to function as a team. If you don't both stay about the same distance from the net after the first exchange, you've created gaps and angles for the other guys to shoot for. Hit the ball down the middle when you can in doubles, because that reduces their chances for angles.

233

*Saturday, May 4 — Montreal*

One break that this tournament has gotten is that the Canadiens have been eliminated from the hockey play-offs so that the tennis can get some attention.

I really want to see this tournament make it, too, because if you give guys enough incentive they'll stop tanking matches on tour. We're only cutting our throats by not making doubles attractive for the players, because it's a good spectator sport, and we risk turning people off from everything, singles and doubles, if they find out that guys are tanking out there.

We play Hewitt and McMillan tonight in the semis. They're the favorites and getting better all the time, because Hewitt was out almost all of last year with a torn Achilles' tendon, and he has been coming back to form slowly. Lutz is playing on a bad leg too, from the injury last July in Boston.

He and Stan are up against Newcombe and Davidson in the other half of the draw. Lutz and Smith are almost all offense. Stan, with his great reach, poaches a lot. Neither Roscoe and I are much good at that, so we seldom try it. Stan is one of the best, although Emmo had the best instinct for crossing, and Pasarell and Stockton are a couple other guys who are good at it. It's a tricky business. If you go a split second too soon, the opponent has half an empty court to hit into; but if you go too late, you fake out your own partner and cause almost as much damage.

Stan is a big enough intimidator just standing at the net. He plays close and with his reach he can be a regular eraser. Lutz is much shorter, of course, but he plays a lot like Smith at the net because he is strong. Generally speaking, if either Smith or Lutz can just get their racket on the ball to volley, they can muscle it into an offensive return.

Newcombe is strong enough to do the same thing, and he has all the shots from the forehand court (what the Aussies call "first court"). Emerson has been a great first-court player too, the *best*, but he had to make up in speed what John can do with his strokes. Newc gets a very high percentage of his first serves into the corners in singles, so he takes a little off of it, and seldom misses in doubles. You'll never find Dave-O poaching when he plays with Newc; there's no percentage in it. John's first volley is too sound.

Many people were surprised at the Davis Cup finals last December when Newcombe played doubles with Laver instead of with Rosewall, who was fresh, held out of the singles. But Newc has played with left-handers in the second court for almost all of his career. Remember, doubles is a game of angles, and Newcombe will get a return angled differently from an opponent if the opponent is hitting back a left-hander's shot. Angles beget angles.

The Australian temperament also gives almost any Aussie combination an edge. Newc told me once: "If I think Dave-O did something wrong, I'll tell him, and he won't get mad. He knows I'm just trying to win the match. You bloody Yanks let things ride all the time, and so you have much more jealousy on your doubles teams. We bring things out in the open."

Well, Newcombe and Davidson made the finals. They beat Smith and Lutz in four sets. Stan doesn't play as well in doubles when he's going poorly in singles, and he's been somewhat off lately. And Hewitt and McMillan are in the finals. They beat us in straight sets — it was five, four and four, and they really just toyed with us.

I love to watch Hewitt and McMillan play. I swear, if you just saw them warming up somewhere — Hewitt bald and with a little pot belly and so slow, and McMillan, skinner than me, with that silly cap and hitting everything like he was cleaning a rug — you'd think you and anybody else on your block could handle them. There is nothing more deceiving in tennis, in sports, than these two guys.

They've been playing together almost completely since 1967, so they know each other's every move so well that it doesn't make the slightest difference whether they even talk to each other off the court. McMillan is such a calm guy that the Hewitt temper doesn't affect him, and, for that matter, Hewitt doesn't carry on quite so much in doubles. He can even relax and enjoy it sometimes. Once tonight Frew had to tie a shoelace, so Hewitt picked up his racket, put a handkerchief on his bald head and, with a silly grin, stood there swinging with both hands on the racket to mimic his partner. I don't think Frew even noticed.

But the usual Hewitt came out on another occasion. On a fairly key point in the first set, I hit a forehand to Hewitt that hit the tape and jumped several feet, right over his racket and into the corner. Well, it was a lucky shot, but out of reflex a lot of people applauded. Bob grumbled and started walking back to receive serve, when he happened to look up into the players' box, which was directly at the end of the court, and see Kathy and Nancy Tanner, applauding politely. That infuriated him, and he snarled, "You bitch," loud enough for the people at that end of the arena to hear quite well.

The outburst really doesn't bother me because I know it's just Hewitt carrying on indiscriminately, but the funny part of it was that Lamar Hunt had just gotten into town. He was making like the President at the Army–Navy game, moving around the players' box judiciously so that he would spend an equal amount of time with the wives and girl friends of all the players. Well, when Hewitt cursed Kathy and/or Nancy, poor Lamar was sitting right behind them with Delaille Hewitt. It wasn't long before he decided to get the hell out of there and go sit with the press.

I don't think Bob missed a half-dozen returns in the whole match tonight. It absolutely demoralized Roscoe — no matter what he hit, it came back, and usually low and down the middle, the perfect return. Then our next shot would have to be hit up — and zap, there would be Frew, like a specter, to pop over from nowhere and two-hand volley it out of play. Unlike Roscoe and me, they complement each other so well. McMillan, in the backcourt, has the speed and takes the calculated risks; Hewitt hits all the shots and provides the consistency.

Hewitt may be, absolutely, the slowest player on tour. He sure ain't no speedy Gonzales. He gets hit a lot. All of us make a great to-do about apologizing profusely when we do hit someone with a shot, but the truth is, of course, that it's a very clever thing to do — and anyway, we all get a fiendish delight out of hitting a guy. Hewitt is so slow that he must play far back from the net, but he can do so much with the racket that he makes up for that deficiency. He and Frew can get the balls back and work their way to the net together so that they cover Hewitt's lack of speed.

236

One thing we didn't do tonight was to try to vary the service angles to Hewitt — if only to get him out of the groove. The Aussies will try that a lot — move a couple feet one way or the other when serving, just so that the ball will come at you differently. McMillan, like Lutz, has a fine backhand cross-court chip return, and if you want to gamble against that, you can play a stretch of "Australian doubles" (also called "tandem doubles"). In that, both the server and the net man line up in the same half of the court, the server's side — an "I" formation. That situates the man at the net exactly where the chip backhand has been coming. The problem, of course, is that it leaves the other side of the court wide open, so that the server must sprint to cover that side as soon as he serves. If the receiver can hit down the line, into the alley, there is no way the server can get to the ball in time, but even if the receiver pulls this off a time or two, you have, hopefully, gotten him out of his backhand cross-court rhythm.

Hewitt and McMillan were so far superior tonight, though, that a little strategy wasn't going to save us. In fact, the way they're playing, they should eat up Davidson's backhand and win the championship tomorrow.

*Sunday, May 5 — Montreal / Toronto / Chicago / Dallas*

Laver and Borg are the only other singles finalists to have arrived so far, but they had worked out by the time I got in, so I just practiced serves for twenty minutes by myself. I'm seeded third after Newcombe and Nastase, and I drew Borg in the first round, which is a little silly since we've been playing each other all year in the Green Group, but since there's four of the eight of us here from one group it was almost inevitable that a couple of us would play each other. By the way, Newcombe and Davidson lost to Hewitt and McMillan this afternoon.

*Monday, May 6 — Dallas*

My brother's birthday. Happy birthday, Johnny.

Gorman is the alternate here, on standby if any of us is suddenly incapacitated. Okker beat him out for the last spot by a few points.

Gorman played with the Red Group in South Africa a few weeks ago, and he was telling me his impressions of the trip. He and Jimmy McManus went out to Soweto for six hours one day. Now there's a couple of guys who really care.

I practiced twice today — against Stan in the morning and Kodes in the afternoon. Everybody's been playing every bloody day since January, and it's senseless to go out here and bust your ass in practice now — it's too late. You just have to hone an edge and get yourself psyched up.

*Tuesday, May 7 — Dallas*

Newcombe and I went out to a club this morning to pose for pictures with some Cystic Fibrosis kids. CF is our official ATP charity. I'm also personally the Easter Seal honorary chairman of Dade County in Florida. There's always somebody who wants to use your name — and I understand this — because we are visible and our identity can help a cause. I'll do what I can. I'm pretty active in helping the National Junior Tennis League too, for example, and last year I was informed that if I made a personal appearance in Indianapolis the Lilly Foundation would donate a really hefty sum to the NJrTL. That's the kind of quid pro quo I understand; I said I'd be on the next flight to Indianapolis. But you've got to be selective.

Lamar Hunt had a big party tonight at his house, the Hunt Hilton. It used to be owned by Jimmy Ling back when L-T-V was selling for a million times earnings. Damndest house you ever saw. It's valued at something like two million.

Okker is scheduled to play tomorrow night against Newcombe, but he's still off playing World Team Tennis. Nothing ever fazes Tiny Tom. Somebody pointed out to me that I'm the only player ever to have qualified for all four WCT singles as well as both WCT doubles championships — plus a couple of years ago, when the schedule changed, I also won a sort of midseason final in Rome. That's a very nice little distinction to own.

*Wednesday, May 8 — Dallas*

My match against Borg is not till tomorrow night, so I watched Stanley play Rocket tonight. Incredible match — Stan in four. Laver couldn't produce the big shots when he had to. So WCT is still the only major championship he's never won. Newcombe just ripped through Okker in the other match.

I passed a note to Lamar today pointing out that there were no black ballboys or black linesmen. Lamar takes hints without the need for any more prodding; they'll be blacks here in those capacities next year. You'll see.

*Thursday, May 9 — Dallas*

It's still early afternoon. I just came out of a three-hour meeting about next year's WCT schedule. Hunt and Davies were there for WCT, with Kramer and Dell and all eight of the quarter-finalists *except* Borg. I really felt sort of stupid at times, sitting there for so long with a match tonight.

Well, Borg beat me. Three straight sets. I feel awful. I'll talk about it more tomorrow.

*Friday, May 10 — Dallas / Las Vegas*

I just could never get going last night. It was 7–5, 6–4 and then 7–6 with a sudden-death tie-breaker. The kid just climbed all over me. He had incredible timing and a really good serve. Nobody ever gives him much credit for his serve, but it's a good one. And I didn't serve well at all.

I'm very disappointed — not that I lost but at how badly I played. I really wanted to win WCT. Well, now Wimbledon.

Kodes beat Nastase in the other match last night. That was a helluva upset; Kodes hadn't really played well since last Forest Hills. Nastase has had his aura of invincibility shredded lately, and since he's not a player who can overpower you, he needs that winning image.

I believe there's a simple barometer to how well Nastase's playing.  If things are going well for him, he's playful on the court, sticking the ball in his mouth, laughing, even mocking and teasing his opponent, but in a friendly way.  But when he's off, as he is now, as he was against Kodes, the theatrics turn sour and mean. It's just a slight difference, but suddenly he really *is* Nasty.

*Saturday, May 11 — Las Vegas*
*and Sunday, May 12, and Monday, Tuesday, Wednesday,*
*Thursday, Friday, Saturday and Sunday*
*May 19 too — Las Vegas*

There are no clocks in this town, and no such thing as calendar days, as we know them, so there's no sense in splitting the diary up every midnight, the way it is properly and formally done in the real world.  It all runs together here:

Caesar's Palace is paying out something like a million dollars for this tournament . . . lots of celebrities.  Diana Ross is in the main ballroom.  I dated her two or three times a while back before she got married so she spotted me one night at the show and reached out and grabbed me and said, "Arthur, get up here with me," and, being the good sport and the bad singer that I am, I did.  I suppose it's only fair that a tennis player make a fool of himself singing, since all these singers and actors and comedians make fools out of themselves playing tennis.  And let's see: I had a long talk with Paul Anka, and I had breakfast with Andy Williams and Sidney Poitier and I had lunch with Lena Horne.  And I saw her show with Rich Little, and Shirley Bassey and Sergio Franchi, and one time I even saw Howard Cosell at a blackjack table.  I went over to talk to him, and he immediately started screaming: "Don't touch me, don't touch me.  All athletes keep their hands off me."  I can't decide whether Rich Little does a better imitation of Richard Nixon or if Howard Cosell does a better imitation of Howard Cosell . . . Cosby and I finished second in our flight in the pro-celebrity.  Dick Savitt, the 1951 Wimbledon champion, and Hank Greenberg won our flight.  Savitt is a stockbroker and he still has terrific ground strokes.  Sometimes back in New York I work out with him, but I don't think I've ever had a conversation with Savitt lasting more

240

than thirty seconds. He talks like a machine gun. All of a sudden, he'll pick up his racket and say, "Gotta go, kid, gotta go," and he'll be gone. He has the same seat at Forest Hills every year, one four or five rows up behind one of the stadium courts. I always look for him, and it's always very reassuring to find him. Sometimes I'll see him on the way to the courts. Without breaking stride, he'll say: "Bend your knees, kid, for God sakes, bend your knees on the forehand volley" — and zap, like that, he melts back into the crowd. If a year passes and I don't see him again, here he comes once more through the crowd at Forest Hills. No *hello*, no *hi, how are ya?* Just: "Bend your knees, kid, for God sake, bend your knees on the forehand volley" and then he's gone again.

There was a costume party one night and a cocktail party another. The president of Caesars Palace came in riding on a baby elephant. . . . One time I saw Eddie LeBaron standing at the bar at the Las Vegas Country Club. Remember Eddie LeBaron? He was the little guy who played quarterback for the Washington Redskins back when I was growing up in Richmond. God, did I hate the Washington Redskins. All their games used to be televised into Richmond and all over the south. Eddie LeBaron, Scooter Scudero, Gene Brito, Chuck Drazenovich. All white, every one of them. The Redskins, playing in the blackest city in the country, stayed all white longer than any other pro team because the owner, George Preston Marshall, didn't want to offend the whites in his Dixie TV network.

We had the usual quota of ATP meetings. A lot of guys are not supporting this tournament the way they should. It's our big association moneymaker, but guys are commuting to WTT matches and treating it all half-assed. We have got to get our stuff together and start living fully up to our obligations — I mean that . . . I got this letter dated May 6:

> DEAR ARTHUR ASHE,
> I am sick and tired of your losing in the finals. When you get up Sunday morning, you look at yourself and say "today I'm going to be a champion, nobody's going to stop me. He won't be able to send me a thing I can't handle. I'm going to run him all over the court and when I get through, there won't be anything left of him but a bundle of sweaty socks. Today is my day!"

241

Do it Arthur, be the champ.  Don't be friendly, don't be a good loser.
Be the champion.

YOURS TRULY,
ELAINE FROCK

Elaine, I better say something to myself about the wind too.  It
was gusting forty miles per hour when Riessen beat me in the quarters, and Roscoe and I lost a couple of hours later to Pasarell and
Ramirez . . . But I shot a 41 for nine holes one time, which ties my
best ever, and I was actually one under after five. . . . Ash Resnick,
who is the assistant to the president of Caesars Palace, Joe Louis
and I played nine holes once.  Louis has about a ten handicap, but
he played a helluva lot better than any ten.  One time Resnick
found a penny on a green and he flipped it over to Louis.  "Hey,
Joe," he said, "put this Lincoln in your pocket."  Joe tossed the
penny into a sand trap.  "Well," he said, "Lincoln freed me a long
time ago, so I'll free him."

On the way home, Resnick suddenly pulled up in front of the
Hilton and told the doorman, "Hold it, I'll be right back."  Joe and I
followed him in.  He went to the baccarat table, won $5000 in two
and a half minutes, picked up his money, stuffed it back into his
pocket, went to the car, tipped the doorman and drove us home
. . . It cost me $300 to learn to play baccarat, but it is really a good
game.  I won $350 doubling up on roulette — you know, playing
the even odds and doubling my bets whenever I lost.  It's an old
game, but it can destroy you if you hit a run of bad luck.  I figure I
can take seven straight losses before I quit, and that's never come
up yet . . . I never saw so much money in my life as around here.
In baccarat, you know, there's no chips, just cold cash lined up on
the table.  I'd see some middle-aged woman playing the damn
game for an hour or more at a time with a stack of hundreds in front
of her — and never really paying attention.  Poitier, who doesn't
gamble at all, thinks that it gives people a real charge just to see
somebody else lose a lot of money, especially if it is real bills.  I saw
a guy lose $15,000 in cash in a half an hour.  I struck up a conversa-
tion another time with the guy standing next to me.  I still don't
know his name, but he has on a white shirt and red shorts and we
chatted every time we passed each other in the hotel.  The last time

I saw him he said he was down $40,000, but it didn't seem to bother him.

I got to get out of here. I'll be sleeping home tomorrow night in Gum Spring, Virginia, and after ten days here, that's like reentry from the moon.

# 21

## *"The hardest thing I ever had to do"*

*Monday, May 20, 1974 — Las Vegas / Atlanta / Richmond*

I stopped off in Atlanta for a few hours to play a benefit match with Congressman Andy Young for the National Junior Tennis League, and then I changed clothes at the airport, bought a couple of those country hams that hang there for my father and got an Eastern flight home. My brother picked me up.

We hadn't seen each other in more than a year and a half. Johnny is looking real good — so big and powerful. He's got a black belt in karate. He's twenty-six now, a staff sergeant, on his way to assignment at Parris Island, where he started off his career almost ten years ago. He finished high school in the marines. Johnny's more like my father — more direct and open, family oriented, good with his hands.

*Tuesday, May 21 — Richmond*

I gave a couple of National Junior Tennis League clinics down in Battery Park. I changed at the house of an old high school teacher of mine, Pop Williams, who taught history and civics and coached football at Maggie Walker; a couple of friends from my old class, 1961, came by to see me at Mr. Williams'.

We had an extraordinary class. There were about two hundred

244

kids in it, and some of them are in jail now; some of them are on dope. But such a number have gone on to some achievement that I think it should be cited.

We were war babies — born in '43 for the most part — but so were the classes on either side of us war babies, and they were nothing special. We were ten or eleven years old when the Supreme Court ruled against segregation, but deliberate speed being what it was in Richmond, we never knew what it was to attend an integrated school. We did have some outstanding teachers; at that time, some of the most promising blacks in the south went into teaching simply because so few other avenues were open. I remember especially Marvin Powell, our science teacher; Miss Ransom, who taught geometry; and Miss Austin, who taught algebra — and whom I had a crush on. They made academic work exciting, something to be proud of. Perhaps more than anything, they stirred us, a group of us, and then we egged each other on.

My best friends, for the most part, had little or nothing to do with athletics. I was probably very lucky that I didn't start off hanging around with jocks. My best friend of all was Ralph Williams. I had known him since I was five years old, and we still see each other occasionally. He's a tenor who lives in Washington now. Pamela Wood Fraley, whom I knew from the kindergarten on, is now a soprano in Boston, and Isaiah Jackson, whose father was always my doctor, is one of the most promising young conductors in the country. Joey Kennedy is a jazz musician with a master's degree in music.

John Fleming is an architect in Detroit; Junius Williams is a lawyer, and for a while he served as one of the top aides to Kenneth Gibson, the mayor of Newark; Conway Wilson works for the Department of Health, Education and Welfare. I'm not sure where Archer Mitchell is now, but I know he got his doctorate in nuclear physics; Willie Banks earned one in physics; Elaine Terry Walker went to Boston University and is now a journalist; and Charlene Pollard, my first date, also has a master's in something.

All of those classmates, and me, all have one thing in common: we left Richmond. It is a much more conservative city than much of the south that is located even deeper into the Confederacy. It's sad for Richmond that the kids I'm talking about, the brains and

245

leaders of my class, left the city. The only one who stayed is Jennifer Robinson Green who married a very radical lawyer in town. And Brother Green is shakin' 'em up, I understand.

And I'll mention something else that we all shared: a light skin. Of all those top members of the class of '61 that I've mentioned, not one is really dark. Many are so light they could nearly pass for white; the darkest ones are about my shade. Being very black, in terms of color, is still to be a disadvantaged minority in the midst of a disadvantaged minority. But it is changing, thank God.

But my class of '61 at Maggie Walker was so very special that it was quite difficult for me to leave after my junior year when Dr. Johnson arranged for me to go to St. Louis, where I could obtain greater tennis opportunities. I wanted to graduate with my friends. Dr. J just said, "You have to do this, Arthur." And so I did, and it was the best for me.

*Wednesday, May 22 — Richmond / South Hill, Virginia / Richmond*

Johnny and I drove down to South Hill, near the Carolina line today, to see our Grandmother Taylor, my father's mother. She has outlived two husbands but still lives in the same big house that we used to visit every summer. It needs a little fixing up, but otherwise Ma seems to have everything under control, as ever. She was just thrilled because she hadn't seen the two of us together for years. It was a terrific time, and we all laughed a lot.

*Thursday, May 23 — Richmond / Capahosic, Virginia*

Capahosic is located at the mouth of the Rappahannock River, where it flows into the Chesapeake. The great Indian chief Powhatan sold it to the white man three hundred and fifty years ago for two "great guns" (cannon) and a grindstone. For all the history of Virginia, it's been generally overlooked that there are still a couple of Indian reservations left down in this area — for the Powhatan and Pamunkey tribes. I've come down here with Johnny and Daddy to fish in the Rappahannock River — which, as any Virginia schoolchild knows, is the real river that George Washington chucked the dollar across.

We're staying at a cabin owned by a friend of my father's named Doctor Day. "Doctor" is his first name, and he was a policeman, so he was always Officer Doctor Day; he and my father and Brenda's father, Frank Randolph, were, as far as I know, the first three special black police officers in Richmond.

Officer Day's cabin here is comfortable and isolated — no phone at all. We're going to stay overnight.

*Friday, May 24 — Capahosic / Richmond / Washington*

Up at five, good fishing till ten, and then Johnny drove me to the Richmond airport, Byrd Field (very few airports left, named "field" are there?) and I flew up to Washington and worked till nine o'clock in the office at Donald's law firm.

*Monday, May 27 — Toronto*

There is a football field at Dusable High, across from Kathy's apartment, and I ran there this morning, and then we went over to Hamilton. On the way we passed a school, and Kathy pointed to it and said: "I was beat up outside there for being Jewish." I would have to say that the fact that she is Jewish, in a minority, has enhanced our relationship.

I'm not going to get up on a soapbox, but I'll tell you for sure that more people of one race ought to go out with those of another. Even if you did it just once, for an evening, it would help us all to understand better. The first time I went out with a white girl was when I was a sophomore at UCLA. There was a dorm dance, and I sort of ended up being with this girl, and somehow I eventually got up my nerve and asked her out afterward. She wasn't even a student; she was a dental assistant, and altogether blasé about the whole thing, as if she went out with black guys all the time, which maybe she did. Me, I was frightened on the one hand and positively titillated on the other. Really, everybody should try it, at least once.

247

*Tuesday, May 28 — Toronto*

I saw my first World Team Tennis match. The Buffalo–Toronto team, which stars Okker, beat Chicago 25–24. It all seemed very weird to me. I didn't necessarily dislike what I saw, but I'm still not sure what I did see. It isn't tennis, whatever it is. It was more like the Harlem Globetrotters; it just didn't seem like the real thing. But maybe it'll find its place.

*Wednesday, May 29 — Toronto / New York*

Yesterday's news was very sad and disappointing to me: Senator Fulbright lost in the primary. I used to hate the guy. I hated all southern politicians. But I found out Fulbright had to toe the public segregationist line to get elected — which doesn't excuse his voting record, but it does explain it. We blacks have a hard time understanding that, especially if we weren't brought up in the south. I know Senator Fulbright will never make the ACLU's top ten, but look, half a loaf is better than none. Besides, Senator Fulbright was getting better all the time.

I met him last year down at Okker's resort, Mullet Bay in the Netherland Antilles, and we played golf together. Very bright man and a helluva nice guy. We can't stand to lose people like that from the Congress.

*Thursday, May 30 — New York / Boston*

Originally, I was supposed to meet Kathy in Paris tomorrow, coming from Frankfurt. She's on a Toronto–Boston–Paris flight tonight, so instead of flying direct from New York, I'm going to take the shuttle up to Boston and walk onto her flight. It should be a pleasant surprise for her. Then again, maybe I'll be the one surprised.

*Friday, May 31 — Paris*

Yeah, she really was surprised. She just flipped when she saw me coming down the aisle.

248

*Saturday, June 1 — Paris*

I had trouble waking up again and had to struggle out to the Racing Club to practice. Tonight, Kathy and I had dinner on the Left Bank at a place called Le Proucope, which was built in sixteen-something and is supposed to be the oldest restaurant in the world.

My French is no better than ever — and Berlitz still has my deposit. Maybe next year I'll keep a diary in French.

*Sunday, June 2 — Paris / Frankfurt / Wiesbaden*

I was on French television with Pierre Darmon and then hopped a plane to Frankfurt and took a cab to Wiesbaden. It cost forty marks — $16. Talk about inflation. And I can remember when it was four marks to a dollar; now it's only two and a half.

I'm staying at the Hotel Nassauerhof, which is one of my favorites. Massive rooms, huge baths, and the personnel never changes. I called up the air force to check the details of my appearance tomorrow and found out the damn thing had been canceled — and it's strictly my own stupidity. The Monday date was never firm, and I was supposed to call in advance to check.

So, I went over to the casino to play roulette. The casino thinned out before long. The Germans are always off the streets and home by midnight. You know, they're early risers. They really do work their asses off. So I went back to my room and read for a long time — *Magister Ludi* by Herman Hesse. Crealy and Parun are also into it, and they're right too: it may be the best novel I've ever read, or, anyway, it's made the strongest impression. To tell you the truth, maybe I like the hero so much because he reminds me of Torben.

*Monday, June 3 — Wiesbaden / Frankfurt / Paris*

I found out at the desk that there was a bus, costing only five marks, that I could take to the airport instead of the forty-mark taxis. The bus was to leave at eleven o'clock from the town square, and so I was on about five or ten of. After a few minutes, I heard the clock in the church tower begin to toll the hour.  As soon as the driver heard that, he just instinctively closed the door and drove off for the airport.

I loved that.  That is the quintessence of German confidence in their efficiency — to completely trust a church tower clock.  Fifty years from now, if I try to explain Germany to anyone, I'll just tell them this vignette.

*Tuesday, June 4 — Paris*

I had a hit this morning at the Racing Club with Dickie Dell, and afterward I saw Georges Goven, who is just in seventh heaven because his wife had a son.  Kathy commented how European men genuinely like their children, while American men tend to want kids — especially sons — largely as an extension of their ego.  I saw what she was driving at, but her opinion was too sweeping for me to swallow whole.  From what I've seen, most American fathers would really like to spend more time with their kids, they would like to like them more, but their ambition, the American success ethos, keeps them apart.  To my mind, the American male ego feeds much more on business success than on children.

*Wednesday, June 5 — Paris*

My first round match was against Ivan Molina of Colombia, who beat me at Toronto last year.  He also teamed with Jairo Velasco to beat the U.S. in the Davis Cup at Bogotá in January, so he was a helluva guy for me to open with on clay.  But I beat him 7–5, 3–6, 6–3, and Gorman beat Velasco too, so the U.S. has avenged its Davis Cup defeat, sort of.

You know, I've been over here almost a week, and I still haven't got established in a regular sleeping schedule.  Tomorrow, if it kills me, I'm going to get up early.

*Thursday, June 6 — Paris*

Well, I got up early.  And I played very well — beat Jun Kuki of Japan one and two.

250

Something most unusual happened in the locker room today. While Edison Mandarino was playing, his very expensive Rolex watch was stolen from his locker under circumstances which suggest very strongly that it had to be an inside job, that another player probably took it — not for sure, but quite probably.

*Friday, June 7 — Paris*

Roscoe and I played our first doubles in a long time and beat a pair from Hungary 6–1 in the third, so Kathy and I went out to dinner with the Tanners and the Lutzes. It's funny, I always drink a great deal more wine over here than I do in the States. Everybody does. I think it's because wine is viewed strictly as a status item in the U.S., while in France and many other countries, it's merely part of the everyday life.

*Saturday, June 8 — Paris*

Only the first two rounds of singles here are played best of three; thereafter best of five — and I had to go four today to take Antonio Munoz 4–6, 6–1, 6–4, 6–4. It was tight all the way against a clay-court specialist. So, I'm in the round of 16, which is especially gratifying because this is not only the premier clay-court tournament in the world, but also because Roland Garros has the slowest clay of any courts anywhere.

The rallies are long and patience counts so much. You must keep returning deep and look for a way to work yourself to the net. But I do believe that you can play with a little more variety on clay than is generally assumed. For instance, when you get into one of those long rallies with a clay-court player like Munoz or Molina, they get into a groove, point after point, and sort of lull themselves to sleep. Particularly if they get a little cocky, if they have you love-thirty or something, you can sneak up to the net and they're liable to plop you a nice fat sitter up there that you can kill. They're not expecting you to move up, so you catch them completely off guard. That can shake them up a little, too, and knock them out of their routine. I must employ a little variety because I'm simply not going to out-steady a class clay-court player.

251

*Monday, June 10 — Paris*

An assassination: Orantes beat me one, two and two and it wasn't as close as the score indicates. It was so ludicrous that one time in the second set when I hit a beautiful approach shot and followed it to the net, he passed me so cleanly that all I could do was stand there and laugh — out loud. The French must have thought I had gone round the bend. Well, I'm still in the doubles.

*Tuesday, June 11 — Paris*

Roscoe and I lost 9–7 in the third to El Shafei and Franulovic. We just didn't play well when we had to. I have got to start getting into better shape for Wimbledon, so Kathy and I are going to spend just one more day here and then go on to Nottingham where I can begin practicing on the grass.

*Thursday, June 13 — Paris / London / Nottingham*

Nottingham is up in the midlands, about a two-and-a-half-hour drive from London. This is Enoch Powell country, which is like saying a place is George Wallace country in the States. But beautiful up here today — plenty of sunshine, plenty of grass courts — and nobody to play with. I've outsmarted myself; no other player has arrived yet. Also, Kathy and I have colds, with a little temperature and some laryngitis. What a beautiful time to get sick — right before Wimbledon.

*Friday, June 14 — Nottingham*

Roscoe got in today, so at least I have someone to hit with. And Kathy and I were both a little better; my laryngitis has improved somewhat.

*Saturday, June 15 — Nottingham*

The goddamn cold is just hanging on, and so is the laryngitis. We did go downstairs to have dinner with the Pasarells and with

Erik van Dillen and his fiancée. There was a slot machine in the lounge and when Kathy heard the bartender call it "a Jew box," she just hit the ceiling. We've both been going stir crazy anyway.

*Sunday, June 16 — Nottingham*

Kathy had something of a relapse today, so I called a doctor in. He also examined me, but there wasn't a helluva lot he could say. We've both got a flu and neither one of us is desperate. And I've got a match tomorrow.

*Monday, June 17 — Nottingham*

The good news, I think, is that it rained today, so my match against Hans Pohmann has been set back a day.

Charlie came in and did our laundry this afternoon. Isn't that a real friend for you?

Later this afternoon, I went down to the bar to get a drink. I had to get out for a while, and a little liquor will probably be good for me. When I was at the bar I learned about an old friend of mine from UCLA who is getting a divorce. I tell you, I think more and more that marriage as an institution is on its way out. Very few people seem to be able to handle it anymore.

*Tuesday, June 18 – Nottingham*

Well, I beat Pohmann. I was even feeling a little stronger today. It was my first match on the grass since Forest Hills, and I really didn't know what I was doing, but then, neither did Hans. Charlie lost to Newcombe 8–6 in the third. Damnit, he plays these fantastic matches, but somehow loses most of them.

*Wednesday, June 19 — Nottingham*

Kathy and I both seem pretty much through with the cold at last, but Vilas beat me 7–5, 7–6 this afternoon. Tonight I just worked on some new ATP rules and guidelines, and then I read some more Herman Hesse. I've finished *Magister Ludi,* but now I'm reading *Steppenwolf.* Well, we're still in the doubles.

*Thursday, June 20 — Nottingham / London*

All right, I broke up with Kathy this morning. I just woke up and decided that it was the best thing to do. I don't want the responsibility of having to worry about her, and us, anymore, and the chemistry has ebbed. I don't know when it did, but it has, and if there's one thing you can't fake, it's a feeling, especially if the feeling has been there before.

So I just said, well I think we had better call it off, and she knew I meant it, so there wasn't really much for her to discuss. She knew I had made up my mind.

Kathy called a friend of hers in London, and I took her to the train station. I would have driven her to London, but we're still in the doubles. It was a very uneasy parting. After all, it's been almost two years. When I helped her on that train, that was one of the hardest things I ever had to do in my life. And then I just stood there and watched the train go away down the track.

Also this afternoon, we got beat in the doubles.

# 22

# *The Championships*

*Friday, June 21, 1974 — London*

So the year is done. I'm back at the Westbury for Wimbledon. I figure I traveled more than 72,000 miles in the United States and Canada and almost 93,000 in the rest of the world. 165,000 miles in a year to play a game. I played twenty-five tournaments and I made nine of those finals and won three. But I didn't win any major titles, which was my goal. I'll be thirty-one next month.

I practiced twice with Okker today, but I'm not hitting the ball at all well, and I'm worried. Ray Moore was one of the people I had dinner with tonight, and that only reminded me that I haven't really served well since I beat him in the quarter-finals at Denver two months ago. What a great time for my serve to leave me: the WCT finals, Las Vegas, the French, Wimbledon. Christ.

You can tell. I'm still recovering from yesterday too. It would be easier to forget if we'd just start playing.

*Saturday, June 22 — London*

I hit again with Okker, and we practiced at Wimbledon itself. There's been a serious drought, and the courts are in the worst shape I've ever seen them, although they're still in far better shape than any in the U.S.

But it just doesn't make any difference.  For the first time in my life, I'm not prepared for Wimbledon.  The cold is still hanging on, and the breakup with Kathy, and I just can't get psyched up.  I spend a whole year looking forward to this, and when I finally get here, I'm not ready to play.

*Sunday, June 23 — London*

An unbelievable day.  Everything just keeps getting worse.  We have found out that World Team Tennis, together with Connors and Evonne Goolagong, are going to sue the French and Italian tournaments for $10 million for banning WTT players from their tournaments.  Goolagong and Connors won the Australian title, and so they both had a shot at the Grand Slam until the French locked them out.  But the really awful thing is that they're also suing Dell and Kramer, claiming that they conspired with the French and the Italians to bar the WTT players.  Which is just crap.

The suit has also been directed at Commercial Union, the international insurance company which puts up hundreds of thousands of dollars a year for a Grand Prix of tennis.  CU has been thrown in, like the kitchen sink, just because the French and Italian championships happen to be included in their list of Grand Prix tournaments.  What earthly good is it to sue people who are putting huge sums into the game?  Some vice president at Commercial Union is bound to say — what do we need this for?  Let's put our promotion capital into golf or skiing or horseshoe pitching.

George MacCall told me flat out once that he would resign as commissioner of Team Tennis before he would ever sue ATP, or Jack or Donald, but I'm trying to remain sympathetic to his position; I know he's caught between the hawks and doves in his league.  And Little Evonne is a child in these matters; I'm sure she doesn't have the faintest idea what is going on.  But I swear, every time I passed Connors in the locker room today, it took all my will power not to punch him in the mouth.  It's sickening.  He and Riordan could be such a good part of tennis, but will they only be satisfied when they have wrecked the whole game?

I'm in the middle of this thing more than ever, too, because tonight I was elected president of the ATP.  Cliff stepped down, al-

256

though he will remain on the board. We twisted Newcombe's arm, and got John to run for vice president, and he was elected. Angie will give him hell for that, but he's the best player in the world now, and he's held in such personal esteem by all players that his presence gives us more clout. Newc was the first big name to sign with WTT, but now he is signaling that when the chips are down, he stands with his colleagues and not his employers.

Jaime Fillol, the most respected Latin player, was elected secretary, and Jim McManus stayed on as recording secretary and treasurer. We have a tremendous cross section on the board: Drysdale and Ray Moore from South Africa; Tiriac and Bengtson from Europe; and Stan from the U.S. Cox and El Shafei resigned, both of them citing the fact that being on the board kept them away from their families too much. This job is going to be tough for me. Cliff has not done well as a player since he assumed the presidency.

Now that I'm president, I've also got to watch what I say and differentiate between Ashe the player and Ashe the ATP president. But I'm going to devote myself to this job. When I give it up a year from now, I want ATP firmly established as a responsible force in the game. It certainly can be. We were only formed in August 1972, and we're already up to 145 members, from ninety-two a year ago. The only players not included are the Russians and Czechs among the Communist countries and Connors and a couple of others in the rest of the world.

But right now, the suit dominates my thinking. The significance of it supersedes Wimbledon. Mostly, however, I just feel so awful for Donald. I've never before had anybody do such a horrible thing to a best friend. $10 million!

*Monday, June 24 — London*

At last, the first day of Wimbledon. I haven't played here since '71 — last year there was the Pilic dispute, and the year before Wimbledon banned WCT players. As terrible as everything is in my life, the start of Wimbledon is some kind of a rejuvenation, a confirmation.

I was scheduled as the fourth match on my court, but after months of drought, it came up mean and drizzly today — not bad enough to cancel play, but enough to drag it out.  Not until 7:30 did the referee, Mike Gibson, finally call play off, so that I hung around all day, like a cocked gun, waiting for someone to pull the trigger.

Notwithstanding the weather, the grounds were jammed today. Most tennis tournaments wither on the vine early in the week, but at Wimbledon, the early days always attract the largest crowds. The courts here are well separated, so that the fans can walk around and select any number of good matches to watch; it's a tennis smorgasbord.  In fact, since there is a tendency to play the British players on Centre Court and Number One in the early rounds, some of the best matches can be found on the outside courts.  Also, this year some players are speculating that Mike Gibson might punish players like myself, who were instrumental in the ATP withdrawal last year.  The locker-room gag is that if Pilic makes the men's finals, the match will be scheduled for Court Four, with a quarter-final mixed-double going on Centre Court.

Part of the reason that Wimbledon attracts such great attention is that it is a bona fide, certified British tradition, and British traditions are just a bit more traditional than anybody else's — just as British royalty is a bit more royal.  Given a head start, the British can always make their things seem more important than anybody else's.  Wimbledon, for instance, is known here as "The Championships," which is one of the great preemptive titles of the world. How do you top that?

Besides tradition, Wimbledon also possesses that companion trait of continuity.  Forest Hills, for example, is almost as venerable as Wimbledon, but it is difficult to accept it with the same reverence when you have college kids serving as locker-room attendants. Wimbledon, by comparison, has one fellow named Peter who has been here for years, possibly generations, and all he does is escort players to the Centre Court or Number One.  The only fresh face I've seen around the locker room this year belongs to an elderly newcomer who serves the Robinson's Barley Water — orange, lemon or lime.  There is still no guy to serve ice with the Robinson's Barley Water, largely because there is not enough ice to bother with.

The locker room has been done over in recent years and Newcombe convinced them three or four years ago to give players five minutes to warm up instead of three. The more important thing, however, is not what the particular rules may be, but that they are abided by. Five minutes to warm up does not mean five minutes and ten seconds.

There is one other major change this year. Previously, the players have been transported to and from the grounds in large black limousines, flying the distinctive purple and green flag, piloted by chauffeurs; but this year our transportation consists of a fleet of Leylands, medium-sized British station wagons. Now that may sound like a loss of prestige, but the British very cleverly compensated by obtaining pretty young drivers. I don't know about the girl players, but none of the men is bemoaning the demise of the limousines — we're all too busy asking the drivers out.

The British sound so good, you don't even mind when they say *no* to you. What Shaw said about the Americans and the British being two peoples separated by a common language must be all the more true. Because Americans just use the language, without really caring for it, I doubt if we could have made English the preeminent tongue in the world the way the British did. We seem capable only of spreading marketable items, from Coca-Cola on up, while the British really do carry more lasting things, like culture or language.

Before we leave the subject of language, I would like to speak briefly on behalf of *bloody*. In America, we don't have an all-purpose mild curse word like *bloody*. If we had had a *bloody* in our vocabulary, President Nixon wouldn't have had all those expletives deleted and would probably have the Judiciary Committee on the run right now.

I would also like to submit some other new British words that I have just learned for adoption into the American language. I especially like *niggle*, which, I understand, is to be mildly annoyed. I was niggled, for instance, that I had to hang around the locker room all afternoon without ever getting on the courts. And *twee*: an adjective, meaning sort of cutesy-poo sweet. What I like especially about *twee* is that it sounds just how it means. You wouldn't call anyone twee unless they really were. The same can be said for *gnomey*, which means sort of super tacky. It is derived from those people who dress up their lawns with little plastic animals or

259

dwarfs — flamingos and deer and elves and gnomes. Thus, if you are the type of person who prefers that sort of decoration, you are *gnomey*.

For the British, Wimbledon is identified as "The Fortnight." It is an event. Americans have the impression that England is tennis-mad, but no, it is merely Wimbledon-mad. Other tournaments draw poorly. But tennis does, however, always remain in the British subconscious throughout the year. The British tennis press travels all over the world, filing stories back to London. While only a handful of other journalists — Judith Elian of France, Rino Tommasi of Italy, Bud Collins of the U.S. — see big-time tennis regularly, as many as half-a-dozen London writers cover us throughout the year. The *New York Times* won't send a man to Montreal for the WCT doubles championship, but Fleet Street will have a squadron cross the Atlantic.

As a result, tennis players become part of the everyday landscape in Britain, and when Wimbledon comes our names are very familiar to the readers. And, since the BBC puts Wimbledon on one or the other or both of its networks for most of the day (plus the reprise, "Match of the Day," later in the evening) you can't escape tennis. There is a play showing over in Piccadilly starring Maggie Smith, and in establishing the characters and the setting early on, one of the principles says to another: "Oh, I understand Ginny is doing well at Wimbledon." Immediately, everybody in the audience knows very well that the small talk is about Virginia Wade. So Wimbledon is a real dent in the whole public consciousness, and it is not just an athletic show overlaid with social attributes, in the way that Ascot or Henley tends to be.

Of course, I'm hardly suggesting that Wimbledon is without social pretensions. The Fortnight is a prime social focus, and the ladies dress for the occasion. Nonetheless, Wimbledon is foremost a national phenomenon. In fact, I think it can be argued that Wimbledon captures the imagination of a complete country more so than any other athletic event, simply because it attracts the interest of both sexes in a way that other great competitions do not.

Virtually every British schoolgirl is taught to play tennis, so that the whole female population is conversant with the game in a way large numbers of women are not with soccer or baseball or what-

260

ever.   The base of Wimbledon is female; I'm sure there's no sporting event in the world that attracts women in such numbers. (They all must be issued autograph books along with their first bras too; British women lead the world in autograph books per capita.)

The matches at Wimbledon don't start until two in the afternoon, because The Championships are held right after the summer solstice, and at this high latitude, the matches can be played in natural light until nine-thirty or so.   In the afternoon, for the first few hours, the grounds are like a large ladies' lounge.   You don't begin to see a few friendly male faces until five or six or so when the husbands begin to get out of work.   Not until well after tea does Wimbledon begin to obtain the coarser sounds and jostling of the masculine arena that we are all more used to.

In the afternoon, a guy like Roger Taylor was a matinee idol here before he was a tennis player.   Glossy photos of the players do a brisk business, like bubble-gum cards for our American boys.   This year the security forces are already girding to handle the additional hordes of schoolgirls who will be pouring out here tomorrow to see Borg, as if he were David Cassidy.   But this kind of teen-age swooning aside, the women here are knowledgeable fans.

Last February, when we were playing a WCT tournament at Albert Hall, the promoters figured they could squeeze in another payday if they scheduled a matinee between the two losing semifinalists for third place.   They got some tour groups of suburban matrons to pile onto buses and come into London to see the match. Well, it ended up a complete disaster — something like 6–1, 6–1 in half an hour of bad tennis, and those ladies were storming the ticket windows afterward trying to get their money back.

In most places in the world, you'll go to some party, and if a beautiful woman comes up to you, she'll ask you why that cute Nastase wears powder blue shorts and carries on that awful way he does; at Wimbledon, she'll come up and ask you why Nasty isn't getting as much effectiveness off his cross-court underspin backhand when he's returning second serve against left-handers.

The people of every nation are unique, but I especially love the British.   How can you not love any people who adore flowers so and, on the other hand, devised the London taxi, which is the most efficiently designed mechanism ever created by man?   I've often

261

thought very seriously — as I am again right now — about taking a flat and living over here for a year or two. It doesn't really make a helluva lot of difference where I live in the world, and so I might as well stay in the most civilized place for a time.

*Tuesday, June 25 — London*

I was up at nine-thirty. My daily cycle works best if I go to bed around one and get up around nine-thirty. It was another dreary day, but I was the second match on Court Four, and we were able to start around three. I played an Austrian named Hans Kary, whom I'd never met before, and I beat him rather easily — four, two and four — but even though I won without ever losing my serve, I wasn't pleased with it and had no confidence in the damn thing.

I'll tell you, at times like these, I really feel empathy for the week-end player when he has service problems and can't figure out where he's gone wrong. Here I am, supposedly one of the best three or four servers in the whole bloody world, and I don't know what the hell I'm doing wrong.

After the match I came into the locker room, and Nastase chose this time to make one of his periodic assessments of my color. He also had Kodes in tow with him. "Hey, Negroni," he called. I kind of wrinkled my brow in reply. "Well, what am I going to call you, Negroni? You're black. But don't worry," he added then, quite solicitously, patting me on the shoulder, "you're not too black."

"Not so black as Amritraj," Kodes said with a big smile, getting his two cents in.

"No, no, no," Nastase said. "Not that black. You're just like candy. Candy Man, we'll call you."

"Candy Man," said Kodes.

If the whole world were collapsing, I think Nastase would still be sponsoring interludes like this one.

Late in the afternoon, Roscoe and I beat Crealy and Parun, the French champions, two, three and four. We really played quite well, and I'm gratified, if nothing else, to have gotten through the

262

first round in the minimum of six sets. Sometimes you can get worn down in the first rounds of a long tournament, like a bull being worked over by picadors, and then you are no match when the real competition comes along. Rosewall has gotten a great break — the only player to have played two rounds already. I'm supposed to meet him in the round of sixteen. Usually I don't like to look at my draw in a tournament, because it distracts you by making you think ahead, but Wimbledon is such a fishbowl that there can be no secrets. Barring upsets, I know exactly who I'm supposed to play, all the way to the finals. And what a draw I've got. I must beat Roscoe in the third round just to get to Muscles so I can play Newcombe so I can play Smith. And then I get to the finals. If, if . . .

I went directly from the courts to the Westbury for an ATP board meeting. It was a good, hard meeting and we came to grips with a lot of realities. The main thing we decided is that everybody's got to bend a little and stop looking out just for number one. For instance, at one point, I really laid into Newc. There are thirty-one members of ATP playing Team Tennis, which means that one hundred and fourteen are not. "And damnit, Newc," I said, "face it — it's not even close to thirty-one guys that count. It's really just you and Okker, Muscles, Roche — the few big names. You're the only ones that matter to WTT. We can't put our whole association on the line for that."

Newcombe sat there looking at me with his mouth open, and I had to take pains to let him know that I bear no grudges against Team Tennis. So then we decided to send out a delegation of four ATP board members who also play WTT (Newcombe, Drysdale, Tiriac and Moore — smart cookies, every one of them) to meet with the owners and try to get them to drop the suit. In return, we will promise to use our best and most persuasive efforts toward getting the French and Italians to ending the ban against WTT players. Everybody in tennis is just going to have to stop being so selfish.

*Wednesday, June 26 — London*

It was one o'clock before our meeting ended last night, and so I had this strange sensation of being relieved when I woke up and looked out the window this morning and saw that it was pouring down rain.  Of those players on the board, I figure that three of us — Newcombe, Smith and myself — have a good chance to win this tournament, and Newc was scheduled to play the first match today against a tough opponent — Geoff Masters.  Newc is staying at a house way out in the suburbs, and so I'm sure it was past two o'clock before he got to bed last night.  It would have been on my conscience if he'd gotten up tired, gone to the courts and been upset by Geoff.

As it was, the rain held up his match until late in the afternoon, and then Newc beat him.  I sat around most of the afternoon waiting for my court to dry, before Mike Gibson finally called everything off at seven-thirty.

All this dampness has kept my cough going wonderfully.  The one good thing is that I'm so caught up in the excitement and the turmoil that I haven't had time to think about my broken romance.

*Thursday, June 27 — London*

I'm playing Kakulija, the number two Russian.  We were the first match on Court Number One, and I ran through him 5–1 before the rain came.  We waited for an hour and a half (with the court covered), then we came back and tried again.  I broke him again to run out the set at 6–1 and we played to four-all in the second before it really started pouring and Mike Gibson gave up the ghost and called off the rest of the day's program.

So, I spent most of another day in the locker room.  Borg has the locker next to mine.  The lockers here are arranged horizontally, like drawers, so that it somewhat resembles a morgue, and to continue the analogy, Bjorn is like a cadaver.  He finished beating Snake Case today and was mumbling "I'm so lucky" afterward — which I've heard often enough not to pay any more attention to — but now he really does appear whipped and drawn.  He seems to have no heart for the game now, and he has to be smuggled around and in and out of secret entrances less the teeny-boppers reach him and do whatever teeny-boppers do if they ever should reach one of their idols.  The other day, when I was playing Kary, Borg started his match on another outside court, and the place started going bananas all around me and generally disrupting the tournament, so now they must schedule every Borg match on Centre Court or Court One, where the bobbies can keep the chaos to a minimum.

Actually, I don't think Bjorn minds all the fuss, but he is simply exhausted from playing all year and from the publicity pressures that have accrued since he reached the WCT finals and then won in Rome and Paris. I think, subconsciously, he would find defeat here to be a satisfying escape. Holecek beat him last week at Nottingham, and Bjorn came off smiling. There was no way he should have played that tournament; it convinced me that every player should be allowed one preemptive withdrawal a year.

We had a brief but very important ATP meeting tonight, in which we made two resolutions:

One, officially, the ATP will use all its best efforts to get the French and Italian bans lifted against WTT players, and two, any suit against individuals in the leadership of the ATP is a suit against us all, and we are all required to help pay any such expenses (if it comes to it, we even discussed putting on a tournament, with all proceeds going to help pay the legal fees for Jack and Donald).

The end result of this is that whether Connors likes it or not he is now in a position, effectively if not literally, where he has sued just about every player in the game. Would you like to have to play people you've sued?

*Friday, June 28 — London*

I finally beat Kakulija, one, four and three. We played on One again, which is the fastest court at Wimbledon, but it has dried out so from the spring drought that it was bumpier than I ever recall. Right after we finished, the showers came again, and now the whole schedule has gone haywire. Like it or not, Gibson is going to have to hang tradition and start matches at noon or earlier. Roscoe hasn't even gotten his second-round match in, so that the soonest we can play will be Monday. We can't play any doubles before

265

then either. Hell, some of the girls haven't played a single match yet, and we're already five days into the tournament.

Donald and I went out to John Marshall's tonight and saw the rough cut of the film about my South African trip. Excellent. Really well done. And they've already sold it to the BBC.

*Saturday, June 29 — London*

Jack woke me at eight-thirty and told me to come right up to Donald's room. George MacCall was there, ready to sign a paper that would terminate the WTT involvement in the suit. WTT simply isn't in a position to devote its time and resources to a long and debilitating legal action. There's a couple of teams in that league where the paychecks are already bouncing higher than tennis balls, and every team is losing big.

I'm convinced that WTT made a large mistake in trying to "liven" up the action artificially. It's one thing to have no-advantage games, even to put in substitutes and to have cheerleaders and mascots, but it's another to hoke the whole thing up, to *create* controversy and dramatizations. The players have been encouraged to put on an act. Tiriac, who is the player-coach of the Boston Lobsters, told me that when they played the New York Sets, where Manolo Santana was coaching, he and Manolo got up after a close call and started screaming and shouting at each other in Spanish as if they were arguing the call or a fine point of tennis law. Actually, Tiriac was just pointing out some of the more intriguing possibilities that he had in mind for a good-looking girl in one of the front rows. After a while, Tirry said, "All right, we've given them a show, Manolo, let's sit down."

Tennis doesn't need that kind of crap.

A deeper, more substantive problem WTT has is that the result is determined too greatly by the women's competition. The top fifty, even the top hundred men in the world, can be expected to play fairly equally for a short set. The odds are that, on most days, Newcombe isn't going to beat someone like Raz Reid any more than 6–3 or 6–4. But there is a huge disparity in female talent after the top half dozen or so. Billie Jean can beat somebody like Marcie Louie 6–1 or 6–0 almost every day. As a result, the teams with the

266

best girls are a cinch.  Dennis Ralston coaches the Hawaiian team, the Leis — the big dirty joke in tennis is that the Leis will merge with the Houston EZ Riders and become the EZ Leis — and he has Snake Case to play men's singles, and Snake is better than many other of the male players in the league — but the Leis have the worst record in WTT because none of their girls are good enough. Every time Snake takes the court his team is down five or six points.

The problem is exacerbated by the fact that if anybody in the league tries to correct the imbalance by somehow giving the men a larger role in a game, then Billie Jean will scream sexist.

This afternoon I went out to Queen's with Dennis and he worked on my serve.  As I had suspected, my toss was off.  Charlie and Stan and I all have a pause near the top of our serve, so that if our toss is not just right, we are inclined to rush the action of the stroke, or hold it back too long.  When my toss goes off, it throws my whole rhythm haywire, and when you lose that groove, you start to struggle and expend a great deal more energy.

I hit volleys for a half-hour too.  I'm really not dissatisfied with the rest of my game, so I might still come around if I can just get my serve back.

I won forty-three pounds at the Playboy Club at roulette tonight.

*Sunday, June 30 — London*

It's amazing how people can talk themselves into something and then reinforce a false opinion.  Everybody is saying that the rain delays will help Newcombe because it will condense the last rounds into a few days' play, and that since Newc is such a big, strong guy, this will profit him.  Virtually every newspaper has played this same angle — and everybody you talk to is repeating the theme. The facts are completely opposite.  Newc is big and strong, sure, but there's no correlation between strength and the kind of sustained energy that everybody's talking about.  He might yet win, but if he does, it will be in spite of the rain schedule, not because of it.

El Shafei and I worked out this afternoon at Queen's.  He had a

267

good win the other day over Jurgen Fassbender, a tall, good-looking German who tells German jokes and who is the best up-and-coming ladies' man on the circuit. Also a very good grass player. Izzy always somehow beats players better than he is and then gets upset himself by nobodies. He plays Borg tomorrow, and he has a good chance because he does play his best against the best and also because Bjorn is so down.

I hit with Izzy because I needed some practice against a left-hander in preparation for Roscoe tomorrow. I've had time to think about playing him, and I know what I have to do. First, I've got to be consistent with my serve. Roscoe doesn't have a great return, so that he wants to go for blazing winners off your second serve. Don't give him the chance. And don't get shell-shocked at how hard he hits it. He's going to bust a few past me, and the best way to combat that is to expect it, and then, when it happens, just to take it in stride. If people think I am expressionless, they ain't seen nothing yet. Tomorrow, I am going to be the ultimate poker face.

Roscoe beat me in Denver for the first time the last time we played, and while that hasn't any real relation to our match tomorrow — he was just blazing balls in the altitude — it was psychologically crucial because now he knows that he can beat me. I've got to get him doubting again.

*Monday, July 1 — London*

I'm sorry it all has to end like this. I mean Wimbledon, of course, but this book too. There isn't even much reason to talk about the match, except that it will be the last one in the book. It was planned to cover through Wimbledon, 1974.

We were out on Court Seven. It was windy at times and the sun was wicked serving on the one side — but what the hell, that just says that Roscoe adapted better than I did, and that's what this whole thing is all about. He served much better than I, on both sides of the court. I went right back to throwing the ball up all wrong. I don't know what the hell's the matter with my toss. I swear, I haven't served well since that match against Ray Moore in the quarter-finals at Denver in April.

But look, I had my chances. At two-all in the first set, I had five

268

break points on him — five of the bloody things — but he served out. And then at 5–6, my serve, I had him 30–15, then 30-all, then I hit a goddamn forehand volley long and a backhand volley into the net, and there's the set. I only hit about a thousand volleys over the weekend.

He won the second set 6–3, with one break, and not long after that, I could see the press begin to gather, one by one, like vultures, assembling up on a little balcony that overlooks court seven. Until today, not a single seeded player had been eliminated, but Izzy was also whipping Borg up on number one.

To start the third set, I double-faulted on the very first point and lost my serve at fifteen, and he held and was serving for the match at 5–4 when I finally broke him. I did it with a backhand cross-court that hit the chalk. We held serve to eight-all, then, and I clubbed him seven points to two in the tie-breaker for the set.

Now, suddenly, I was confident. I felt good, sure I could win. Roscoe had to be doubting. He was still playing a match he had won, and my serve was coming back. So, what do I do? I lose my first service game at love, my next at fifteen, and like that, I'm down 0–5. Izzy had mopped up Borg by now, so the press had returned in force to catalogue my defeat. And at this point, damn if I don't straighten up, break him and come back to 3–5, thirty-all on his serve. But it was too far for me to go. He held: 6–3 in the fourth. I was out of Wimbledon in the round of thirty-two.

It's tougher losing when you don't expect to. I feel embarrassed that I lost to Roscoe because I feel I'm a better player than Roscoe. He hasn't done what I have. But I don't mean that, after the match, I was embarrassed to face other players in the locker room, anything like that. The embarrassment is all within.

Everything in this game is within. There's never anyone to console you, because nobody cares that I lost today, not really. Oh sure, I want Charlie to win, and Stan, and I'm sure they root for me too, because we've known each other for so long and been so especially close, but I can't afford to get involved in their wins and losses. You can't do that. I practiced with El Shafei over the weekend, so sure, I'm glad he got a big win today, but I wouldn't have really cared if he lost. And Izzy doesn't really care what I did. We

269

must be dispassionate.  Hell, believe this or not, but I'm glad for Roscoe.  As soon as it's over, it's incidental that it was me he beat.  It's just: El Shafei got a big win and Tanner got a big win.  Good, they're my friends.  And Ashe and Borg got beat.  Tough, and so what: you've got to remember that half of us get beat every day.

But my losing hurts me.  I take defeat harder all the time.  I just wanted to be left alone after the match.  The girls kept jamming their autograph books at me, and I turned them away.  "I'm sorry, I really don't feel like signing now," I said.  I rarely do a thing like that.  I saw the press, but I didn't want to.  After a defeat, they make me feel as if I'm on trial.

Sympathy for myself comes next.  I methodically took off my clothes and showered and sat there and felt sorry for myself.  Just you, all alone.  That's why it's even more wonderful when you win, when out of one hundred and twenty-eight players, you are the one who adapted better than anyone else.  But nobody in the locker room cares then either.  You win alone, just as you lose alone.

Only after the embarrassment and self-pity does the disappointment begin to set in, and then, at last, when I'm removed by time, when I've finally gotten out of the locker room, I can begin to see the defeat in cold technical terms.  This evening, as always after a hard loss, I waver between two extremes, between the emotional and pragmatic solutions.  First, I decide that I must break my game down and go out like a tiger and practice every component part three hours a day.  I will overcome my weaknesses, *defeat* them.  And then, on the other hand, I say to hell with it.  Why don't I just give it up and take a job at Philip Morris and collect my gold watch thirty-five years from now?

That's the way I lose, and everybody must learn to lose, because you can't play the game if you can't take the losing.  Most guys lose in character.  Nikki might throw a racket just to get it out of his system.  Nastase will jabber compulsively in defeat, talking incessantly about why he lost.  Rosewall and Roche never say a word.

As far as I can tell with Okker, he has forgotten about the defeat before he reaches the locker room.  Lutz and Pasarell lose as hard as anyone.  Sometimes you'll see the tears in Charlie's eyes, and he'll say things like, "I'll never play Wimbledon again."  Drysdale is perhaps the most philosophical.  He just wants to sort it out in his mind why he lost, where he failed technically, and once he has that filed away for future reference, it is all forgotten. Newcombe, when he hit his bad patch last year, was a great loser. He was losing to guys like Gerken and Holecek, but he would come back to the locker room, unemotionally, and would sit down and analyze his defeat, much like Drysdale. Hewitt, the loser, is, of all the players, most at variance with the person that the public sees on court. He leaves everything out between the chalk lines and is a subdued, even gracious, loser.

It's tougher for the single guys — I think, anyway, maybe because I'm single. My chief focal point is tennis. I have a lot of other interests, but no one single counterbalance, like a family. Defeat is always hardest for me the next day, because it stays with me and swells. The married guys seem to have more of a safety valve. How many times have I seen a guy come off the court, really way down after a hard loss, and he walks out of the locker room, and his pretty little daughter runs up to him, and it's all forgotten.

And I can't drink it away either. I'm not a guy for chemical crutches. I'll have dinner and gamble a little.

I'm sorry the book had to end like this.

*Tuesday, July 2 — London*

You won't believe this, but I played roulette last night at the Playboy Club. I was playing the double-up system, betting 1-through-18, and 19-through-36 came up seven straight times. First time ever. It certainly wasn't my day.

I just learned I've been invited to appear on the Barbara Walters' show when I get back to New York next week. The theme of the show I'm appearing on is "Success, And How You Made It." Great casting, huh? Hubert Humphrey is going to be another guest. Maybe we can talk about Wimbledon and the '68 election and call it "Success, And How You Missed It."

I told you that it was harder the day after a defeat. I just keep telling myself that whatever happened yesterday, there are still only five or six guys in the world with better overall records than me. And there's still Forest Hills this year.

Hell, I've got a lot of years left. Look at Rosewall. I keep myself in good shape and I don't have any weight problem. I do hate the practice. That's the only negative. But I don't mind the training. I love to run, and I love this life, even if I take the losing too seriously now. But it's an awfully good outlet for your frustrations when you can make a living holding something in your hand and hitting things with it. That's very healthy. Then, when I do finally quit, whatever I do next after that, first I'm going to take a year off and do nothing — just read all the books I've always wanted to and go to all the places I've never been.

But, what the hell, right now I'm still in the doubles.